"Kentucky Lion: The True Story of exciting books that I have read in a . couldn't put it down until I finished it. It is filled with history and is a very well-written story about the efforts of a man and his commitment to stop the evil practice of slavery. I got to personally meet Abraham Lincoln and Mary Todd through the novel, and historically it was so poignant. The book gives the reader a personal view of the inner life of those trying to make the world a better place. I was able to feel the emotions of the slaves and those who sought to keep slavery and those who sought to end it. This book truly gives readers insight about the different feelings of society at that time. There were no fence-sitters. I give a standing ovation to the authors. It will make a great movie and I will buy my ticket now.

- Rosey Grier, former NFL
  football great, actor,
  and minister

"Kentucky Lion: The True Story of Cassius Clay" is a wonderful, artistically written account of one of this country's most dramatic eras in history, and in particular of one man who held his courage above those fears that have always separated color and class. This book proves very well that the truth is audacious"

- David Patch, theatrical
  producer and winner of the
  prestigious NAACP Image
  award

Authors Richard Kiel and Pamela Wallace have expertly fashioned an epic drama revolving around the life of 19th century anti-slavery hero Cassius Clay. Full of historical tidbits and illuminating insights, it is as exciting and colorful as it is informative.

- Dr. Tim LaHaye, co-author of
  the best seller "Left Behind"
  and the continuing book
  series

Thanks to the devotion of Richard Kiel and Pamela Wallace, the public has the opportunity at last to learn about one of history's greatest participants.

- Daniel Pruett
  Vanderbilt University

KENTUCKY LION

The True Story of Cassius Clay

By
Richard Kiel
And
Pamela Wallace

ISBN - 13: 978-0-9794948-1-9
ISBN - 10:   0-9794948-1-8

Library of Congress Control Number: 2007940603

Cover Art by Jeffrey Marshall

For more information on this book, or for direct sales, please visit
http://www.richardkiel.com

Acknowledgements

I'd like to thank my producer friend the late Arch Hall Sr. for bringing the story of Cassius Clay to my attention. My wife Diane for letting me spend endless hours on the project and for proof reading it for me. The publisher Brian Forbes at Morrison McNae, LLP for his decision to get behind the project. Ray Willey for his support and Pamela Wallace for the wonderful job she did in rewriting and polishing my 25-year labor of love.

I want to thank photographer Tim Webb for taking many of the photos in the photo section. Photographer Dennis DiSilva for my author's photo. I would like to thank the Filson Museum in Louisville, Kentucky for maintaining a fine collection of that period.

I would especially like to thank Jim Shannon, Denver Music and Ed Shepard for helping me to locate the memorabilia and getting permission to photograph it.

Finally, I would like to thank the State of Kentucky and it's Department of Parks, monuments and shrines that has preserved the Whitehall Mansion for visitors to see as they drive through Kentucky near Richmond and Lexington.. It's a beautifully renovated huge and magnificent three-story home that takes you back a century when you walk inside and they have a very informative staff, library and gift shop.

PART ONE

A Dream of Freedom

PROLOGUE

White Hall Plantation, Kentucky, 1823

Two twelve-year-old boys, their shirtless, sweating bodies glistening in the sunlight, wrestled with playful determination in a grassy meadow on a hot summer day. One boy was black, with ebony skin, and wore tattered white cotton breeches held up by a thin rope "belt." The other was white, with dark hair and eyes, and wore breeches of an expensive, heavy fabric. On the ground nearby, bass and perch, caught in the crystal clear water of a nearby stream, hung on a short line.

In the distance, on a low rise, sat an imposing three-story house, built of brick, laid in Flemish bond, with heavy range work of marble and limestone. That house defined the relationship of these boys, and the future laid out for each of them.

The white boy, Cassius Marcellus Clay, was the son of the owner, General Green Clay, one of the wealthiest men in the state. General Clay's empire included distilleries, taverns, farms and a ferry across the Kentucky River. George Smith was the son of slaves who were fortunate enough to work up at the "big house" instead of out in the fields.

"Cash" and George had grown up together practically since birth and were best friends. They spent long summer days fishing and swimming. And long winter evenings playing chess, a game Cash's father taught him and that Cash taught George. Cash attended a nearby school in an unchinked log cabin. Most slaves weren't able to read because they weren't allowed to learn. But Cash had made certain that George learned along with him.

A few minutes earlier that day George had caught one more fish than Cash, but Cash claimed his were bigger. The competition ended with Cash suggesting that they Indian wrestle. He had a lot more experience with that than George did, since he often

9

wrestled with his two older brothers. In spite of being younger, he usually won those competitions with his brothers, because he was already bigger than they were. For the same reason, he usually won his wrestling bouts with George.

George was breathing hard as he tried to bait Cash with a show of confidence. "This time I'm gonna win," he boasted. "I let you win before, jus' to show you what a nice guy I am."

Cash grinned, and a hint of the devilishly handsome man he would grow into was apparent. "Sure, George. It had nothin' to do with me being stronger or anything."

George just grinned back. He was still grinning when Cash made a quick move, flipping his friend over onto his belly. But as George hit the hard ground, his face slammed into a small rock and his nose began bleeding profusely. Ignoring the injury, George shot back, "Good one, Cash. But not as good as this." He moved quickly, reversing their positions. Now he was on top of Cash. Blood dripped from his nose onto Cash. When George took one hand off Cash to try to wipe away the blood from his nose, Cash managed to break free and jump to his feet. Now they stood facing each other.

"Sorry," Cash said with a grin and a shrug. "I had to do that. You were bleeding all over me."

With that, both boys broke into laughter. No matter which one of them got slightly hurt in these tussles, he took it with good humor, understanding that it wasn't intentional. The goal was to win, not to inflict damage. At least not damage that was too serious.

Just then they heard someone approaching on horseback. By the time they looked around to see who it was, it was too late. George jumped as a whip snapped across his bare back, making a God awful sound as it cut through his flesh, and he yelped in pain.

Harry Anderson, a tall, burly man who was foreman for Cash's father, was ready to lash George again, even harder if necessary. "You get on home to your shanty, boy, or I'll really whoop you good!"

George stood utterly still for a moment, paralyzed by fear.

Furious, Cash stepped between George and the foreman. At nearly six feet tall and two hundred pounds, Cash wasn't much shorter than Anderson was on horseback. "What did you have to do that for?! I was just about to win, fair and square."

Anderson was torn between anger at this boy challenging his authority, and the knowledge that he'd better treat him with respect. His tone was tight but obsequious as he responded, "You all right, Master Clay? I saw the negra boy on top of you and figured you was in trouble."

Cash's words came through clenched teeth. "I'm fine. And how many times do I have to tell you not to call me 'master?' The Bible says we are not to call anybody 'master' or let them call us 'master.'"

"Yes, sir, Master Clay."

Cash shook his head in frustration at the man's stupidity. "You shouldn't have whipped George. He's my best friend. Don't ever lay a hand to him again."

George had remained silent throughout this exchange. He knew better than to interrupt a conversation between two white people. But he smiled slightly when Cash called him "friend."

"He's a slave, Master Clay, and it looked like he was gettin' the best of you. Big Master Clay would be real upset if he found out a negra was beatin' on you. You'd best be gettin' home or you'll be late for dinner."

"His name isn't negra or boy!" Cash insisted. "His name is George! He wasn't beating on me. We were just wrestling. And don't you be worrying about my father finding out. I'll tell him myself."

An hour later, Cash and his family were seated in the dining room. Bessie, the head servant, a large black woman dressed in a maid's uniform, complete with a white lace collar, with lace at the sleeves, stood at the head of the large formal dining table. An enormous brass chandelier hung over the exact center of the table. Everyone but Cash was dressed formally. He had simply thrown on a wrinkled shirt over his dirt and blood-stained pants.

At the head of the table sat his father, a tall, imposing figure. Though in his sixties, Green Clay still had the chiseled good looks he passed on to his son. He was a distant figure because he was gone so much on business. But he was Cash's hero, and a true hero of the War of 1812. He led 3,000 Kentucky volunteers to the relief of Fort Meigs. Cash grew up hearing the thrilling story of his father cutting his way through enemy lines to get to the fort, and then successfully defending it against the combined 1,500 British troops and 5,000 Indians led by the famed Tecumseh. Cash's dream was to someday distinguish himself on the field of battle as his father had done.

At the end of the table was his mother, Sally, a still-beautiful woman of fifty. His mother's strong Baptist faith and her belief that truth was the basis of all moral character had a profound impact on Cash. For all his life he would retain a powerful respect for honesty, literally beaten into him by his mother, who didn't believe in sparing the rod when her children misbehaved.

Bessie addressed the patriarch of the family with familiarity but deference. "Would you like some more peach cobbler, Master Clay?"

"No, thank you, Bessie. But it was mighty good." His own tone was courteous and respectful.

Cash's older sister, Sally, named for her mother, gestured to Bessie that she didn't want any more, either. His older brother, Brutus, gave a perfunctory, "No, thank you."

Cash's oldest brother, Sydney, said, "I'll have some more." He took after their mother, and had a soft appearance that made him pale in comparison to his rugged little brother.

Bessie served him, and then turned to Cash. She smiled warmly at him as she asked, "How about you, Young Master Clay?"

Cash tried to respond with the same grace and courtesy as his father. Though the youngest of the general's children, he was the most like him. "No, thank you, Bessie." Then he turned to his father. "Can we talk about something that's bothering me, father?"

"Of course. Let's move into the study."

As father and son left the table together, Cash's brothers watched with undisguised jealousy. These private talks, while rare, were part of a pattern that made it painfully clear to them that Cash held a special place in their father's heart.

In the study, Cash politely waited for his father to take a seat behind his large desk, before sitting down, facing him. The general pulled a cigar out of a silver box and lit it as he waited for his son to speak.

Gathering his courage, Cash asked bluntly, "Father, do you think it's right to own people like we do?"

"Of course. We paid for them. It's perfectly legal." His tone was matter-of-fact, devoid of emotion. Like most people in that time and place, he didn't question the status quo.

"Why do you ask?"

Cash knew that his father, like his mother, believed strongly in the Bible. "I'm not talking about whether it's legal to own slaves. I'm talking about whether it's right."

His father's eyes narrowed as he studied his son. "Does this conversation have anything to do with what was going on between you and that negra boy today?" he asked pointedly.

Cash realized that Anderson had beaten him to the punch, leaving him at a disadvantage. But he was determined to have this out. He knew that his total obedience to the scriptures was the best way to reason with his father, who prided himself on being a genuinely religious man. "The Bible says that in heaven we'll all be the same -- bondsman, free man, gentile, Jew, rich man and poor man."

The General nodded agreement. "You do know your Bible, son. I have to give you that." His warm tone hardened as he continued, "But what does that have to do with you consorting with the negras?"

"If it's God's will to treat us all the same in heaven, then why do we treat the -- "He paused, then went on, pointedly using the more respectful pronunciation of the word, " negroes -- different here?"

His father didn't have an immediate response. He was a stern commander, but a thoughtful man who strove to be reasonable. "Cassius, I admit I do not have a good answer to your question. But I promise you, I will think about it until I can give you the kind of answer your provocative question deserves."

Cash knew it was best to quit while he was ahead. It would do no good to continue arguing with his father.

"Thank you, Father."

He rose to leave. His father gestured to him to wait. "One more thing, Son. I am . . . proud of you. Very proud, indeed."

As Cash left the study, he passed his mother who was coming in. She went inside, closing the door after her. Cash hesitated, then consumed with curiosity, leaned toward the door so that he could hear what was being said inside.

He heard his mother ask, "Did you resolve whatever problem it was that our son wanted to talk to you about?"

His father responded slowly, "I believe there will be a resolution. But it may take some time." Then he added, "When God gave us young Cassius, He gave us a very special gift."

Sally agreed. "He's the only one who takes his Bible lessons seriously. I expect he'll do great things one day."

"Yes. And I intend to do all I can to help give him that opportunity."

Bursting with pride at his parents' words, Cash hurried away before they might catch him snooping and change their high opinion of him.

His photographic memory had served him well that night, enabling him to recall the pertinent details from scripture.

As he went to his bedroom, he wondered what his father meant by saying he was going to give him the opportunity to do great things. At twelve, Cash didn't fully appreciate the fact that his father's position as one of the wealthiest men in the state would make it possible for his biggest dreams to come true. He couldn't yet articulate what his dreams were. But there was a stirring in his soul when he watched what his friend, George, had to endure as a slave. It was just plain wrong to treat people so badly. Of that, he was already certain.

CHAPTER ONE

Two Years Later

It was late summer, so hot and humid that the air was heavy, oppressive and damp as a wet dishrag. Pausing occasionally to wipe the sweat from his face with a crumpled handkerchief, fourteen-year-old Cash, now well over six feet tall, carefully tended the miniature garden that was a hobby of his and his older sister, Eliza. There were lots of wildflowers with colorful names – fleabane, angelica, tickseed, heal-all. His favorite were Indian pipes. He had found them growing on the banks of the stream where he and George went fishing, and he transplanted some in the garden.

Working nearby was a beautiful young mulatto slave, Mary Carter. As Cash awkwardly tried to tie up sweet pea vines, he kept sneaking glances at Mary. Whenever she would happen to look up, he would quickly look away, trying to appear as if he were focusing intently on anything other than her.

Seeing him struggle with the tangled vines, Mary took them from him. Their hands briefly touched. Mary didn't seem to notice or care. But Cash did. He felt a jolt of electricity through his husky young body and had to force himself not to react.

"No, no, no, not like that," Mary insisted. "Too tight, it dies. Too loose, it falls down, gets trampled on. Gotta give just the right amount of support. Like this."

As she showed him, he grinned mischievously. "You always were a bossy little thing, Mary."

"Not bossy. Just right." She finished tying up the vines. "There. All this little plant needs is some help so's it can stand up an' reach the sunlight. It'll be blooming 'fore you know it."

Cash looked at her, trying to keep his expression matter-of-fact. He was having a hard time dealing with the powerful feelings that came from being so close to Mary. Those feelings had started coursing through him a few months earlier when he noticed that Mary's body, once thin and uninteresting, was suddenly growing full and round in places that were very interesting, indeed. She was his age, fourteen. And if she'd been white, and a member of his class, his budding romantic feelings for her would have elicited nothing more than good-humored teasing from his family and friends. If his feelings persisted, both families would have talked seriously of an alliance.

But even though Mary had sparkling hazel eyes and light, caramel-colored skin, and could easily pass for white, she was still a slave. And that one fact made all the difference in the world. Cash knew that he had no business having those kinds of feelings about a slave. There was no future in it for either of them. His father felt strongly that it was wrong for white owners to take advantage of their female slaves. And even if that wasn't the case – if Green Clay was one of those men (and there were many) who considered it a privilege of ownership – Cash still wouldn't have acted on his feelings. He didn't want to force a frightened and unwilling Mary to lie with him. He wanted . . . something much more. He wanted her to look at him as he looked at her – with longing and delight and a desperate desire to know her down to her very soul.

Still, he couldn't stop looking at her furtively. And wondering what it would be like to hold her in his arms and kiss her full, soft lips. Powerful feelings rocked his body. Feelings that he had no control over. He wondered helplessly, does she ever have these kinds of thoughts about me?

The sound of footsteps interrupted his thoughts. His father came up to them. By the concerned look on his face, Cash sensed that his father was aware of Cash's attraction to Mary. And he wasn't happy about it.

"Mary?" The General's tone was carefully matter-of-fact.

"Yes, sir?"

"I want you to go over to Mr. Payne's for a bit. Help out while his wife's recovering from her confinement."

Mary's carefree expression changed abruptly at the mention of Payne. She looked nervous, frightened even. "But . . . Mr. Clay . . . I got to finish tying up these sweet peas."

16

"Cassius can do that." He smiled wryly at his son. "He must've learned somethin', all the time he spends in the garden with you."

Cash flushed at the clear meaning behind his father's pointed words and even more pointed look.

The General turned back to Mary. "Now tell your momma where you're goin' and get on over there."

Mary hung her head in abject submission. "Yes, sir."

Reluctantly, with a brief glance back at Cash, Mary walked away. In that moment when their eyes met, Cash saw clearly how desperately she did not want to go. Was it because of him? he wondered hopefully. Did she want to stay here, to be around him? Or was there some darker reason?

The General's tone still carried that tone of suspicion and disapproval as he continued to his son, "Think you can handle those sweet peas, Cassius?"

Cash forced himself to smile half-heartedly. "I'll try, sir." When his father left, Cash turned his attention back to the sweet peas. But his mind was on Mary. Why had she looked so frightened?

Hours passed. Cash was tired from the effort to string the vines just as Mary had instructed. He sat back on his heels, squinted up at the sun that beat down mercilessly, and then looked back at the fragile vines. He remembered Mary's words. All they needed to thrive was a little help from the sun . . .

The peace and quiet of the moment was shattered by the sound of hysterical sobbing, growing louder as it came closer. Looking up sharply, Cash saw Mary running toward him. She carried a bloody butcher knife and her torn and disheveled clothes were covered with blood. Throwing herself into his arms, she buried her face in his chest, so distraught she couldn't speak.

His eyes ran over her body quickly, enormously relieved to see that she didn't appear to be hurt. But where did all that blood come from?

"Mary! What is it?! What happened?!"

Still sobbing uncontrollably, it was a moment before she could raise her trembling face to his. At that moment, as he looked into her eyes, he knew he would never forget the look of helplessness and terror that he saw there. It pierced his heart.

"Oh, Master Cash, that awful Mr. Payne tried to take me!"

The word "master" jolted Cash back to the reality of the situation. She was a slave and she had just committed a heinous act that could lead to her death. "What did you do, Mary?" he asked, trying to sound much more calm and reassuring than he felt.

With tears streaming down her face, her voice choked with emotion, she explained haltingly, "Soon as I got there, he sent me out to the barn to get eggs. I heard about him from some other womenfolk. How he used 'em. I knew he'd be followin' me, so I hid a knife in my dress."

Now Cash understood why she hadn't wanted to go. But she'd had no choice. "Did he hurt you, Mary?" Cash asked gently, sickened at the thought of what such a man might have done to her.

She shook her head vehemently. "I told him no . . . but he kept comin' after me . . . even when he saw the knife, he wouldn't stop . . . " She broke down completely, unable to continue. Cash held her tightly, trying to comfort her. But both of them knew there was no real comfort to be had in this desperate situation.

"What about Payne?" he asked, sensing the answer and dreading it.

Mary didn't answer. She just looked down at the knife still in her hand. Suddenly she dropped it then covered her mouth in horror at what she'd done. And what it meant would happen to her.

Finally, she looked up at Cash and whispered hoarsely, "I think he's dead . . . Oh, Master Cash, what are they gonna do to me?!" The answer was written all over Cash's anguished expression. Still, he tried to hold out some hope. "I'll talk to my father, Mary. He never would've sent you there if he'd known what Payne was like. Don't worry, everything will be all right." He finished in a tone of grim determination, "No one's gonna do anything to you."

It was hard to say which of them – Cash or Mary – needed to believe that more.

One month later, after a short trial in the county court, during which Mary wasn't allowed to testify in her own defense, the jury foreman read the verdict. "We, the jury, find the defendant not guilty!"

Standing in the dock, trembling with fear, Mary nearly fainted with relief. The Clay family, all of whom liked Mary very much, reacted with joy. Both Mr. and Mrs. Clay had stood by her steadfastly. Because of their position in the community, that had a significant impact on the jury. And Payne's sordid reputation had contributed significantly to this verdict.

Now Cash caught Mary's eye. For an instant, the tumult in the courtroom seemed to subside, and it was only the two of them sharing a look that spoke volumes. For the first time in a month, Cash saw a hint of the smile that had enchanted him.

But Payne's friends and family erupted in anger and outraged disbelief. The judge had to bang his gavel repeatedly and order them to come to order. "The prisoner will be released into the custody of her owner. In accordance with the law, she will be taken out of the State of Kentucky and sold to the highest bidder."

Cash's euphoria dissolved in an instant. Mary looked stricken, then screamed, "No! Oh, my God, no!" Her eyes went to Cash again, beseeching him to help. But he could only stare at her helplessly. There was nothing he or even his father could do. The law had spoken. His eyes followed a sobbing Mary, her wrists tied, as she was grabbed firmly by the arm and lead stumbling out of the courtroom.

Outside, Cash watched with a sick feeling in the pit of his stomach as Mary was shoved violently into a wagon and driven off. She wouldn't even be allowed to see her family one last time, to say good-bye. Seeing Cash, she screamed, "Master Cash! Please don't let them take me! Please! Master Cash!"

Cash couldn't bear it. He started to run after the wagon. He had no idea what he was going to do, but he was determined to do something. Then his father stopped him, physically restraining him. He tried desperately to break away, and it took all his father's considerable strength to hold him back.

Cash turned on his father in impotent fury. "They can't do this! She's not guilty!"

The General responded firmly, "I'm truly sorry, son. There's nothing more we can do. At least her life is spared." Meeting his son's confused, lost look, he went on gently, "It's the law."

Cash blurted out defiantly, "What kind of law is it that finds a girl innocent, then tears her away from everyone who loves her?!"

"I know it doesn't seem fair. But under the law, there must be consequences when a slave kills a white person. Even in self-defense."

Cash's anger only intensified in the face of his father's attempt to reason with him. "He tried to rape her! She was just defending herself! If a white woman did the same thing, she wouldn't be driven off!"

His father sighed heavily. His drawn expression revealed the depth of his feelings about this tragedy. "I feel responsible. If I hadn't sent her over there . . ." He shook his head, trying to shake off the guilt that haunted him. "But the law's the law."

Cash watched the wagon disappear in the distance. Mary's tortured expression as she begged him to help her would forever be seared in his memory. He knew he would never see her again. And she would never again see her loved ones. General Clay would have to go home and tell Mary's mother and father, who had been worried sick about their daughter, that she was gone forever. Whatever fate awaited her would remain a mystery to them until the day they died.

Cash's expression hardened. In that moment, the carefree boy seemed to age into a bitter man. His voice was hoarse as he said, "It may be the law, father, but it isn't justice. And if it's the law, then it needs to be changed!"

For the rest of his life, he would never forget the poignant image of a distraught Mary being sent away. Nor would he forget how impotent he felt because he couldn't help her when she needed him most. At that moment he found his life's calling. He had already decided that slavery was morally repugnant. But now he felt a burning passion to deal slavery a deathblow. Even if it meant committing the worst sin anyone could commit in Madison County at that time – going against his own people.

CHAPTER TWO

Three months after Mary was dragged from his life forever, Cash was sent to boarding school at the illustrious St. Joseph's Academy in Bardstown. The leading families of the South sent their boys there. Among the students was one whose name would go down in history – Jefferson Davis, future President of the Confederacy.

The school had the look of a fine Catholic university. Ivy covered the brick walls, and a huge bell tower and stained glass windows gave it a stately and traditional look. Cash studied international diplomacy with a French priest named Fouche. He loved the South, but he was curious about the rest of the world, and looked forward to traveling one day. He enjoyed talking to the Spanish-American students and the French Catholics from Louisiana. They were so different from the people he'd grown up with. Far from being put off by other cultures, he was fascinated by them.

At his father's suggestion, he began corresponding, in halting French, with his well-known, highly respected older cousin, Henry Clay, who was Secretary of State under President John Quincy Adams.

One day in 1828, when Cash was in his third year at the school, he strolled down a walkway into a courtyard. By his side, a new friend, Thomas Lancaster, jabbered non-stop. "How'd you do on your tests?"

Lost in thought, Cash didn't pay attention. He was used to ignoring the talkative Thomas. Belatedly he realized his friend had just addressed him. "I don't know."

Cash's attention was caught by a very large young man who was even bigger than the strapping Cash. He was bullying a much smaller, younger student. A familiar, deeply physical feeling of revulsion engulfed Cash as he watched this show of force. When the bully pushed the frightened young man, Cash hurried over to them. Driven by a silent rage, he punched the bully hard in the nose, sending him crashing to the ground. Looking down at the

21

figure sprawled there, holding his nose and groaning in pain, Cash said in a grim voice, "Now you know how it feels."

While other students looked at him in admiration or bemusement, he continued walking across the courtyard.

A few minutes later he entered a classroom and took a seat. The stern-looking, middle-aged professor asked, "Do we have a Cassius Marcellus Clay present?"

Cassius stood up and answered, "Yes, sir!"

"You're wanted in the dean's office immediately, Mr. Clay."

There was a murmur of curiosity among the other students as Cash left. He tried to look nonchalant, but the truth was he was worried. Students were never called into the dean's office for good reasons, but only when they were in trouble. Could the dean have heard already of the altercation?

In the dean's outer office, Cash saw the bully sitting there, his shirt and tie covered with blood. Cash steeled himself for the lecture he fully expected to get. He was about to take a seat on the far side of the room from the bully, when Dean Ashgrove came out of his private office. "You needn't sit down, Mr. Clay. We have just received an urgent message that your father has taken ill. We've arranged for a carriage to take you home immediately."

The bully smirked at Cash's grim news.

Cash couldn't believe it. Even at seventy-one, Green Clay was a strong, commanding presence. It was inconceivable that he could be ill. So ill, in fact, that Cash was being called home. It seemed impossible. Of course he would recover. Cash couldn't bear to think about any other outcome.

Determined to put things right before he left, Cash said, "Before I leave, sir, I'd like to explain -"

But the dean cut him off. "I seriously question whether this is the right place for you, Mr. Clay. Think about that while you're away. And decide if you should return."

As Cash took his leave, he had already made up his mind. Despite the fact that he had loved going to school here, any place that tolerated the mistreatment of the weak by the strong wasn't for him. He wouldn't be coming back.

Several months later, on a dark, rainy afternoon in October, and a large crowd gathered at the small cemetery on the grounds of White Hall. George stood behind him, offering silent comfort.

Sally Clay's face was covered by a heavy black veil to hide her tears, but her muffled sobs were clearly audible.

Green Clay had died of cancer. Cash had nursed him devotedly, while he stoically put his business affairs in order. Now the man whom Cash admired above all others, was gone.

The preacher, a white-haired, patrician-looking man who'd known the family for most of his life, spoke in a deep, sepulchral tone. "We commit this mortal body of our good friend, General Green Clay, to the grave. Ashes to ashes, dust to dust, but with the blessed assurance that one day this good man will be caught up in the clouds to be with his Maker and Lord."

When the preacher finished, several people approached the family, and murmured the usual condolences. He was such a good man . . . He surely will be missed . . . If there's anything I can do to help, Miz Clay, anything at all . . .

Cash listened to the sincere words, knowing that his mother, brothers and sister felt as bereft as he did. There was nothing anyone could do to help. The man who had dominated their lives, who was larger than life itself, was gone. And nothing could fill that void.

The next evening the family sat in the library. The sound of thunder and heavy rain lashing the house contributed to the forlorn atmosphere. Everyone listened as the attorney read the will. Cash's eldest brother, Sydney, sat up straight, an air of confidence mitigating his grief. As the first-born son, he had great expectations.

The attorney read aloud, "Being, at the time, in good health and of sound mind, I, General Green Clay, hereby write down in my own hand my last will and testament. To each of my children, I bequeath the sum of fifty thousand dollars, and to my wife the balance of my cash until her death. At that time, the balance of any cash remaining, along with the farming lands and the main house, including all livestock, horses, carriages and all other assets will revert to my youngest son, Cassius. From the moment of my death until this transfer occurs, Cassius will act as trustee for my wife and oversee the estate and all its assets, including the slaves. I want to feel that somehow I will have made a difference. I am confident that with the wisdom that God has imparted upon my youngest son, that he will carry out that mission on my behalf."

Sydney couldn't believe what he was hearing. To be passed over in favor of the youngest was unthinkable. He took it as a posthumous humiliation and rejection by his father. Concerned for Sydney, his mother reached out to touch his arm reassuringly. He was so furious, that he jerked his arm away from her, refusing to be placed in a position lower than his younger brother.

The attorney continued, "The farming operation will be owned jointly by all the children and administered by my oldest son, Sydney."

Sydney's rigid expression relaxed slightly. That was some degree of vindication, at least. But it wasn't enough. It wasn't what he believed he deserved.

The attorney droned on in a monotone, "To my head servant, Bessie, who has served us so faithfully and well for so many years, I bequeath the sum of one thousand dollars."

Bessie was in the midst of serving drinks to the family when she heard these words. She dropped the tray and nearly fainted.

"To George, Luther and Henry, I bequeath the sum of five hundred dollars each. And to all the workers on the Clay plantation, the sum of three hundred and fifty dollars each. Although this is not a great deal of money, it will provide enough for each of you to buy the materials to build your own home on a five-acre parcel of the Clay Plantation, which I have instructed my attorney to deed to you upon my demise."

If anything, Bessie was even more thrilled with this good news than with her own. She grabbed Cassius by the arm. "Can I go tell them, Master Clay?"

He winced at being called "master." But he told himself it wouldn't be for long. "Sure, Bessie, but call them all together. There's something else they need to know."

At that moment, a furious Sydney rose to leave. Cash tried to stop him, but Sydney just pushed him away and stormed out.

Within an hour, every slave on the plantation was gathered in front of the house, their faces lit by torchlight. Cash came out of the house and stood in front of them. Though only eighteen, he seemed to have grown from boy to man in the last few months as he became his father's caretaker and their roles were reversed. The surprising, deeply affecting terms of his father's will, had completed the transformation. His father thought he was mature enough to shoulder the enormous responsibility of the vast estate. Cash intended to live up to his father's belief in him.

His father had also laid down another responsibility, a moral one. While the words in the will were ambiguous, Cash was certain he knew exactly what his father wanted him to do. And he intended to do it without delay.

He began, "You have heard by now what my father has provided for all of you." Shy murmurs of gratitude could be heard. "Well, there's one more thing. You are all set free. I have just signed the necessary papers." At their looks of disbelief and incomprehension, he went on, "You are all free to go."

For a moment there was nothing but stunned silence. The now former slaves were motionless, hardly daring to breathe. There were no cheers, no applause. Cash couldn't believe their lack of response. They must not understand, he thought. "I said you are no longer slaves to this plantation. You are all free men and women, every one of you. You are free to go!"

There was still no reaction. "Don't you understand?" he demanded. "You're free!"

Finally, an older field worker found the courage to speak on behalf of all of them. "But we got no place better than this to go, Mr. Cash. Can't we still work for you and farm our own little bit of land, too?"

Cash was flabbergasted. And then he understood. If they could stay here as free men and women, then they had no need to go. "Of course you can stay," he said. "For as long as you choose to. But from this day on, you are all going to be paid a fair wage for your work."

Now the crowd roared its approval. Cash looked over at George, who smiled broadly at him. Then George began to clap. Soon everyone was applauding Cash as he stood there, looking out at them, and he found himself struggling to control the emotions overwhelming him.

At that moment, he thought of Mary, as he often did at unexpected times. The freedom Cash was able to grant these people had come too late for her. Nothing he could ever do would make up for what had been done to her. In the midst of the joy surrounding him now, he felt only a bittersweet pleasure. But as he looked at George, and saw something shining in his friend's eyes that he'd never seen before – the incandescent light of freedom – he knew this was, nevertheless, a wondrous thing.

CHAPTER THREE

L exington, known then as the Athens of the West, was the cultural and business center of Kentucky. There were lovely residential areas, with old mansions. Pleasure carriages -- gigs, barouches, coaches -- took members of Lexington society on pleasant drives in the late afternoon. Well-to-do citizens enjoyed the delicious pastries of Swiss chef Mathurin Giron at his Confectionary and Saloon.

Lexington boasted the finest college in the state, Transylvania College, founded in 1780. The year after his father's death, Cash enrolled there. He took classes in many subjects, but his favorite was oratory, in which he excelled. He closely followed the great political issues of the day, especially the issue of slavery, and wanted to be able to argue his abolitionist opinions forcefully and persuasively.

In a small room in the dormitory, Cash and his old friend George sat at a table, playing chess. At nineteen, each had grown up to be strong, handsome young men. Cash held a chess piece in his hand, thinking hard about his next move. George was winning, and Cash needed to pull off a brilliant move.

"I'm sorry I ever taught you this game," Cash said with a wry grin.

George took some tobacco and a paper from a pouch in his pocket, rolled a cigarette, lit it, and then took a long drag on "I sure envy you, Cash, bein' able to go to a fine school like this."

Cash met George's look. He knew his friend was genuinely glad for him. And that made the comment all the more poignant. "Once I graduate, George, I'm going into law, so one day you'll be able to go to a college like this."

George shook his head slowly. "Come on, Cash. You're tryin' to make me feel good. But we both know there's no way someone like me will ever be able to go to any school with you all. Let alone a fancy one like this. If they won't allow girls, they're sure not gonna allow – he exaggerated the word – "negrooooos.""

Cash got that stubborn look that George had come to know well as they were growing up together. "Mark my word. It will happen."

George didn't argue further. There was no point in that when Cash had made up his mind about something. But he didn't believe it. The fact that he and the other workers at White Hall had been given their freedom had been a dream come true. George didn't allow himself to have any other dreams. As his momma would say, wanting anything more, like a real education, would just be "crying for the moon."

Without saying anything further, he stubbed out his cigarette in an ashtray then tossed it into a nearby wastepaper basket.

Later that night, as Cash slept in his bed and George slept in a big chair with his feet propped on an ottoman, flames shot up in the wastepaper basket, where the cigarette butt had been smoldering. The basket was full of papers, and soon smoke began to fill the small room. Cash stirred, began to choke in his sleep, but didn't awaken. George snored.

Suddenly, from out in the hallway came the sound of young men shouting, "Fire!" and pounding on the door. Cash awoke with a start. Immediately, his eyes began to sting from the smoke, and his coughing got worse. He could see the fire in the wastepaper basket beginning to spread to the desk and chairs. Stumbling out of bed, he went over to George and pulled him to his feet. As they opened the door into the hall, the influx of fresh oxygen turned the small fire into a rapidly growing inferno, feeding on the wooden walls.

Outside, students poured from the building. Through the windows the flames could be seen growing with terrifying rapidity. Cash and George made it to a stand of trees about fifty yards from the building. They were still coughing badly. But Cash knew the worst problem wasn't the smoke they'd inhaled but what would happen if people learned who had accidentally started the destructive fire.

"George, you have to go. Now. Before they start asking questions."

George was horrified at the damage he had inadvertently caused. "I'm sorry, Cash. I didn't mean for this to happen."

"I know," said Cash.

"Will they blame you? Will you get in trouble for this?" George asked in dismay.

"Don't worry about me. I'll be okay. Hurry now, and be careful."

As George reluctantly left Cash to deal with the consequences of one careless act, Cash felt far less confident than he had tried to appear to George. He would take the blame for this disaster. And it would almost certainly mean expulsion from the school, if not criminal prosecution. His law career could be over before it even began. But if George took the blame, the consequences would be much more dire. At the very least, George would be viciously whipped and imprisoned. At worst, he would be hung.

The next day the dean of the school, looking grim, stepped up to a podium in the packed auditorium. Surveying the tired, worried-looking students, he began, "Until we can rebuild the dormitory, you all will be transferred to private lodgings nearby."

He began reading from a list. "Ashcroft." The student came forward to receive the name and address of his host family. "Clay." Cash responded, not quite meeting the dean's piercing look. Nothing had been said to him yet about the cause of the fire that everyone knew had started in his room. But he knew it was only a matter of time before he'd be called to account.

"You will be with the Robert Todd family," the dean said, handing him a piece of paper with the address. Cash took it, and as he walked away, the dean continued, "Burgess."

Later that morning Cash stood at the front door of an elegant, two-story brownstone. The beautifully landscaped front yard was resplendent with maple trees, the leaves a riot of brilliant fall colors. Taking the big brass doorknocker in his large hand, he rapped twice. A moment later the door opened and a pretty girl of thirteen appeared. She had a heart-shaped face, dimples and dark brown eyes. But to Cash she was just a child.

"Can I help you?"

"Yes. My name's Clay. Cassius Clay. I've been assigned to stay here for awhile." He added, "I'm sure it won't be for long."

She smiled and the dimples deepened. "You're the student we've been expecting." With surprising composure in one so young, she held out her hand and said, "I'm Mary Todd." She added with a twinkle in her eyes, "I'm sure you're welcome to stay as long as you like."

She gestured to him to come inside. At six feet, three inches tall now, he towered over her as he brushed past her. He followed her down the wide hallway.   At the rear of the hall, she opened a door and stood aside for him to get a look inside. "This will be your room." It was nicely furnished, with a comfortable looking bed. Most important to Cash, there was a good size desk. "Very nice," he murmured.

She led him to the end of the hall and into the great room. A fire was blazing in the huge brick fireplace, and there was an entire wall of bookshelves filled to the brim. Cash immediately went to examine the books. "We have all the classics," Mary said proudly.

"Do you think it would be all right if I . . . that is . . ."

"Of course. That's what they're here for -- to read. Not just to look at." She moved on into the dining room that opened off the great room. "Come on, I'll introduce you to Ma."

Cash was surprised at the way she referred to her mother. He'd never heard anyone use that word before. Noting the magnificent furnishings, including a massive oak table that could seat at least ten people, Cash said, "You have a beautiful home."

"Why, thank you, Mr. Clay. I'm glad you like it."

Mary led Cash into the kitchen. There was a huge, wood-fired double oven stove with warming racks above, and a long sink and counter area. Two middle-aged women, one white, one black, both in white aprons, worked side by side at the counter. As Mary introduced her stepmother to Cash, he couldn't help noticing that the woman was as plain as her daughter was pretty. The servant, Bertha, was about as large a woman as Cash had ever set eyes on. "Ma, this is our young student guest, Mr. Cassius Clay." Gesturing to the servant, she added, "And this is Bertha."

Cash summoned his best manners. "Pleased to make your acquaintance, Mrs. Todd . . . Bertha. Can I help with anything?"

Mrs. Todd smiled warmly. "You surely can, young man. I need some wood brought in for the stove. And Bertha could use some help chopping ice for the dessert. Let me show you where we keep the wood."

As Mrs. Todd took Cash outside to the woodpile, Mary moved close enough to Bertha to whisper excitedly, "Bertha, I'm going to marry that handsome young man some day."

Bertha frowned in disapproval. "How can you say something like that, Miz Mary? You just met him."

"Maybe so, but I know what I like, and I like what I see. He's tall and good-looking and he has all kinds of muscles!"

"My lands, girl, you're only thirteen years old! That young man's already in college."

"Tall, good-looking and smart, too. All the more reason to marry him," Mary responded impudently. "By the time he finishes his education and is ready to think about marriage, I'll be seventeen.

30

Just the right age to get married and have lots of children."

They heard Mrs. Todd and Cash returning. Mary finished quickly, "Now don't you be telling Ma what I just said or she'll be having kittens. And whatever you do, don't say a word to Mr. Clay, because if you do, I'll just die."

The door opened and Mrs. Todd came in, followed by Cash, whose arms were filled with logs.

Mary moved to hold the door open for him. "Let me get the door for you, Mr. Clay," she said with a winsome smile.

Mrs. Todd went to a cupboard and took out a brown pottery crock of blueberry preserves. The mouth of the crock was sealed with beeswax. She handed it to Bertha. "This'll be good on our biscuits at supper." She turned to Cash. "Are you partial to blueberry preserves, Mr. Clay?"

"Yes, ma'am. They're my favorite."

"I put up those preserves," Mary interjected quickly. "Bet you'll find they're the best you've ever tasted."

"Mary!" her mother admonished her. "Don't be braggin' on yourself."

But Mary wasn't at all chastened. It never hurt, she felt, for a girl to let a man know she was a good cook.

When Cash returned to school the next morning, he had made up his mind what he was going to do about the fire. Without waiting for the dean to call him into the office, Cash went in first thing and asked to see him. The dean was immediately available, and Cash was ushered into his office.

Without preamble, Cash began, "I accidentally started that fire, sir, by throwing a cigarette in the wastepaper basket. I thought it was out, but clearly I was wrong. I'm more sorry than I can say."

Cash's contrite attitude didn't seem to have any effect on the dean's grim demeanor. "It was obvious the fire started in your room, Mr. Clay. I've already told the authorities as much. They'll be here some time today to speak to you. Rebuilding the dormitory will be a huge financial burden to the school. Your apology does nothing to lessen that burden."

"I'm aware of that, sir. That's why I want to offer to pay to rebuild it. It's the least I can do."

The dean eyed him suspiciously for a moment. He knew the Clay family was wealthy, but could this young man really speak for them?

As if reading his thoughts, Clay went on frankly, "My father passed away last year. I control a large portion of my family's financial assets. I don't have to ask permission to use them as I see fit."

The dean hesitated. Without having it spelled out, he understood perfectly well the deal that Cash was offering. In return for financing the new dormitory, there would be no charges filed relating to the fire. Cash didn't blink as he met the dean's look. But inside he wasn't nearly as confident as he appeared. His very future hung in the balance here. If he was convicted of a crime, his good name would be compromised.

The dean blinked first. "Very well, Mr. Clay. When I receive the estimate on the rebuilding costs, I'll give them to your attorney. I assume he'll remit a check for the full amount forthwith."

"Yes, sir. I assure you there will be no delay."

"In that case . . . I will let the authorities know there is no reason to take further action at this time."

Without saying another word, Cash turned and strode out of the room. Only when he got outside the building, away from prying eyes, did he allow himself the luxury of a huge sigh of relief.

CHAPTER FOUR

1831

The two years that Cash had spent living with the Todd family were among the happiest of his life. He worked hard at his studies, but also found time to participate in Lexington's active social whirl – dancing under the high, ornately decorated ceilings of the ballrooms in the finest mansions, attending the races at the new Kentucky Association Track, and enjoying social evenings in the fine old homes. He was a highly sought-after, eligible bachelor, attractive and well-spoken, with a respected name and large fortune. Though he escorted several attractive young ladies, none caught his fancy for more than a brief period.

Cash and Mary Todd had become good friends. He didn't notice how much she had matured from the thirteen-year-old who first opened the door to him. She was now fifteen, and she saw herself as a young woman, even if he continued to see her as a delightful child. Moreover, she was a young woman with a very strong attachment to him. She was as determined as she'd been the first day they met that some day she'd be his wife. Because she wanted this so badly, it didn't occur to her that perhaps he might feel differently.

Cash was intent on his studies one day when Mary stuck her head around the half-open door to his room and startled him out of his concentration. "Some friends and I are going hickory nut hunting after church tomorrow. Want to come along?"

"Is it gonna be a bunch of girls?"

Mary was clearly taken aback by his pointed question. "Pretty much." Then she grinned impishly. "Unless you go. Then there'll be a strapping young man in the group."

Cash considered the invitation for a moment. He was exhausted from studying and could use a break. Who knows, he thought, maybe I'll meet an attractive girl. He looked at Mary. "Sure, why not?"

Mary tried to appear nonchalant. "Fine." But as she turned to leave, she thought excitedly, Wait till I tell my friends! They're going to be so surprised!

The next day after church Mary's friends and Cash went to a nearby area where there were hickory trees. The bunch of giggling girls stared at Cash as he sat on the ground and cracked a huge collection of hickory nuts with two large rocks. They seemed to think he was utterly fascinating. Cash did his best to ignore them. To him they were just silly little girls. To Mary's consternation, Cash seemed to view her as just being one of them.

Finally growing bored with Cash's lack of response to them, the girls, including Mary, wandered off to look for more nuts.

Then a young woman closer to his own age, but still dressed in plain, loose cut school-girl's attire, passed by. Cash noticed her immediately. Her eyes were a soft gray-blue, large and fringed with dark lashes, her full mouth was inviting, and her long, luxuriant hair was a rich, golden auburn.

"Want to join me?" he asked. Seeing her hesitate, he added persuasively, "I sure could use some help cracking all these hickory nuts."

She blushed prettily then said shyly, "There's no place to sit."

Cash made a seat for her with his long legs. "You may sit here if you'll be mine."

He expected her to decline. Or perhaps tell him he was being much too familiar, and flounce away. That was certainly what she should do as a proper young lady. After all, they hadn't been introduced and didn't even know each other's name.

Instead, to the surprise of both of them, she hesitated then boldly sat down in his lap. Her dark hair lightly brushed his cheek, and the sweet scent of her perfume mingled with the heady aroma of hickory nuts and spring grass. "I guess I'm yours," she said, without a hint of shyness.

Their eyes met, their faces were only inches apart. She felt light as a feather on his lap. The forwardness he'd shown only a moment earlier dissolved, and he was at a complete loss as to what to say or do. He only knew that he wished she'd stay there forever.

The unmistakable romantic tension between them was broken by the return of the girls. Abruptly, the young woman jumped up from Cash's lap. Mary Todd looked at them in shock and dismay. Her jealous feelings were painfully apparent to everyone.

The older woman chaperoning the group, Mrs. John Allen, who was Cash's cousin, took in the entire situation in an instant. Clapping her hands to get everyone's attention, she told the girls it was late and they must be on their way home. They hurried off, an unhappy Mary Todd with them.

The young woman sitting on Cash's lap, got up slowly, gave him a sidelong glance, murmured "Good day," and sauntered off.

Mrs. Allen turned to Cash. "Cousin Cash, I see that you are much taken with Mary Jane Warfield."

Cash knew the name. Her father, Dr. Elisha Warfield, was a member of the medical school faculty, and prominent in horse racing circles. This young woman who had so brazenly flirted with him was from one of the first families of Lexington. Her social position made her behavior all the more surprising – and intriguing.

Before Cash could ask any of the questions whirling around in his mind – how old is she? Does she have a beau? – Mrs. Allen said tartly, "Whatever you do, don't marry a Warfield. If you do, you'll be sorry for the rest of your life."

Cash was shocked. He couldn't believe she would say such a thing. It was both rude and presumptuous, uncharacteristic behavior for his normally sweet-natured and soft-spoken cousin.

"Why?" he asked bluntly.

She frowned. "I'm sure I can't say," she hedged, apparently regretting her impulsive words.

But his cousin's frank advice would ring in his memory for the next forty years . . .

Months later, Cash graduated from Transylvania. He was putting the last of his clothes and personal possessions into his trunk when Mary came into his room. Since the disturbing scene between Mary Jane and Cash, Mary had changed from the brash girl who was clearly smitten with him, to someone quieter, more reserved. Cash spent most of his free time outside of school with Mary Jane, so Mary didn't see much of him anyway. But now as she looked at his trunk and thought of him leaving, she felt a sharp jolt of loss.

"Where are you going?" she asked, trying to keep her tone lighter than she felt.

"I thought I'd go on up and check out Yale University. They say it's the best school to graduate from if you're going to practice law."

"So you've definitely settled on the law, then?"

"If I want to change the law, I need to study it first," he responded.

"How long will you be gone?"

"A couple of years to finish my post-graduate work, then off to Louisville or even one of the big eastern cities. It depends on which law firm will have me."

Cash looked at her with compassion. He knew now how she felt about him. He'd known it the moment he saw the hurt, jealous look in her eyes when she saw him flirting with Mary Jane. He regretted how hurt she would be by his next words. "I don't expect to come back here, Mary."

Mary had been determined to handle all this in a mature manner, to impress Cash with the fact that she was now a sensible young woman and not a flighty girl. But she couldn't help herself. She burst out, "You can't go, you just can't! It isn't fair! I've hardly seen you! You spend all your time with her! And now you're going away forever!"

"Mary, I'm so sorry . . . "

She burst into tears and ran out of the room, thoroughly humiliated by the spectacle she'd made of herself. Cash started to go after her, to try to help somehow. Then he stopped. He realized there was nothing he could do or say to make Mary feel better. His pity would only make her feel worse. The best thing he could do for her was to leave as quickly as possible and let her begin the painful process of putting her feelings for him behind her.

He was extremely fond of her in the way he would have been if she'd been his little sister. He hoped that before too long, some other young man would capture her heart, and she'd find the happiness he couldn't offer her. That way, when he married Mary Jane after graduating from law school, Mary would be okay.

He couldn't say exactly when he'd made up his mind that he wanted to spend the rest of his life with Mary Jane. Perhaps it had happened in the first moment their eyes met. He only knew that his life would be incomplete without her. He hadn't felt this way about any girl since his first love -- the young slave, Mary -- had been dragged out of his life forever.

For a long, lonely time he was afraid he'd never feel that way again. But he did now. And it was all because a lovely, outgoing young woman had thrown convention to the wind and responded to his impudent suggestion with an irresistible impudence of her own.

After graduation, Cash traveled extensively. He arranged meetings with some of the greatest men, and women, of the time – including President Jackson. Being a Henry Clay Whig, Cash's political beliefs were the opposite of Jackson's. But the President was nevertheless polite to him. And Cash was thoroughly impressed by the President's moral courage as he dealt with affairs of state.

Cash also met with Martin Van Buren, Daniel Webster (who had the largest private library Cash had ever seen), John Greenleaf Whittier, Julia Ward Howe, and many others. He was eager to learn all that he could from each of them.

The one subject he was most eager to discuss with these distinguished people was slavery. He wrote to his brother, Brutus, "The slave question is now assuming an importance in the opinions of the enlightened and humane, which prejudice and interest cannot long withstand. The slaves of Virginia, Kentucky and in fact all the slave holding states must soon be free!"

Once he was settled at Yale, Cash carefully observed how the economy of the North, with its free working class, worked in comparison to the slave-holding South. In the North, education was common, not just reserved for the ruling elite. There was prosperity all around, and relatively few signs of the kind of abject poverty that existed in the South. Besides being a moral issue, Cash realized that slavery simply didn't work economically.

Like Henry Clay Cash realized that prosperity in the South depended on free and educated workers. Though his cousin was a slaveholder, he was also a gradual emancipationist who called for the abolition of slavery within a generation. Cash agreed with this time table. It would be too disruptive to abruptly cast slaves out into the world to fend for themselves. First, they desperately needed something that had been denied to them – education.

That fall Cash was in his dormitory room at Yale when his roommate, Bill Jenkins, rushed in excitedly. "How'd you like to go with me an' Pete to New York over the weekend?"

Cash didn't need to think about that. "Sounds like a great idea. I need a break."

"We're leaving right after class tomorrow. Pete has his own carriage, and we can be in the city by Saturday night."

"You're on. I'll be packed and ready to go."

"Are you going to the lecture tonight?" Bill asked.

"I don't see why I should. I'm already against slavery, so what's the point?"

"They say that Garrison is one hell of a speaker. It might be worth it just to hear how he presents his closing argument."

Cash considered this. "Persuasive closing arguments are a big part of what successful lawyers are made of."

"And politicians," Bill added.

Cash responded emphatically, "A low-down politician is something you'll never catch me becoming."

Bill laughed. "That's how a lot of people feel about lawyers, in case you haven't heard."

That night Cash sat in the packed auditorium, listening avidly to William Lloyd Garrison. He studied Garrison's demeanor, determined to learn from him. He noticed that the charismatic speaker was careful to make eye contact, at least briefly, with everyone in the room. At least it sure seemed that way. Cash was also impressed with the way Garrison used illustrations and graphics to make his points.

"It is one thing to say you oppose slavery," Garrison intoned in a commanding voice that captured and held the attention of everyone in the room. "And another to do something about it. To do nothing is to join forces with the slaveholders, as they feel you don't care one way or the other. It isn't right and you know it! What are you going to do about it?! Join us and help us do something to stop this horrible sin called slavery!"

With that, the meeting ended. Garrison joined some other people who were signing people up for different tasks, including being a part of a system to help slaves escape to the North and freedom.

As they rose to leave and walk back to their room, Bill turned to Cash. "What did you think?"

"He's a damn good speaker," Cash allowed. He had been deeply affected by Garrison's words. He felt as if those words had combined with his own bitter experience to arouse his very soul. But Garrison's violent approach was disturbing.

Cash added hesitantly, "But what he's proposing is anarchy."

"Sometimes we have to break the law in order to change it," Bill insisted. "Remember the Boston Tea Party?"

"That was a whole different situation. Rebellion was the only answer. But the end of slavery can be brought about in different ways. Through education, for example."

Bill clearly wasn't convinced. Cash pressed on, "We put an end to slavery on our plantation. And financially we're doing better than ever. But our workers didn't have to worry about where they would go or what they would do. They were each given a plot of land to sustain themselves."

"If everyone had your compassionate heart, Cash, slavery would end tomorrow. But most people aren't like you. It's going to take someone like Garrison to get people fired up enough to change things."

"The answer is to change the law," Cash argued, with the passionate conviction he brought to all serious debates. "Not break the law."

"But who's going to do that?" Bill demanded. "Certainly not you, since you despise politicians."

Cash rarely lost an argument, but this time he was lost for a response.

The truth was that even though what Garrison proposed was radical by most Southerners' standards, Cash couldn't get the man's words out of his thoughts. They touched something deep within him that had been building for some time. But he wasn't yet ready to take such a giant step of following Garrison, for it would put him at odds with nearly everyone he knew back home.

The next evening the three young men were riding in Pete's carriage, headed for New York. But it didn't look like they'd make it to the city that night. Pete's horse sounded as if it was on its last legs.

"We'd better stop somewhere and buy another horse," Cash said, only half-jokingly.

"He'll be all right," Pete insisted. "He's sounded worse than this before."

They were just coming up to a large white church. A sign out front said, "Anaconda Baptist Church. Revival service every

Saturday night. Reverend William Peakes presiding." Dozens of carriages stood outside. "Maybe we could borrow one of those horses," Bill suggested with a laugh.

"Sure," Cash said, grinning. "Stealing a horse outside a church. Great lawyers we're gonna be if we take to crime before we even graduate."

At that moment, the carriage came to a stop. The horse simply refused to go one step further.

"So much for a good time in New York," Cash said dryly.

"Looks like we're gonna have to get saved if we're gonna get us another horse from these people," Bill quipped. The three young men got out of the carriage and walked toward the church.

"Well, I know more about the Bible than both of you combined," Cash boasted.

Inside, they took seats in the last pew. Old Bill Peake was in top form. His powerful voice rose and fell, as he alternately cajoled and threatened his congregation. "Some of you think you're Christians because you come here to church every week. Or because you read your Bible and maybe have memorized a few verses."

He glared at the crowd as if challenging each and every one of them to dare argue with him. As Garrison had done the night before, Peak made eye contact with everyone – including Cash. Most people averted their eyes from his piercing look. Not Cash. He looked right back at him, unflinching.

"Some of you think you're Christians because you don't drink or smoke or swear. Well, my dog don't drink, smoke or swear and that don't make him a Christian!"

He paused to let the significance of that statement sink in. Then he continued, "Jesus said the way you could tell if someone was a Christian was when he saw others in need and did something about it. It isn't enough to walk past people who are hungry or need clothes on their backs, and to pat them on the head and say, 'God bless you.' No! That's not being a Christian! If you can do something to help someone and you do nothing, you're not a Christian."

Something began to stir deep inside Cash. Something he didn't want to acknowledge. As Peake went on, Cash began to feel more and more uncomfortable.

"You say you want to do the right thing. But sometimes, for some reason, you just don't. Well, my friend, you need to ask Jesus to

40

come into your heart. He'll give you the courage and the strength to do the right thing, no matter how hard it is."

He paused, took a deep breath, then finished in an exhausted but triumphant voice, "Everyone please stand and raise your hands and ask Jesus into your heart. Ask him to change you and to remove your doubts and fears and give you the courage to do the right thing. I promise he won't fail you."

Throughout the sermon, Bill and Pete had waited impatiently for Peake to finish speaking, so they could find someone willing to sell them a horse. But Cash stood up with the rest of the congregation, his hands in the air, his lips moving in silent prayer.

Garrison's words echoed in Cash's mind. It's one thing to oppose slavery and another to do something about it! At that moment Cash could see George's doubting expression as Cash promised that one day Negroes would be able to attend a fine college. It'll happen, George, I promise. Then he saw Mary, the young mulatto slave who was his first experience with what he thought at the time was love. He heard her desperate voice calling to him as a wagon took her away from everyone and everything she had ever known and loved. Master Clay! Please don't let them take me. Please, Master Clay!

Cash reeled under the onslaught of emotion that these memories brought. He felt sick at heart and profoundly ashamed at how naïve and ineffective he'd been. He cared deeply about both George and Mary, but he hadn't really done a damn thing for either of them. He certainly hadn't helped them in the way they most needed his help. At that moment of epiphany, he felt that the "good seed" that Garrison had watered, and which his own bitter experience had sown, aroused his whole soul.

"Cash? Cash? You all right?" Bill asked. Cash looked at him, not really seeing him. "We'd best find someone who'll sell us a horse or we'll never get to New York."

Cash pulled himself together. But his voice was a little ragged around the edges as he spoke. "You two go on. I think I'll just make other arrangements, if you don't mind. I can catch the stage back to school tomorrow."

"Where will you stay tonight?" Pete asked.

But Cash had already left them and was walking up to Rev. Peake.

The Reverend watched the tall young man, who towered over nearly everyone else, coming toward him. Cash stopped in front of him and said with heartfelt emotion, "I just want you to know, reverend, that what you said touched me more deeply than any words I've ever heard before."

"It wasn't me or what I said, young man. It was the Holy Spirit talking to you. We all have a purpose in life. Mine is to be a vessel for God's spirit to speak to young people like yourself. You have a purpose – a greater purpose than you ever could imagine. God put you on this earth for a reason. He brought you here tonight so you could figure out that reason and fulfill His purpose."

Bill had followed Cash. "Excuse me," he interrupted. "Do you know where we can buy a horse for our carriage?"

Rev. Peake smiled. "Yes, I do. I have a horse you can buy. And a room at my house for this young fellow. Just follow me in your carriage."

The three young men walked behind the reverend as he made his way through the crowd as it exited the church, men and women leaving through separate doors.

"What happened in there?" Bill asked Cash. "Did you tell him we needed a horse and you needed a place to stay?"

Cash was lost in thought and didn't respond.

They got into the carriage. When Pete snapped the reins, the horse started trotting briskly, as if nothing was wrong with him. "Looks like Old Thunder got over whatever was ailing him," Pete said in amazement. "I think we can make New York tonight, after all."

"Just catch up with the reverend," Cash said. "I'll ride with him to his house."

Bill started to argue, "But . . ."

Cash went on firmly, "I'll see you back at school."

"I don't understand," Bill said in frustration.

Cash looked at him and said calmly, as if it were the most reasonable thing in the world, "I just figured out something that should've been obvious. Just being a lawyer isn't enough, if I want to help get rid of slavery. I need to go where the power is. And that means becoming a politician."

Bill was flabbergasted. "But you're close to getting your law degree!"

"Oh, I'll get my degree, all right. It's a handy thing to have, when you're making the laws. But mark my words; I'll do something about slavery."

Bill said, "I grant that you have all the attributes of a successful politician. You're smart, you can give a speech like nobody I've ever heard, and being rich doesn't much hurt, either. But your antislavery position will kill any hope you have for a successful political career."

"I don't agree," Cash insisted confidently. "But if you're right, so be it. My principles are more important than my ambitions."

Bill just shook his head in bemusement at his friend. He'd never known anyone with the force of character that Cash presented. If anyone could achieve a distinguished political career in spite of an unpopular stance on slavery, it was Cash Clay.

Pete had pulled up beside the reverend's carriage, which had stopped. Cash jumped out and got in the carriage with the reverend. As they pulled away from a stunned Pete and Bill, Cash called out, "Have a good time, boys!

CHAPTER FIVE

1832

Cash graduated with honors and was chosen by his Yale classmates to give a speech at their graduation ceremony. Standing at the podium in University Hall, he was an impressive figure. His thick, dark hair and eyes contrasted with his fair skin. A high-collared velvet coat and white shirt with a cravat framed his full, sensitive mouth and strong chin. Sporting a mustache now, he looked like the fully-grown man he'd become.

Now he gazed out at the sea of faces before him – professors, fellow graduates, families and friends. Normally he wasn't nervous about public speaking, but giving the commencement address to this impressive gathering did test his composure a bit. Especially since he knew full well that what he was about to say would displease, even enrage, many of the people in this audience. He was about to give his first antislavery speech to a public gathering.

The previous year he had written to his brother, Brutus, that slavery must be eradicated or it would lead to the dissolution of the government at some point in the not-too-distant future. He wrote, "The glove is already thrown down. The Northern and Southern champions stand in sullen defiance."

But putting his views in writing, and proclaiming them before an august gathering, were two very different things. He felt an unaccustomed nervousness as he stood before this group who waited expectantly to hear what he had to say.

In the front row sat his mother, sister, brothers and George. Cash met George's encouraging look and felt better.

He began, "Today, as I stand before you, I ask, do you not have any painful thoughts that disturb your conscience? Are there none somewhere today, who are cast down and sorrowful, who dare not approach a place like this; those who cannot put their

45

hands to their hearts and say, 'Oh, Washington, what do you mean to us? Are we not also supposed to be free men?'"

He paused to let the meaning of his words fully get through to the audience. Then he continued with even more passionate conviction, "God said, 'Foolish man, lay down thy offering, go thy way, become reconciled to thy brother, and then come and make thy offering.'"

Cash's family and George applauded again in support. Cash continued, "You need not the eyes of God to see that differences of interest are at work in this vast territory. Washington saw it; we see it. The glove is already thrown down; the Northern and Southern champions stand in sullen defiance."

He paused then finished in ringing tones, "I hope that a blinded people will not rest secure in their lies and deception, until the birthright left us by our Washington is lost! Till you awake one day to find yourself surrounded by the rotting ruins of what was once a great nation!"

He was done. He stood there for a moment as utter silence engulfed the room. Then his family and George stood and applauded vigorously. At first they were the only ones doing so. Then others joined in, and soon the majority of people were standing, with tears in their eyes, clapping resoundingly.

But many people remained seated and looked disapproving. Cash's words were heresy to them.

Moments later the ceremony was over and the graduates exuberantly threw their caps in the air in time-honored tradition. They went to meet their families, as did Cash. As he walked up to them, Brutus stepped forward to greet him first and extended his hand. "Congratulations, little brother. That was quite a speech." Then his mother hugged him tightly. "I'm so proud of you, son. If your dear father were here, he'd say the same."

Cash was glowing with pride. "Thank you, Mother. That means a lot." He turned to George and after a moment's hesitation, the two old friends hugged warmly. "I'm so glad you could be here, George."

George grinned. "Your brothers insisted I come, even though it's planting time." Then he whispered to Cash, "They pay us all cash money now. Everybody – Bessie, Luther, Henry, the whole McDaniel family and Aunt Emma."

"They've learned that a free economy works better and harder than a captive one," Cash whispered back.

George glanced around the huge auditorium in awe. "This school's even bigger and nicer than the other one!"

Cash's exuberant expression turned sober. Neither George nor any other black man had the opportunity to take advantage of all that this place offered. "It will come, George," he said with conviction. "I promise you that before I die, your day will come."

At that moment, Mary Jane Warfield ran up to Cash, threw her arms around him and looked at him with utter adoration. "I thought we'd never get through the crowd!"

Looking down at her, Cash felt flooded with relief. Finally, after four long years, they could get married and she would be his.

Mary Jane's parents had lagged behind. Now they joined the circle of people surrounding Cash. Dr. Warfield shook Cash's hand and said warmly, "You have my congratulations, son."

Cash hadn't yet told Mary Jane's parents of his intentions toward their daughter. He was relieved to see that apparently Dr. Warfield, at least, approved of him. Her mother, he knew, was another matter entirely. Mary Jane had told Cash that her mother would have the final say about any engagement, and she could be quite difficult. He wondered now if that was what his cousin had been referring to when she'd warned him not to marry into the Warfield family.

Standing a few feet away, Mary Todd and her mother watched Cash accept congratulations all around. Mary's expression was pained as she saw the way Cash looked at Mary Jane. The passage of time had not lessened her feelings for him. She was a grown woman now, but no other young man had captured her heart. And she was convinced no one else ever would.

Mrs. Todd eyed her daughter thoughtfully for a moment, then said carefully, "Instead of going right back to Lexington, why don't we visit Elizabeth in Springfield?" Mary's older sister was married to a successful young attorney there. "John knows a great many eligible young men in the law and other professions. You could have a very gay time, indeed."

Mary didn't respond. She didn't care about any "eligible young men" her brother-in-law might know. She only cared about the young man standing so near to her. The young man she couldn't have.

Her mother went on determinedly, "In fact, there's one young attorney John spoke very highly of. Abraham Lincoln, I believe his name is. John thinks he'll go far." As Mary remained silent, her mother finished, "Yes, I definitely think we'll have a nice, long visit in Springfield."

A week after graduation, Cash, accompanied by George, finally returned to White Hall. His mother and brothers had returned immediately after the ceremony, but Cash had last-minute business to attend to. Now, as the carriage carrying Cash and George drove past the sweeping bluegrass lawn, down the road banked with towering magnolia trees, toward the home Cash hadn't seen in so long, he felt a wave of emotion. He loved this place almost as much as he loved the people who lived there.

The carriage pulled up to the front entrance and Luther and Henry greeted Cash enthusiastically. "Welcome home, Mister Cash," Luther said, smiling broadly. Cash returned the warm smile. How wonderful it was, he thought, to be called "mister" and not "master."

Cash started to walk inside, and then stopped as he saw George heading toward the old slave quarters behind the house. "I thought we'd have dinner together. Play a little chess later on."

Despite the profound changes here, George still knew his place. "I best leave you to have some private time with your family. I'm sure you have a lot to talk about."

Watching George disappear around the side of the house, Cash realized that things hadn't changed entirely. It still wasn't all right for a black man to sit at a white man's table and break bread with him.

Sally Clay had remarried and moved away from White Hall, as had Cash's brothers and sister. While Cash was in school, Brutus had served as overseer of the farm and other holdings, and had managed well. For Cash's homecoming, Sally, Brutus and Sydney had returned for a visit.

Later that night the remains of a veritable feast – roast beef, a huge ham, and a large turkey, along with side dishes – were still on the dining room table as Cash and his family lingered over coffee. Brutus, seated at the head of the table, said to Bessie, "I'll have another glass of that French brandy. How about you, Cash?"

Cash smiled. "No, thanks. I'm still working on my third piece of blueberry pie."

Brutus gestured to the food as he spoke to Bessie. "Take what's left of all this out to your people. Along with that blueberry pie, before my brother makes himself sick."

Bessie said gratefully, "Thank you so much, Master Clay."

Cash frowned. He hated that Bessie felt the need to address his brother that way. And he was disappointed in Brutus for not correcting Bessie and reminding her that he was no longer her master.

Brutus sipped his drink and puffed on a cigar. He was trying hard to step into their father's shoes. Cash loved his brother, and looked up to him in many ways, as a younger brother should. But he knew those shoes were far too big for Brutus to ever fill them.

Looking at Cash, Brutus asked, "Well, brother, now that you have your law degree from that fine university, what do you plan to do with it?"

"I'd like to run for state representative in the fall." Glancing around at his family, he said, "I assume you all approve."

Both of his brothers roared their approval. Sydney said, "Approve?! Why, we're all absolutely delighted. You'll have the family backing you all the way, and you know what that means."

Cash did, indeed. His family's backing ensured that he would be one of the Lexington area's representatives in the state legislature by the following fall when the next election was held.

Cash's mother spoke up. "That's a worthy goal, son."

Brutus said excitedly, "I can think of a dozen things that need to be changed. First, there's this new tax on tobacco. Then you have the ground tax based on the area that's fenced on your land . . ."

Cash listened quietly as Brutus listed all the things he'd like to see him do. Cash didn't bring up the one issue he cared about more than any other. The issue that was his entire reason for getting involved in politics. The abolition of slavery . . .

The next day Cash rode over the "farm," as even large plantations were called in Kentucky. There were bountiful crops of tobacco, corn, wheat, hemp and sugar cane in the bottom lands. Cattle and sheep grazed in lush pastures. Brutus had managed well while Cash was away at school. But Cash was master of White Hall and was eager to take on full responsibility for it. He knew he'd have his hands full, managing the farm and running for political office. But he was completely confident that he could handle both. At that moment he felt that with the gifts a generous God had given him – wealth, social position, intellect and robust strength -- there was nothing he couldn't do. Including eradicate slavery.

But before putting his ambitious plans in motion, there was something equally important he had to attend to. And he knew just how he intended to do it.

For the remainder of the summer Cash took every opportunity to spend time with Mary Jane and her parents. He was confident that Mary Jane returned his loving feelings, although she'd never exactly said it in so many words. But he wanted her parents to accept him. Mary Jane had an extremely close relationship with them and probably wouldn't defy them if they told her this wasn't a suitable match.

So Cash danced attendance on Mary Jane, and did his best to impress her parents with his maturity and sterling character. And when he felt his position was strong enough, he made his move.

One early fall day Cash picked up Mary Jane at her parents' imposing new sixteen-room brick mansion, built in classic-revival style, and called "The Meadows." He had told her they would go hickory nut gathering. They drove in his carriage out to a nearby wooded area, where the trees had turned brilliant shades of gold, crimson and orange. As he had been doing when they first met, Cash sat on the ground and used two rocks to hull the nuts that Mary Jane gathered and brought to him. A sudden case of nerves made him postpone the speech he had carefully prepared, until there was an impressive pile of hulled nuts.

Cash looked up from his task when Mary Jane laughed suddenly as she watched two chattering gray squirrels chase each other up a nearby tree. Her dress was as expensively tailored as usual, but she'd thrown off her bonnet, and her disheveled hair hung down her back. At that moment, she was the most adorable creature he'd ever seen. And so lovely she made his breath catch in his throat.

He rose and walked over to her, taking her hands in his. As she looked up at him curiously, he forgot all about the speech he'd spent hours preparing. Instead, he said what was in his heart. "Mary Jane – you know I love you. You've known it from the first moment I laid eyes on you. Will you marry me?"

She didn't even pretend to be surprised. She'd expected this proposal ever since Cash's graduation. The only unexpected aspect was how long it had taken him. For a moment she considered letting him dangle for a bit on the end of her line. But she was just as besotted with him as he was with her, and she couldn't make herself pretend otherwise.

"Yes, Cash, I'll marry you," she said simply, her eyes meeting his.

He let out the breath he'd been holding. And he did something he'd wanted to do since that day when she had plopped down in his lap. He kissed her, tenderly, but with a passion barely held in check by the proprieties that had been drilled into him.

It didn't occur to him that that perhaps they should discuss what their married life would be like. He simply assumed that Mary Jane would share his views, especially about slavery. And that she would, of course, whole-heartedly support his political ambitions. After all, this was his life's calling. Surely, the woman he loved to distraction would appreciate how important this was to him.

Later, he asked her father for her hand in marriage. Dr. Warfield, who had known this moment was coming as surely as the changing of the seasons, gave his ascent. Only later did Cash learn that Mrs. Warfield, a proud and imperious woman, was furious that he hadn't first asked her for her daughter's hand in marriage. By then, it was too late to heal an unintended breach that would grow wider over the years. The seeds of alienation and distrust sowed by Mrs. Warfield would eventually bear fruit.

One week later posters declaring "Cassius Clay for State Representative" were nailed to trees all over the county. A picnic was held in the town park, with free food supplied by Cash. Delivering his first speech as a political candidate, Cash used a copy of the Constitution, a small Bible, pistols and a Bowie knife to emphasize the points he made. The crowd responded enthusiastically. His campaign was off to a rousing start.

Later, at the barbershop, a newspaper was passed around. The customers read with interest the full-page ad extolling the strengths and virtues of Cassius Clay.

There was a bright full moon on election night. Cash galloped down the road toward White Hall. Even with the light of the moon and the kerosene lanterns hanging on either side of the front door, it was still dark.

When he arrived at the entrance and dismounted, Luther, Henry and George were waiting on the front steps. Luther asked anxiously, "Mr. Cash, what's the word?"

Cash flashed a smile at the men, but didn't answer. He flung open the door and entered, closely followed by George, only to find his family waiting. They had gathered at White Hall to celebrate what they were confident would be an overwhelming victory.

"Well?!" Brutus demanded. Cash let the question hang in the air dramatically for a moment. Then he burst into a huge grin. "We won!"

His brothers cheered, his mother and sister took turns hugging him, and George beamed at him.

"What was the margin?" Sydney asked. "How many votes did you win by?"

"Three to one!" Can you believe it? Three to one!"

"This calls for a celebration," Sydney said. "Bring out the champagne."

Just then Bessie and Aunt Emma came in with a bottle of champagne in a bucket of ice. Brutus said with a laugh, "I'm way ahead of you, brother. I told Bessie to be ready and waiting."

When glasses were filled and passed around, Brutus gave a toast. "Here's to our little brother, Cash – our new state representative." He noticed that Cash didn't have a glass. "Where's your champagne? Aren't you going to celebrate with us?"

"I'm getting to work as a representative right this minute. I've got to write an acceptance speech to give at the courthouse in the morning. And I've got to start planning my agenda." He looked meaningfully at George, "There's a lot of hard work in front of me to make some changes happen."

George felt a surge of hope. If anyone could make profound change happen, Cash could.

The next morning Cash alighted from his carriage in front of the courthouse in the town square. A waiting crowd gave him a big round of applause as he helped his mother down. Brutus and Sydney followed. Cash noticed George in the crowd, and they exchanged a triumphant smile.

Before Cash could address the crowd, the county clerk, wearing a sober expression, confronted him. "We had no reason to question that you were old enough to run for office, Mr. Clay. A big, strapping young man like yourself. But Mr. Palmer," he gestured toward a man Cash knew only slightly, "insists I ask you now – what exactly is your date of birth?"

Cash was confused. "Why?"

"Because you have to be twenty-five years old to in order to take office."

Cash's expression was stricken. "I . . . I won't be twenty-five for three months."

"I'm sorry, young man. But you're going to have to wait until the next election and run again, if you really want to be state representative. For now, Mr. Hutchings holds onto the position."

The clerk turned and hurried away, wanting no further part in this unpleasantness.

Feeling like he'd just had the wind knocked out of him, Cash turned to his mother. "We'd best be getting home. There's nothing we can do about this."

He helped her back into the carriage. As he got in, he caught George's perplexed look. His heart sank even more. He could live with his own deep disappointment here. But he couldn't bear the thought that he'd disappointed his best friend, who had counted on him to try to make things right.

Brutus and Sydney just stared at him in helpless sympathy.

Looking out the window of the carriage, Sally Clay's attention was caught by Palmer, who was looking at them and smirking. Next to him stood Hutchings. The now-triumphant representative said something to his companion, and they laughed as if sharing a particularly good joke.

Sally said to Cash, "You don't think . . . no, surely they couldn't be that immoral."

"What, mother?"

"Is it possible that Representative Hutchings and Mr. Palmer knew all along that you were too young?" She shook her head. "No, that's just too wicked to even think about. Why would anyone do such a thing?"

Cash's tone was hard. "To guarantee that Hutchings would win by default. To make us spend a great deal of money on a futile campaign." He forced down his rising anger. "But it's my own fault. I should have been aware of the age requirement. I made it easy for them to win."

There was utter silence in the carriage. Neither his mother nor his brothers had any idea what to say. Suddenly, Cash went on in a less defeated tone, "But there are a lot of people here. And I'm going to take advantage of that."

He got out of the carriage and stood before the crowd that hadn't yet dispersed. They hadn't heard the exchange with the clerk, and were still waiting for Cash to make his acceptance speech. Seeing this, Hutchings was surprised. He said to Palmer, "What does he think he's up to? The clerk told him he's history."

Palmer, too, looked mystified, and just a little bit worried.

Cash stood before the crowd, looking cool and confident now. He spoke in a voice loud enough to carry to the people furthest away. "Friends, neighbors and fellow citizens of the great state of Kentucky, I have a confession to make. In my zeal and desire to become your elected representative, I failed to wait until I reached the necessary age of twenty-five, which is three months from now."

The crowd responded with shock and dismay. Disappointment and anger – some at the law and some at Cash – rippled through the audience. "No!" someone shouted. Someone else called out, "What difference does it make if you're old enough, Mr. Clay? You're big enough to do the job." A chant began, "We want Clay! We want Clay!"

Cash's attention was focused on George. Seeing the hurt and disappointment in George's expression was painful.

Cash motioned to the crowd to quiet down, and then he went resumed speaking, "I have let you down, and I am profoundly sorry. But the law is the law. Mr. Hutchings is a good man and I'm sure he'll continue to do a good job as your representative for the next two years."

Someone shouted, "We don't want Hutchings! We voted for you, Clay!"

"I'll be running again next time," he vowed. "And if you vote for me again, I promise you that I'll work even harder and do an even better job for you than I would've done now." He paused for full dramatic effect, and then finished in a shout, "I will be your representative! And I will make you proud!"

The crowd shouted their appreciation. As people rushed up to Cash to shake his hand and slap him on the back, Cash noticed Hutchings and Palmer slip away together. But his attention wasn't on them. It was on George, who continued clapping, long after everyone else had quit.

CHAPTER SIX

1833

One month later a lavish dinner party was given at Whitehall, and the Warfields were there. Mary Jane was the focus of all attention and interest – especially from the male guests and Cash's brothers. She was stunning in a crimson satin gown with almost scandalously low décolletage.

When dinner was nearly over, Cash banged his spoon against his empty crystal wine glass, bringing everyone to attention. "I want to thank Mr. And Mrs. Warfield and Mary Jane for being our honored guests this evening." He exchanged a loving look with her then went on, "Mary Jane and I wanted you all – our closest friends and family – to be the first to hear our good news. We are engaged to be married!"

There were expressions of surprise and joy from the people gathered around the table. Sally Clay was delighted and not at all surprised. She had expected this announcement to come as soon as her son graduated from law school. She smiled at the young couple. "I am so very happy for both of you, my dears." To Cash she said, "You couldn't have chosen a more . . ." She searched for just the right word.

Before she could finish, Brutus interrupted. "More ravishingly beautiful bride!"

There was audible agreement from the men, and a hint of jealousy in the looks of the women.

After both Cash and Mary Jane had accepted the congratulations of everyone, Sydney turned to Cash. "I must say, little brother, you have excellent taste in women. But aside from making such a marvelous match, what do you plan to do to occupy your time until you can run again for state representative? Have you thought about returning to run our little farm?"

Brutus was defensive. "Our 'little' farm consists of thousands of acres. I've been running it without any problem for over eight years now."

Cash knew his brother did not want him intruding on his territory. He hurried to reassure him that he had nothing to worry about. "Actually, since I majored in journalism, I thought I'd go to work for the newspaper here in Lexington."

This was a surprise to everyone in his family, and to Mary Jane. It rather surprised Cash, himself. Until that moment he hadn't actually decided what to do during the next couple of years.

Sydney hastened to smooth things over. "Have you thought about starting your own paper? Something a little more exciting than that stuffy old Lexington rag?"

That piqued Mary Jane's interest. She loved the idea of being the wife of a publisher of a newspaper that would undoubtedly be very influential.

Cash replied, "Of course, what journalism student doesn't dream of having his own paper? But it takes a lot of money to start a first-class one. Why, the cost of the press alone would be prohibitive."

Sydney didn't want to appear to be a piker when it came to sharing the family fortune with his brother. And he definitely wanted to encourage Cash to find another area of interest aside from the plantation. "Why don't you go into Cincinnati tomorrow and find out exactly what a press would cost? I've always felt the family should be in the newspaper business."

Cash wanted to make one thing perfectly clear before this went any farther. "I have a lot of ideas about how to run a paper. I'd want to be in charge."

"Of course," Sydney agreed.

"What would you call it?" Brutus asked.

"I don't know. I haven't thought about that." His mind raced with possibilities. Then he said, "How does 'The True American' sound?"

Mary Jane spoke up in support of her fiancé. "It sounds perfect!"

The next two months were spent acquiring a press, hiring an editor and pressman and securing a building. After what seemed to the impatient Cash to be an inordinately long wait, he and Mary Jane together finally read the first edition of "The True

American," hot off the press. The top headline read, "PREMIER EDITION – THE WORKINGMAN'S PAPER."

She said happily, "At least now you won't have to go into that foolish career of politics."

He looked at her in surprise. She'd never said anything to indicate she didn't support his political career. He said firmly, "Just the opposite, my dear. I am now a future politician with my own newspaper. It's a perfect combination to guarantee success."

Mary Jane knew better than to argue head on with her willful and determined fiancé. Changing the subject, she said, "I tried on my wedding gown today. It's magnificent. But you can't see it until Saturday." She finished with a coquettish smile, "You'll have to wait until then to see the lingerie my sister sent over from France, too."

Cash's brief irritation with her was gone in an instant. She was once again the vivacious, irresistible creature he'd fallen passionately in love with.

He couldn't wait until Saturday, when she would become his forever. He foresaw nothing but a bright and shining future ahead of them.

The wedding ceremony took place outdoors, on a broad lawn behind Whitehall mansion. The crowd was enormous. Mary Jane had invited many more people than Cash had. He couldn't believe she knew this many people. There were so many, in fact, that people at the back couldn't see the bride and groom as they exchanged vows in front of a makeshift altar.

A young man climbed up into a tree, and using opera glasses, described to people on the ground what was happening. "I believe he's about to kiss the bride."

He was, indeed. As their lips met, it looked to everyone like the romantic epitome of true love.

Afterwards, the hundreds of guests were all eating, drinking, talking and laughing. Cash and Mary Jane stood together, accepting everyone's best wishes. Holding a champagne glass in one hand, Brutus came up to them. He took the bride's hand in his, and when he spoke it was clear that he'd had too much to drink. "May I?"

She thought he was asking to kiss her hand. "Of course."

But Brutus wasn't about to settle for that. He kissed her lips, hard. Startled, Mary Jane pulled back. Brutus grinned, then turned to Cash, who was glowering at him. "That's a fine woman you have there, Cash. Take good care of her."

"I intend to," Cash said tightly.

"Here's your present from the family," Brutus went on as if he'd done nothing wrong. He handed Cash a key. "It's to the cottage on the pond. There's a fireplace in the master bedroom. Of course, you two won't need a fire to keep you warm tonight, I'll warrant," he finished with a suggestive wink.

To Cash's intense relief Brutus moved off. Cash turned to his bride. "I apologize for my brother's disrespectful behavior." She smiled prettily and whispered in a voice so low that only he could hear, "Actually, sweetheart, Brutus is right. I don't believe we'll need a fire tonight."

Cash felt a thrill of anticipation. "I do love you, Mrs. Clay. By the way, your gown is, indeed, beautiful. But not nearly as beautiful as you are."

Mary Jane felt she could happily bask in the loving look in her new husband's eyes forever. But there were duties she had to attend to as the bride. "I must greet some of our guests, Cassius. You should see all the presents we have to open. But they'll just have to wait until we return from our honeymoon in New Orleans."

A few days later, the newlyweds were in New Orleans, at a small but elegant hotel in the French Quarter. Their room was furnished in the opulent French style, complete with canopied bed. Cash and Mary Jane lay in bed together. He was still asleep when she awoke. She looked at her big, strong husband for a moment in total happiness, then nudged him awake. "Cash, wake up. It's nearly noon. I'm starving. Let's ring downstairs for some breakfast to be sent up."

He opened his eyes slowly and surveyed his enchanting bride. She looked particularly fetching in her white lace nightgown, her hair in charming disarray. "Let's hold off on breakfast for awhile . . ." And he reached out for her.

Giggling, she jumped out of bed and pulled three times on the cord that summoned the serving staff. "Oh, no, you don't, Cassius. We're not spending our entire honeymoon in this bed. There's so much to see and do here -- so many shops with fine things from France and all over the world. Let's have coffee then go out to one of those sidewalk cafes. Please?"

Cash couldn't deny her anything when she looked at him in that beguiling way. "Of course," he agreed reluctantly. He would take her to all the cafes and shops and fancy restaurants she wanted to see. As long as they eventually returned to this room and this bed and each other.

58

CHAPTER SEVEN

Springfield, Illinois, was a small town with a quaint charm. Everyone seemed to know everyone else. People greeted each other politely as they passed on the street, the men tipping their hats to the ladies.

The words "Law Office" were painted on the front window of a small, two-story building. Inside, Mary Todd, who'd been helping out here as a way to keep busy and not think about Cash, stood at a filing cabinet that was nearly as tall as she was. As she searched for a file, her boss, Abraham Lincoln, Esquire, a very tall man with a dark beard, approached her with a letter in his large hand. "There's a letter for you, Mary. It's from Lexington."

She opened it eagerly and quickly scanned the contents, as Mr. Lincoln stood there a bit awkwardly, towering over her. He felt he should leave her to read the letter in private, but he could tell by her response that it was important and he was, frankly, curious. Mary had only worked for him for a brief time, but he was immediately taken with her dainty beauty. Already he was beginning to think they might have a future together.

Tears began welling up in her eyes. She looked up, to see Mr. Lincoln eyeing her with concern. "Something wrong, Mary?"

Quickly, she brushed away her tears. "No . . . that is, it's just news of friends who got married. I guess I'm so happy for them it made me cry. I'm all right."

They didn't look like tears of joy to him. He took her tiny hands in his. "Are you sure you're all right?"

Unable to contain herself any longer, she fell into his arms. He held her, comforting her, until her sobs finally subsided. She stepped back and looked up at him. "You're such a good man, Mr. Lincoln . . . a true friend. I'm so ashamed to behave this way."

"Mary, from the day you started working here, I have been trying to work up the courage to ask you to dinner. Will you join me tonight? And please call me Abraham."

Mary looked at him thoughtfully. He wasn't as handsome as Cash. He didn't have Cash's brash charm. She knew he would never take Cash's place in her heart. But he was, indeed, a good man. She respected and trusted him. Love could grow from that. Or at least a deep and abiding affection. Cash was part of her past, lost to her forever. Abraham presented a possible future. She forced herself to smile at him with more warmth than she actually felt. "That sounds lovely . . . Abraham."

CHAPTER EIGHT

1835

Almost exactly nine months after the New Orleans honeymoon, Cash paced back and forth in the parlor at Whitehall. Outside, crickets chirped in the warm summer night air. But the peace was shattered by a piercing scream coming from upstairs. There was a moment's silence, then another scream.

Cash turned to Brutus. "I'd better go up to her."

Brutus stopped him. "She told Bessie that she didn't want you to see her like this. It's embarrassing enough for her father to see her, and he's a physician."

Cash hesitated. He knew Brutus was right, but it took all his self-control not to go rushing up those stairs to his wife, who was clearly in agony.

In the bedroom, Mary Jane was panting in exhaustion and pain. Her nightgown was soaked with sweat. "No! I can't! It hurts too much! Please, please no more . . ."

Bessie mopped her brow with a cool, damp cloth and tried to comfort her, as she'd comforted two generations of women in this family. "It's all right, Miz Clay. Its little head is out now. It's almost over."

Mary Jane called out anxiously to her father. "Is it a boy?"

Dr. Warfield was preoccupied with the delivery, but he tried to sound patient as he said, "Can't tell yet."

Mary Jane was wracked by another fierce contraction, even worse than the others. She screamed again. Her father ordered her, "Push! Push hard!"

With what little strength remained in her tortured body, she forced herself to push with all her might. Her head and shoulders lifted off the bed as she bore down hard in spite of the pain. "It's coming!" her father said excitedly. "It's . . . a boy!"

Mary Jane fell back onto the pillow, as a wave of profound relief mixed with lingering pain engulfed her. A boy, she thought proudly. A son and heir for Cassius.

Her father put the child, wrapped tightly in a blanket, into her arms. Looking down at the tiny, red-faced infant, she beamed, the pain forgotten. "He's so beautiful! My little Elisha! Daddy, aren't you proud of your namesake?"

He smiled at his daughter and grandson. He was very proud, indeed. But even more than that, he was relieved that both mother and child had survived. All too often, they didn't.

In the parlor, Cash didn't know which was more frightening – the screams or the sudden silence. When he saw Bessie coming down the stairs, he hurried up to her. "Mary Jane?" he demanded anxiously.

"Doin' just fine, Mister Clay. Her and the baby both – a handsome boy!"

Cash felt a profound relief that went deeper than any emotion he'd ever experienced. He thanked God that Mary Jane was all right. And that he had a healthy son.

Bessie went on, "You can see him as soon as I get him all cleaned up."

"I want to see my wife."

"She wants to see you, too, but first she wants to get tidied up a bit. She had a real rough time. That baby was a big one, even for a boy." Bessie hesitated then hesitantly shared news she knew would disappoint Cash. "Miz Clay says he's to be called Elisha."

Cash was caught off-guard. They'd discussed names, and Mary Jane knew he wanted to name the child Cassius Jr., if it was a boy. If it was a girl, he'd agreed to let her name the baby after her mother, even though Mrs. Warfield was still very cool toward him. Mary Jane hadn't said anything to suggest she wanted to change this agreement.

"She told you this?" Cash asked Bessie.

"Told her daddy," Bessie answered.

Cash felt frustrated. He couldn't be rude to his father-in-law. He'd have to accept the name Elisha. He told himself that he would have more sons. But next time he'd make certain Mary Jane didn't take it upon herself to change things he thought they'd agreed on. His relief at knowing his wife and son were all right was tinged with a realization that Mary Jane was capable of a deviousness he never would have suspected.

Over the next ten years, Cash's life revolved around farming, running the newspaper and politics. The political conflict between pro-slavery and anti-slavery forces grew more and more bitter and divisive. As the state representative from Madison County, Cash quickly learned that his support of abolitionism engendered violent disagreement among many of the people he represented.

As Clay had predicted at Yale, northerners and southerners were in "sullen defiance" against one another.

Cash tried to make the pro-slavery politicians he worked with understand that slavery was not only an evil violation of basic human rights but it kept the South from growing economically. But his insistence that slavery was a "fatal disease" set him apart from his own class of wealthy, aristocratic landowners.

His political views and the fact that he was seen as a traitor to his own kind, created problems for Mary Jane. Like her mother, she was supremely social. She enjoyed her position at the height of Lexington society, and resented the fact that her husband's political career impacted that position.

In an attempt to mollify her, Cash agreed to buy a home in Lexington and spend most of their time there, rather than at White Hall, which was rather isolated.

He bought one of the most impressive mansions in the city, the "Lord Morton" house. While Mary Jane happily busied herself decorating the house and enjoying the social whirl, Cash focused on supporting his cousin, Henry Clay's, campaign for the presidency. But in spite of his energetic efforts, his cousin failed to win the Whig party's nomination.

Cash cemented his controversial reputation by opposing the repeal of a law that prohibited the importation of slaves into Kentucky for sale. He denounced slavery as an evil, "morally, economically, physically, intellectually, socially, religiously, politically – evil in its inception, in its duration, and in its catastrophe."

He was engaged in open warfare with the pro-slavers. As he boldly denounced slavery, he tried to ignore his growing realization that Mary Jane did not support his views.

By 1845, Cash had five children, a prominent political career and a thriving newspaper with many employees. After his wife and children, "The True American" was still his first love. Cash was sitting at the desk in his office, writing an editorial, when the assistant editor and publisher, Herbert Whitlow, came in to see him.

"Most people seem to think your campaign is going well. In three weeks you'll be re-elected state representative," he announced confidently.

"Not if Palmer, who backs my adversary, Wickliffe, has his way. He's a very effective speaker, and I hear that every chance he gets, he makes me look like some kind of loony."

He put the quill pen back in the holder and rose. "I'm leaving early today. Wickliffe has a campaign meeting at Russell's Cave this evening, and I hear he's asked Palmer to speak. I'm going to make sure they don't twist around what I've said or use that phony pamphlet again."

"You're going to their campaign meeting?" Whitlow asked in concern.

"Why not?" Cash asked. "Should be a big crowd there. It'll give me a chance to reach some folks."

Before Whitlow could figure out a polite way of telling his boss he thought that was a bad idea, Cash was gone.

That night a large crowd was gathered at a beautiful picnic area next to the creek emanating from Russell Springs. A bonfire lit the darkness and a makeshift platform had been built, with a podium in the center. Several men sat on the platform. Everyone waited eagerly to hear Palmer. Even though he was physically unprepossessing, he was known to be a strong orator.

He stepped up to the makeshift podium and began. "Some of our opposition, like that crazy Cassius Clay, would have you believe that the federal government has the right to tell you, the people of Kentucky, how you should live your life." Palmer grinned, knowing he had the crowd eating out of the palm of his hand. "Clay has the audacity to tell us that the negras should be treated equal and not like the property that we purchased with our hard-earned money."

At that moment Cash was making his way through the crowd to the podium. At six-feet, three inches tall and two hundred and thirty pounds, he had the physical stature Palmer lacked. And despite his relatively young age, he moved with the confidence and determination of someone older and wiser.

Palmer was stunned to see Cash coming toward him. He continued in a slightly more nervous voice, "The next thing he'll be telling you is that the negras should eat at the same table with you. This is absurd! I ask you, do you bring your mule in to have supper with you?"

The crowd laughed appreciatively. Shouts of "lunatic," "traitor," and "madman" could be heard. But Cash forged ahead, joining Palmer at the podium. The speaker was dwarfed by Cash's size and charismatic presence.

The rugged young man looked down at the short politician. "I'll have you know, sir," Cash said disdainfully, "that a Negro is not a mule but rather a person just like yourself."

Palmer was appalled at this statement. He looked out at the crowd. "See what I mean? He's crazy!"

There was a mixed reaction from the crowd. Some people laughed and jeered Cash, while others cheered him for having the courage to confront Palmer.

"Sit down, you crazy nigger lover!" someone shouted.

"Let him have his say," someone else countered.

Cash had never forgotten the lesson he learned in watching William Lloyd Garrison use "props" as he spoke. Reaching inside his coat pocket, he pulled out a copy of the Constitution. He held it up for the crowd to see.

"This revered document, my friends, is for all law-abiding citizens. It says all men are created equal under the law, and therefore have the right to their liberty and pursuit of happiness. All men, not just some of us."

The crowd had quieted down now.

He reached into his pocket again and pulled out a small Bible. He held it up to the audience. "This sacred book is for all those who believe. It says that free men or bond slave, we are all the same in the eyes of God!"

The crowd was utterly transfixed now, hanging onto his every word. Palmer could only listen in mute outrage.

Next Cash took out a pistol and a nineteen-inch Bowie knife that popped out of a spring-loaded scabbard on his chest. "And these are for the likes of those who do not believe in either the law or the word of God!"

Most of the crowd was now firmly behind him, realizing that he had both the law and God on his side of the argument.

Cash gave Palmer a piercing stare that seemed to see through right to his very soul. "I understand, Mr. Palmer, that you have a case in tax court at this very moment where you refuse to pay taxes on your slaves because you don't consider them property like your wagons or your mules. Is that right?"

Palmer stammered, "Well . . . I . . ."

The crowd was enjoying his extreme discomfort now. One of the men on the platform left and joined the crowd in front of the podium.

Cash went on, "In other words, Mr. Palmer, the Negroes are human beings when it comes time to pay taxes on them, and mules when it comes to how you treat them."

He turned back to the crowd. "If all of you could see the success of the Northern industrial cities that are free of slavery, you'd understand that freedom for all means better working conditions and higher wages for everyone!"

Robert Wickliffe, Jr., candidate for the Eighth Congressional District and the choice of pro-slavery interests, was sitting on the platform. He rose and faced Cash. "Ever since you went to that fancy Northern college you not only sound like an Abo, you sound like a damned Yankee!"

Cash was incensed at this insult; the worst that any Southern could throw at another. "I'm no more a Yankee than anyone here tonight! I only want what is best for the South and its people. From what I've seen in the North and in our great South, we would . . ."

Wickliffe interrupted. "As you well know, your party has deliberately changed the boundaries of the Eighth District in order to bring your friend, Garrett Davis, into the Fayette District. That's what we want to talk about here tonight. I have in my hand the very pamphlet that proves that this is so."

"Mr. Wickliffe! Mr. Davis is not here to defend himself, but I have heard his position on this and I know that you do not have any facts to back up your claim."

Samuel Brown, the man who left the platform and joined the crowd, spoke up. "Sir, that is not true!" A burly, hired killer and enforcer for some rich plantation owners, he wasn't intimidated by Cash's size or social position. "You're nothing but a damned liar!" he yelled. And he rushed at Cash.

He had drawn a gun. As he ran toward Cash, he aimed at his heart and fired. Hit in the chest, Cash staggered back, nearly collapsing. But to Brown's amazement, Cash remained standing.

Gathering his strength, Cash now rushed at Brown. The Bowie-knife, held in his upraised fist, glinted in the light from the bonfire.

Brown's eyes were huge with disbelief and fear. Before he could reload, Cash was on him. Brown felt the knife slash through the flesh of his arm holding the gun and he dropped it as a piercing pain tore through him. He felt the warmth of his own blood as the knife slashed deeper inside him, then twisted. Brown's eyes rolled back and he fell to the ground in an apparently lifeless heap.

Cash stood there, panting heavily. He looked out at the crowd who had watched this violent confrontation in shocked silence. "I stand ready to defend the truth!" he shouted, as he gasped for air.

Jack Rogers, a farmer who was nearly as big as Cash, shoved a revolver in his back and ordered, "Drop your knife, Mr. Clay!" Cash hesitated then did so.

A man standing over Brown shouted, "He's hurt pretty bad! Someone get a doctor!"

Rogers added, "And the sheriff!"

To Cash, it was self-defense, pure and simple. But he knew the law might not see it that way. However, at that moment being arrested wasn't his most urgent concern. He began to feel the full effect of the gunshot wound, and he slumped to the ground.

.

CHAPTER NINE

In the Lexington jail the next day a furious Mary Jane confronted her husband. Dressed in a prisoner's uniform and still in pain, he looked nothing like his normal strong, confident self. "You are a lucky, lucky man, Cassius Clay! If the pistol ball hadn't hit that leather scabbard, I'd be a widow right now, instead of the wife of a criminal."

"It was self-defense, Mary Jane," Cash insisted through clenched teeth. The scabbard may have saved his life, but his chest still hurt like hell.

"And what were you doing there, anyway? I'd like to know. You were just asking for trouble, and it surely found you. Thank God Henry has offered to defend you for the sake of the family."

"I don't want my cousin getting involved in this."

Mary Jane wasn't about to be challenged on this point. "You need a good lawyer, and Henry has never lost a criminal case. My brother-in-law, John Speed Smith, is going to help. You'll have two good lawyers defending you. For the sake of your children and your family you'd best start praying that your case is not Henry's first defeat."

Cash looked at Mary Jane as if seeing a stranger. He'd expected her to tearfully fall into his arms and say how glad she was that he was alive. He'd expected her to be filled with righteous fury at the man who'd nearly killed him. He'd even dared to hope, thought not really expected, that she'd understand why he had to address that gathering. Instead, it was painfully clear that what mattered most to her in all this was the disrepute it might bring to their name.

At that instant the infatuation he'd felt for her from the first moment they met began to quietly, sadly disappear. It would be a long time before he could acknowledge it to himself. But when he finally did, he would know that this was the seminal turning point in their marriage.

Cash was arraigned before the circuit judge a few days later, in the Fayette County courthouse with its spire-topped cupola and huge clock with four faces. The courtroom was packed with people who were both for and against Cash, depending on their views on slavery. Far from being impartial, the jury was clearly pro-slavery. Looking at these men, most of whom Cash knew, he realized the odds were definitely stacked against him. Some of them could barely hide their delight in seeing him in this position.

The trial began with an opening statement by the prosecutor. A slightly built, scholarly-looking young man, wearing a prim bow tie and glasses, he addressed the jury for over two hours, describing Cash's behavior in the most florid, condemning terms.

Finally, he concluded, "The defendant that you see here before you," he pointed accusingly at Cash, "tried to murder Mr. Brown in cold blood! He slashed his ear clean off, cut his nose in two, then practically disemboweled him!"

Cash frowned. He'd certainly hurt Brown, but he hadn't done that much damage to the man.

The prosecutor finished, "You must find the defendant guilty of attempted murder or let a violent criminal go free!"

He went to the prosecution table and sat down, flashing a satisfied smile at Henry Clay. He clearly felt confident he would win this case.

Henry Clay, nearly sixty but still an imposing figure, tall, commanding and graceful in manner, rose and moved to the front of the courtroom. Everyone waited with baited breath to hear the great orator. Tension filled the room. Cash's future, perhaps even his life, were in the hands of this man.

Henry Clay and Cash had had serious differences about the slavery issue. Clay, known as "the Great Compromiser" because he tried desperately to craft a compromise that would keep the South from seceding from the Union, wanted to abolish slavery slowly over at least a generation. Cash wanted to abolish it now. But in his cousin's dire time of need, Henry was there.

Standing as close as possible to the jury, he pulled out his pocket watch, looked at it, then looked at the jury. "Two and one-half hours – to tell you what? That my cousin, Cassius, cut up that hooligan, Brown? Well, I'm not going to take so long."

He spoke briefly but eloquently of their common Kentucky heritage and of his gratitude toward the people who had done him the great honor of allowing him to serve them. But mostly he talked of the sacred importance of the law, which everyone must

70

respect, no matter what their differences might be on other issues. He knew that the only way to save Cash was to separate his cousin's political views from the charge laid on him.

"The question which this jury of freemen is called upon their honor and conscience to decide is not whether the political views and sentiments of the prisoner were just or not. You are bound on your oath," he thundered, raising his voice, "to say was Clay acting in his constitutional and legal right? Did he occupy even higher ground than all human enactments – the eternal laws of self-defense – which come only of God?"

He had the jury's rapt attention as he went on, "I'll keep it short and simple. That 'poor man' the prosecutor was talking about aimed a pistol point blank at my cousin's chest and fired with the intention of killing him. The only thing that saved Cassius's life was the fortuitous happenstance of the ball from the would-be assassin's gun striking the knife scabbard that Cash wears inside his jacket. Here, take a look for yourselves."

He took the bloodstained scabbard out of a pocket and held it up for inspection. "You can see where the pistol ball embedded itself in the leather."

Walking over to the jury, he handed the first man the scabbard. As each man on the jury took turns examining this evidence, Henry rested his arm on the wooden barrier separating the jurors from the rest of the courtroom. He looked at each juror in turn, as though sizing him up. They were mesmerized by the dramatic evidence, and by the calm, cool, almost disdainful demeanor of the great lawyer and orator.

Clay went on, "My cousin simply did what he had to do before the scoundrel could get off another shot. If Cash Clay hadn't defended himself, he would be dead right now, instead of sitting in this courtroom, a wrongfully accused man!"

He paused then continued, "I ask you, gentlemen of the jury, what would you have him do? Would you have him turn and run like a coward? Or would you have him do what he did, what any man whose life was threatened, would do?"

Despite his passionate and eloquent argument, Cash couldn't tell from the jurors' expressions if Henry was convincing them.

Henry concluded in ringing tones, "If Cassius Clay had not defended himself, he certainly would not be worthy of our family name!"

With that, he went back to the defendant's table and sat down. His speech in defense of his cousin had taken a scant fifteen minutes, compared to the over two hours the prosecutor had taken.

Judge Andrew Taylor, white-haired, elderly but as magisterial as ever, turned to the jury. "Well, that was short and sweet. Gentlemen of the jury, if you find that the defendant, Cassius Clay, committed mayhem on Mr. Brown in cold blood, then you must also find him guilty. If so, Mr. Clay will most likely be hanged."

Mary Jane, sitting behind Cash, gasped. He didn't turn to look at her. He kept his eyes on the jury, trying to gauge their reaction.

The judge continued, "But if you find that Mr. Brown was about to kill Mr. Clay in cold blood, and Mr. Clay acted in self-defense, then you must find the defendant not guilty. It doesn't matter if you agree with Mr. Clay's political views, or not," he said pointedly, clearly echoing Henry Clay's words. "The question before you today is whether he acted with malice aforethought or whether he was simply defending himself. Now, do you all understand that?"

The jurors nodded.

"Good," the judge finished. "The jury will now retire for deliberation on this matter before them."

The jury filed out, and two jailers pulled Cash to his feet. Now he turned toward Mary Jane, sitting right behind him. He spoke to her quickly, knowing he had little time. "Cousin Henry didn't waste a lot of breath on my defense."

Mary Jane responded tightly, "He did what only he could do. Deliver a compelling argument on your behalf. Now you need to do what you can do, Cassius. Pray!"

That night Cash lay on the cot in the cell with his head resting on his hands. Without speaking, he asked God, Lord, why me? What have I done to deserve this? There was no answer that his heart could hear. It was a long time before he finally fell into a fitful sleep.

The next morning he was still asleep when the bailiff opened the cell door and came over to him. Shaking Cash, he said roughly, "Come on, wake up. The jury has a verdict." Cash rose tiredly, put on his jacket over his prisoner's uniform, and left with the bailiff.

He entered the courtroom, rigid with tension. It was already packed with his supporters and those of Brown. The prosecutor took his place at his table, and Henry Clay took his position at the defendant's table, next to Cash. Neither spoke.

Sally, Mary Jane and Cash's brothers were the last to arrive, before the jury filed in. Cash looked at them intently, trying to gauge their decision from their expressions, but it was hard to tell. Some of them met his look, others looked away. Finally, Judge Taylor was announced.

The judge looked out at the courtroom to make certain everyone was there. Then he banged his gavel and demanded, "Foreman of the jury, have you reached a verdict?"

The foreman, an elderly man named Joshua Willis whom Cash knew to be a slave owner, spoke out. "Yes, we have your honor."

"Would you please hand the verdict to the bailiff?"

Willis did so. The bailiff handed it to the judge. Taylor read it and nodded his head in agreement.

The judge's reaction unnerved him. Cash glanced nervously at his attorney and cousin, Henry, sitting next to him. To his surprise, Henry looked confident.

Sally, Mary Jane, Sydney and Brutus were clearly nervous, as they sat next to each other, grasping each other's hand for reassurance.

The judge handed the verdict back to the bailiff. "Will the bailiff please read the verdict?"

The bailiff took his time opening the folded paper. Then he took a pair of spectacles out of his pocket and carefully put them on. Cash wanted to shout, "Get on with it!" but he restrained himself. Finally, the bailiff read the verdict. "In the case of the State of Kentucky vs. Cassius Marcellus Clay, we, the jury, do find that the defendant acted in self-defense and is not guilty!" Except for Brown's supporters, it was evident that the spectators were clearly on Cash's side.

They erupted in shouts of delight. Sally and Mary Jane embraced, both crying tears of relief, and Sydney and Brutus slapped each other on the back in congratulations. As profound relief washed over him, Cash pumped his fist in the air in a gesture of victory.

Without saying a word, Henry rose and started to leave the courtroom. Cash stopped him. "Thank you!" Henry removed his cousin's hand from his arm with clear distaste. "I had no choice but to help you. You're family. But I don't agree with

73

your radical position on slavery, Cassius. And as far as I'm concerned, your crazy notions about this issue put you in this predicament. You have much to lose if you continue urging the abrupt end to slavery – friends, reputation, even your life. Think about that." And he left.

Cash watched him go with a mixture of gratitude and frustration. He knew he owed his life to Henry, and for that he was sincerely beholden to him. But he hated the fact that his cousin didn't have the courage of his convictions that slavery was wrong and shouldn't be allowed to continue for one moment more than was absolutely necessary. Unlike Cash, Henry wasn't willing to risk his political career, his social standing, his fortune, and perhaps even his life, for this cause.

Cash's family came up to him then. His mother hugged him tightly, and his brothers shook his hand enthusiastically. He looked for Mary Jane, who had left the courtroom the moment the verdict was announced. Now she returned, holding a folded copy of The True American. She handed it to Cash, who opened it to find a huge headline: CASSIUS CLAY INNOCENT! ACTED IN SELF-DEFENSE!

"They had it ready to go," Mary Jane explained. "It'll be hitting the front porch of every house in town before sundown." Before Cash could respond, she went on in a chiding tone, "Cassius, I hope this brought you to your senses, and you'll put an end to all this foolishness about the negras."

His exultation turned to irritation. "Mary Jane, it isn't foolishness. I'll continue to do everything I can to get rid of slavery."

Mary Jane's expression hardened and it was clear she would have argued further, but she knew this wasn't the time or place. Still, she wasn't about to let this go.

Cash was surrounded by more well wishers now. He quickly accepted their words of support, then excused himself and went over to Brown, who was trying to make his way through the crowd out of the courtroom. One of his ears was missing, and his nose had been crudely stitched up where it was slashed down the middle. Looking at the man who'd tried to kill him, Cash felt no satisfaction at how badly he'd hurt him. He said simply, "I regret the wounds that you suffered at my hand. I'm sorry it came to that." And he held out his hand.

Brown just looked at him with anger and hatred. Ignoring the outstretched hand, he turned his back on Cash and left.

74

CHAPTER TEN

1844

The Whig party nominated Henry Clay to run for the presidency against James K. Polk of Tennessee, who represented not only the Democratic Party but the pro-slavery interests. One of the biggest issues was whether or not to admit Texas to the Union as a slave state. Both Henry and Cash were opposed to this. But Cash was far more outspoken than his cousin. He knew that "the Texas question" was a plan to extend slavery and gain leverage in Congress for its supporters.

Henry asked Cash to campaign for him, not just in Kentucky but in the North, as well. Having gone to school there, Cash knew many influential Northerners and was fairly well-known. During an exhausting three-month campaign, Cash received an enthusiastic response from anti-slavery audiences. One time he spoke to a huge crowd on Boston Common, along with orator Daniel Webster.

Cash brought up the Texas issue repeatedly and argued forcefully against it. His slogan was, "Clay, Union and Liberty!" over "Polk, Slavery and Texas."

Instead of being grateful to his cousin, Henry began to feel that his campaign was actually being hurt by Cash's strong anti-slavery views. He urged Cash to be more "circumspect" in his speeches. This, Cash couldn't do.

At the end of the grueling campaign, Cash rode home on a stage. They passed a newly erected Hickory pole, from which hung a skinned raccoon. At that moment Cash knew the results of the election. The Whigs, nicknamed 'Coons, had lost.

His heart sank. All his efforts seemed to have been for nothing. And yet . . . every time he had given a speech, he had sensed an awakening in the crowd. He knew he was helping to persuade people to focus on their highest humanity, not their basest.

After the election, Henry Clay was honored at a dinner in Lexington. Cash attended, although he knew his cousin was still angry at him for not moderating his views during the campaign. Henry was in a sour mood, and didn't bother to hide it. At the best of times, he had an arrogance that could put people off. And it was in naked display on this night.

Henry spoke bitterly about the abolitionists of the North, who he blamed for his defeat, since they had voted for a stronger anti-slavery candidate. He glanced disdainfully at Cash as he spoke, clearly lumping him in with the abolitionists.

Cash had taken a lot of heat from the press and denounced by local bigwigs for his speeches in the North. Despite his genuine fondness and respect for his cousin, he wasn't about to accept being censured by him. Especially since he believed that Henry had lost the election because he didn't have the courage of his anti-slavery convictions. When Henry finished his brief, angry speech, and sat down, Cash immediately rose to rebut him.

"Mr. Clay, whatever errors of judgment, or of patriotism, may justly be imputed to the abolitionists, I think you are the last man who ought to complain; for if I remember aright, you said that the abolitionists should be set apart from, and denounced by all parties; so they but played the role you marked out for them."

The other men at the huge dining table stared in stunned amazement. It was unheard of for anyone to challenge the great man in that way, especially a member of his own family. Henry sat there, silently fuming, but said nothing. From that night on, he and Cash were cool toward each other.

Two weeks later, Cash was a speaker at another political rally. He spoke eloquently. "In our great country, we have an equality of religion. Has equality of religious rights worked? In what other country have so many Bibles been scattered about like good seed? Men are required to hold this great book in reverence in our courts of justice."

He paused then went on, "Its precepts are taught in the public schools in all the states. But there is an exception to these great principles that our founding fathers sought and fought to establish. This lone exception rears its ugly head in the midst of our great republic in the form of slavery."

He looked out at the crowd. People were listening intently. "There are in the South some eight million people. Three million are black and five million are of the same color, teachings and professions as yourselves. Of this number, only three hundred thousand are slaveholders."

The crowd, many of whom weren't aware of these numbers, reacted in surprise. "When you hear a man, then, talk about serving the interests of the South by defending the interests of slavery, strip him of his subtle deception and tell him that he is playing the part of a supple tool of the three hundred thousand slaveholders of the South; while the great masses, black and white, and nearly eight million in number, suffer together as victims of slavery."

His logic was convincing, his eloquent delivery deeply compelling. Cheers erupted. Cash basked in this approval and agreement. He felt he was persuading the grass roots working class, who had been adversely affected by having to compete with almost-free slave labor, to agree with his position. If he had this group on his side, then he believed the tide of support for slavery would turn.

That same evening, George was in the former slave, now workers' quarters, reading The True American to Luther and Henry. The headline read: ENDING SLAVERY WILL BRING HIGHER WAGES TO FREE WORKERS.

He could see that Cash was counting on the real fact that there were a lot more working people in the county than rich plantation owners. The owners might have money, but Cash had a newspaper that could reach everyone.

When George finished reading the article, he looked at Luther and Henry, and saw the light of hope shining in their eyes. He shared that tenuous hope. Maybe, just maybe, his friend would be able to keep his promise made to him so long ago.

A week later, there was another political rally. The mayor of the town where Cash was speaking introduced him to a large crowd of mostly working-class people in the town square. The mayor wasn't particularly anti-slavery. But he was a shrewd politician and sensed that Cash had connected with the voters. He wanted to get re-elected by hanging onto the coattails of this influential man.

"Today," the mayor began, "I have the very great pleasure of introducing the man of the people, a 'true American,' Cassius Clay!"

To the sound of enthusiastic applause and cheers, Cash moved up to the podium. His speech was constantly interrupted by roars of approval and agreement. Finally, he was able to get out his basic message:

"Higher wages, better working conditions, and better living conditions, is what I represent will be accomplished if you vote for me."

Two months later, Whitlow sat at his desk at The True American, reading the day's edition, hot off the press. The headline read: CLAY RE-ELECTED BY LANDSLIDE VOTE IN RECORD TURNOUT.

Cash was at that moment on the floor of the state capitol speaking to the gathering of representatives, all of whom were white males. "But how can you not tax the slaves because they are people and still have a law that says they are merely property, which should make them taxable?"

Representative Pope, one of the most influential representatives, answered sharply, "Because they are Negroes, Mr. Clay! They are different from you and me. They do not have the same amount of . . ." He searched for the right word. ". . . potential, and therefore must be kept in their place."

Cash tried to keep his temper in check as he responded carefully, "That may or may not be true, Mr. Pope, and I respect your views on the matter. But the reality is that they are still people and have been brought here against their will. For better or for worse, they are with us now. One day, Mr. Pope, they will be a part of our governing society, just like you and I."

Undaunted by the jeers of his listeners, and the rising anger in Pope's expression, Cash went on, "We must see that they are educated, so they can take on that responsibility and their rightful place in our society."

The entire House of Representatives was now in an uproar over this "radical" view. Some of them laughed derisively, others shouted their strong disagreement. The Chairman and House Speaker, Lonsdale, banged his gavel several times.

Looking out at his angry audience, Cash knew he would never be able to convince most of them. After all, they were bought and paid for by the wealthy plantation owners, whose marginal lands wouldn't reap a profit if it were not for the nearly free slave labor.

Lonsdale kept banging his gavel until finally there was some semblance of order in the chamber. "I call a one-hour recess!"

While men filed out, Representative Baker came over to Cash and spoke quietly. What he had to say was for Cash's ears only. "You'd better stay away from here for awhile and rethink your approach."

Before Cash could argue, Baker went on, "I share your views, Mr. Clay, and I know several others who do, too. But you're going to have to handle things differently if you want to have a prayer of succeeding. Let's talk about this further over dinner."

That night, Baker and Cash sat at a table in a quiet corner of the Royal Inn Restaurant. Lonsdale and Barnes were also there.

Baker said to Cash, "You'll never convince the majority of the legislature because they're bought and paid for by the very people who are getting rich off slavery."

Cash hadn't considered himself to be naïve, but the longer he was in politics; the more stunned he was by the ugly realities he learned. "Then how can we ever put an end to this terrible practice?"

Lonsdale interjected. "The answer's simple, if you think about it. You must convince the people, not the politicians."

"But I've already done that. That's how I got elected."

"And a remarkable job you did," Baker said. "But now you have to convince all of the people in the entire state of Kentucky."

Barnes added, "They, in turn, must convince their own local representatives."

Cash thought hard about this. "That's a mighty big job."

Lonsdale responded with a grin, "You're a mighty big man. I believe you just might be able to do it. We'll stand behind you when the time comes. Barnes or Baker will second your motion, and I'll call for the vote."

Baker said, "By using your newspaper to send out the message to every constituent in every district that slavery hurts the working class financially, we can get the people behind this. State representatives will have to vote to put a stop to slavery or face losing their . . ." He hesitated, considering whether to use a colorful epithet. He finished pointedly, "seat in the next election."

Everyone laughed, except Cash. He knew what a huge challenge lay before him, and how very much was at stake.

.

CHAPTER ELEVEN

Abraham Lincoln sat on the sofa in front of the fireplace in his modest home. A baby slept peacefully in a cradle nearby. Mary, who was his wife now, came in holding a newspaper and sat down next to him.

"Abraham, I've been reading this paper some friends in Lexington sent. There's someone I think you should meet – Cassius Clay. He publishes the paper and is a state representative. You have a lot in common and I think you might be able to help each other."

Lincoln gazed fondly at his wife. "I'm not too sure I want to meet Mr. Clay, Mary. I believe the last time you got a letter from him, it made you cry."

She was surprised by her husband's insight and sensitivity, though she quickly realized she shouldn't have been. It was so much like him. He was just about the kindest man she'd ever known. That quality had persuaded her to accept his proposal of marriage. She didn't love him in the same romantic sense that he clearly loved her. But she trusted and respected him. And there were worse reasons, she knew, to enter into marriage.

"That was a long time ago, Abraham," she said slowly. Then she admitted with a twinge of remembered pain, "The feelings were never mutual. And besides, those feelings changed when I came to know you and become so very fond of you."

Her words meant more to him than she could possibly imagine. He'd known when he proposed to her that she was in love with another man. He hoped in time she'd come to feel for him as he felt for her. Now it seemed that she was moving in that direction.

He said, "I'm aware that Mr. Clay is one of the richest men in the state. But I have a far greater treasure than all his wealth. I have you, Molly."

She loved it when he called her by that pet name that only he used. She smiled at him warmly, returning his affection, then brought the conversation back to her original point. "Read this and you'll see that you have something very important in common. You both hate slavery."

He took the paper and scanned it quickly. The headline on the front page immediately caught his attention: NO MORE NEW SLAVES IN KENTUCKY! The sub-headline read: House Votes Next Tuesday. Let your Representative Know How You Stand On This Issue.

Lincoln was impressed with this forthright stand on a difficult, enormously controversial issue. "Perhaps when we visit your family in Lexington, I'll meet Mr. Clay," he agreed thoughtfully.

CHAPTER TWELVE

In Frankfort, Kentucky, Baker's area of political influence, Cash began speaking to a large crowd at an outdoor gathering. "Many of you are called 'poor, white trash.' And who are these people who call you that? They are the rich plantation owners who buy slaves so they have almost free labor to plant their fields, cheap labor to wait on them and cook their meals."

Many in the crowd nodded their head in agreement. Cash continued, "And you have to compete in the labor market with these slaves who are working for next to nothing. That's what you get paid when you can find a job – next to nothing, just like them."

Cash was hitting a nerve and he knew it. His voice rose with passionate conviction. "Because you have to compete with this 'free' labor, you end up living in shanties, just like them. It's slavery that's making you 'poor, white trash,' and until you put an end to it once and for all, you will remain 'poor, white trash'!"

The crowd erupted in vociferous agreement and gave him a standing ovation.

This was only the latest of a series of appearances Cash had made in different districts. The representatives who supported his stand on slavery arranged these speaking engagements in their districts. Over and over again he used the Bible, his gun and Bowie knife to great effect when he spoke. His powerful logic on the issue of slavery, and his reputation as an outspoken and eloquent politician was spreading all over the state.

Barnes, whose district this was, and who had arranged for Cash to speak, added his voice once the applause had subsided. "Here's what you need to do. First, I'm going to ask you to get hold of every man who can vote and share with him what you heard this morning. Ladies, talk to your husbands, brothers, and fathers. You don't want your families to be poor forever."

The women in the audience nodded in grim agreement. Every one of them knew what it was like trying desperately to feed and clothe their children, while their husbands searched in vain for jobs that would pay a living wage.

"Second, I need you to write letters to some of the other representatives. Someone is passing out the list of representatives as we speak. Finally, you need to ride up to the state capitol on Monday. We'll have people there to hand out signs, and we need to make a big show of force. That's the only thing those politicians understand. Will you do it?"

Cries of "Yes!" went up from many in the crowd. Cash and Barnes exchanged a pleased look. Their tireless efforts were working.

All over the state, people were talking about Cash's argument. A typical comment was, "The way I see it, it's real simple. We're the majority. The slave owners are the minority. All we have to do is vote out slavery!"

A barber in Lexington spoke to a customer sitting in the chair as he trimmed his hair. "What this Clay is saying makes sense. You have to compete with the slaves, money-wise, in order to get a job. That's why no one south of the Ohio River has any money! Except the plantation owners!"

The customer murmured agreement . . .

Two women shopping in a millinery store were deep in conversation, as well. One said, "Fred's going to vote for Cash Clay's amendment putting a moratorium on slavery. You should get your William to vote for it, too."

On Monday, the streets of the capitol were literally filled with people on horseback. People carried signs reading, "Better our lives," "Put an end to slavery," "Slavery is a sin," "Enforce the old Negro law," "No more slavery," and "If you want our vote, stop slavery!"

An open carriage was stuck in the slow-moving traffic. In it, Representative Pope looked out at the people and the signs, and was livid. His black driver said, "This is as far as I can go, Mr. Pope. I'm afraid you'll have to walk the rest of the way, sir."

His tone was deferential, but Pope thought he sensed a hint of secret pleasure in the driver's countenance.

Pope got out and started walking, shoving his way through the crowd. He was soon joined by Representative Howard Carter. "This is madness!" Pope fumed. "It's that lunatic Clay's doing. He must be stopped!"

Carter, too, was outraged. "They've been here since yesterday morning. My office has received stacks of mail. The halls are filled with people trying to get in and tell me how to vote."

"You're not going to listen to them, of course."

"I have no choice, if I want to keep my seat," Carter said bluntly.

"But what about the people whose money put you in office?"

They had reached the steps of the capitol building and began climbing them. Carter said matter-of-factly, "If I want to stay in office, I'd better listen to the people who pay my salary."

With that, Carter strode ahead, leaving Pope behind.

Pope shouted after him, "They're nothing but poor, white trash!"

Cash stood at the top of the capitol steps, with Barnes, Baker and Lonsdale. They looked out at the crowd, thousands of people, some on horseback or in carriages, most on foot. Cash had heard Pope's loud statement.

He said with a grin as Pope passed him, "That may be, Russell. But for every rich plantation owner, there are a hundred 'poor, white trash' voters."

Then Cash and the others moved inside, leaving Pope fuming even more.

Moments later, Lonsdale rapped his gavel then addressed the assembly. "We all know the nature of the motion before us, and without further ado, I call for the vote."

Pope called out from the floor, "Point of order, Mr. Chairman. There has been no discussion on this motion."

Many of the other representatives grumbled audibly in disapproval. They had no desire to drag this out.

Lonsdale felt confident enough of the outcome to let Pope speak. "The Chair recognizes Representative Pope, who may take whatever time he needs."

Pope began a pompous speech. "Gentlemen of the House, today we have a motion on the floor that can affect the very success of our great state. Why, the farmers could be put out of business if . . ."

A spectator in the packed gallery shouted, "Shut up, you old goat! You're just tryin' to keep us all in the poor house!"

Pope tried to continue, but his words were drowned out by catcalls from the protestors who had filled the gallery.

Outside the capitol building, the representatives' carriages had made it through the crowd and were lined up at the bottom of the steps. The drivers, all of whom were black, stood talking to one another. George was among them. He had come with Cash, but because he was black, he had to remain outside.

"I'd give my eyeteeth to know what's goin' on in there," he said to one of the drivers.

The man laughed. "You go in there and you probably will give up your eyeteeth."

Inside, Pope tried to continue with his statement, but the crowd wouldn't let him. He turned to talk directly to the gallery. "Can't you see? You're all being deceived. This bill doesn't put an immediate end to slavery. It's just enforcing an old law putting a moratorium on any new slaves."

The man who had told him to shut up earlier, responded, "At least it's a start. Heaven knows we need to do somethin' soon or we'll all be poor forever!"

The rest of the gallery roared their agreement.

But Pope refused to give up. "It'll be years before this affects you. In the meantime, farming in this state . . ."

No one was willing to hear him out. Shouts of "Sit down!" and "We've heard enough from you!" drowned him out.

One man shouted, "At least our young 'uns won't have to be poor like us, scratching for a living. You live up in your fancy house, wearin' your fancy clothes, while most of us can't even get a job 'cause of all those slaves bein' here. It's gotta stop!"

Realizing it was hopeless, a furious, frustrated Pope sat down.

Lonsdale rapped his gavel again until there was a modicum of quiet in the chamber. "Unless there's a request for more discussion, I call for the vote."

He looked around for a response, knowing there wouldn't be one. Every representative, even those who agreed with Pope, were silent. They wanted to get re-elected.

Early the following morning, newspapers began hitting the front porches of houses all over the state. Banner headlines read: CLAY BILL PASSES! MORATORIUM ON SLAVERY. The sub-headline read: VOTE NEARLY UNANIMOUS.

At one house in Lexington, a black maid picked up the paper and took a quick look at it. She had only a rudimentary reading ability, but it was enough to let her understand the meaning of these words. She smiled triumphantly, then carefully folded the paper and took it to her master . . .

In the modest home George had only recently moved into, he showed the paper to his wife of less than a year, Orelia. "I told you it was true," he said with a grin. "But you wouldn't believe me."

Orelia asked, "But what does it mean, George?"

"It means that no new slaves can be brought into Kentucky."

"What will it mean for our baby?"

"It's the beginning of the end of slavery in Kentucky."

"But it'll still go on for awhile? Maybe a long while?" Orelia asked, frowning.

George patted her protruding stomach gently and spoke to his unborn child. "Don't you worry, little one, Cash isn't done yet."

CHAPTER THIRTEEN

A t the Lincoln house in Springfield, Mary was just finishing cooking dinner when she heard the front door open and close. "Is that you, Abraham?" she called out.

He came through the door into the kitchen, carrying a bouquet of wildflowers that he'd picked on his way home. As he handed them to her, he said, "I got through early in court and thought I'd take a little time off to spend with you."

She smiled as she took them. "Thank you. They're beautiful."

"Just like you, Molly," he responded, kissing her on the cheek.

As she put the flowers in a vase, she said, "There's a letter from Lexington on the dining room table, with a newspaper article. I think you'll find it interesting."

He went into the dining room and returned with the letter and article. Mary watched his face as he read first one, then the other. When he finished, he looked up at her and said thoughtfully, "I think the time has come for us to visit your family in Lexington. What do you think?"

"I think that's a wonderful idea. And while we're there, you can meet my old friend, Cassius." She added meaningfully, "And his wife, Mary Jane."

CHAPTER FOURTEEN

1845

A group of plantation owners gathered in a smoke-filled room at the Colonial House Hotel. Nearly everyone was smoking a fat cigar and was wearing a tie, vest and gloves. This was the kind of gathering that led to the unsavory image of unethical deals being made in secret.

The unofficial leader of the group, Colonel Morgan, spoke. "We have to do something about this fanatic, Clay. That moratorium on importing slaves is just the beginning. Mark my words, gentlemen, he wants nothing less than to abolish slavery altogether, as soon as possible. Just imagine hundreds of thousands of negras runnin' around, free as you and me. Free to do God knows what. One thing I know they won't be doin' is workin' in our fields."

A black maid came in with snifters of cognac and handed them around. When she got to Morgan, he took the glass then grabbed her around the waist. Startled, she pulled back and hurried out, while the men laughed at her reaction.

One man asked Morgan, "Say you're right. What exactly do you propose that we do to stop him?"

"There's only one thing that'll stop a man like Clay. Hit him where it hurts most. I hear he's a good family man, loves his children. We need to send a signal, not only to him but to anyone else who might share his radical ideas."

The men responded to the blatant threat with uncomfortable silence. Most of them had families of their own. The thought of hurting a woman or child made them feel extremely uneasy.

Sensing their resistance, Morgan said harshly, "Desperate times call for desperate measures. Do you want to lose your wealth, your position, your very way of life?" No one argued with him. He went on, "Are you with me on this?"

Slowly, one by one, each man nodded reluctant agreement.

At the office of The True American, Mary Jane passed the two brass cannons that were aimed at the front door. Going up to her husband's desk, she demanded, "What on earth are those doing here?" Before he could answer, she noticed rifles, shotguns, pistols and sabers hanging on the wall behind him. It was a virtual arsenal, readily accessible. "Cassius, all these guns! What do you need them for?"

He answered carefully, trying not to frighten her, "There have been rumors of . . . possible unpleasantness from an unruly mob. I'm certain they're unfounded. And mobs are cowards by definition. But I thought it best to be prepared."

"What kind of rumors? It's bad enough that half of Lexington society won't speak to us. Now there's worse to come?"

"They're just rumors, Mary Jane. They don't worry me, and I don't want them to worry you. But if anyone should try anything, it would probably be here, at the office. Just in case they try to shut us down, I'm ready for them. If anyone tries to sneak in and blow up the press, they'll get blown up themselves."

She was both frightened and angry. "I've had enough of this, Cassius! When are you going to stop this dangerous nonsense so we can lead a normal life?"

He realized he needed to be honest with her. Nothing less than the hard, cold truth would get through to her. "I'm afraid all of this – being cut off by polite society, people making threats against the newspaper and . . . and me . . . is just the beginning."

Before she could erupt, he hurried on, "But now that we see that people will unite behind this issue, we have to do even more, no matter what the risk. It's our Christian duty, Mary Jane. Surely you see that."

"Your Christian duty is to your family, Cassius! Not to those negras!"

He just looked at her helplessly. There was no way to reason with her, at least not at that moment while she was so angry. But it bothered him profoundly that she didn't share his feelings about this issue. When they married, he thought he would have not only a loyal wife, someone to be a wonderful mother to the children he looked forward to having, but also a helpmate in the cause he felt so passionate about.

He was beginning to reluctantly accept that Mary Jane would never be that helpmate. And it affected his feelings for her in a way he didn't like to think about. He had loved her deeply once. He was trying to hold onto a vestige of that love for the sake of the children.

"Let's talk about this tonight," he said tiredly, "I have work to do."

"Colonel and Mrs. Hastings are coming to dinner tonight," she reminded him tightly.

"You know I don't like that man."

"His wife is one of the few friends I have who are still speaking to me."

"He owns over three hundred slaves," Cash fumed.

"He has a very large farming operation that requires a great deal of labor," Mary Jane pointed out.

"So do we, but we manage very well with free workers rather than slaves."

"That's because they all look up to you as some sort of hero or something," Mary Jane said dismissively. "You've got them working twice as hard as they did before, and they're too ignorant to realize it."

"They work hard because they're rewarded fairly and because they choose to, not because they're forced to do so."

Mary Jane was as tired of this old argument as he was at this point. She said coldly, "I expect you to be home in time to greet our guests, like a proper host. They'll be arriving at seven o'clock."

Without waiting for his reply, she turned on her heel and left.

Cash made it home on time that night. He tried to be polite to Hastings and his rather silly wife, Hortense, but it was hard going. There were few subjects he and Hastings could discuss civilly. And Hortense was only interested in talking about horse racing, which she loved to wager on. That didn't interest Cash.

"Tell me, Mary Jane," Hortense asked, "what dark horse, if any, does your father and his friends favor to win the Derby this year?"

Dr. Warfield and some friends had built Churchill Downs and were at the top of the thoroughbred racing world in Kentucky. Mary Jane said blithely, "My father refuses to tell me what horse he thinks will win for fear I'll tell my friends and it'll reduce the odds."

93

At Hortense's shocked look, Mary Jane hurried to correct her unintentional faux pas. "I can tell you, however, that he hasn't picked a winner since the Derby began," she said with a laugh.

Hortense wasn't mollified. "How do you know that if he won't tell you which horse he's picked?"

"Because, according to my mother, he goes around slamming doors and muttering angrily to himself for at least a week after the race."

Hastings turned to Cash and raised the issue they'd been skirting all evening. "Now that you've achieved your compromise moratorium on slavery, I imagine you'll be getting out of politics and spending more time with your family."

Cash sensed that Mary Jane had shared her dislike of his political career with Hortense, who had shared the information with her husband. Hastings was fishing to find out what Cash was going to do.

Cash flashed an irritated look at his wife then said evenly, "On the contrary, Colonel, we've only just begun. I don't believe the voters will be satisfied until slavery no longer exists in Kentucky."

"Your fiery speeches and editorials are responsible for stirring up the voters," Hastings snapped.

For the sake of his wife, Cash tried to be diplomatic. "The True American is just a reflection of the views of the people. It doesn't mold those views." He added with a wry smile, "I didn't realize you're so interested in my little paper."

The women realized their men were getting dangerously close to a really ugly confrontation. If tempers flared enough, it might actually lead to a duel. Such things weren't all that uncommon. And Mary Jane knew her husband well enough to realize he would never back down from a physical fight.

She hastened to smooth things over, saying quickly, "Would either of you like a drink? We have some lovely French cognac."

Hortense responded, "I'm sure they would, Mary Jane. I know how much gentlemen enjoy an after-dinner libation."

Mary Jane called out, "Bessie!"

But the escalating tension between the two men couldn't be checked by social niceties. Hastings said, "Look, Clay, I'm just trying to do you and your family a favor. I've heard unpleasant rumors."

Cash stood up, towering over Hastings. He was absolutely infuriated that the man would dare to threaten him, even obliquely, in his own home, in front of his wife, who was already worried enough. "Don't try to intimidate me! I've faced one assassination attempt, and that didn't stop me from saying what must be said!"

Hastings glared at him then rose. Without looking at his wife, he said through clenched teeth, "We'd best be going, Hortense."

Hortense rose also and said awkwardly, "I'm so sorry, Mary Jane. I'm afraid that we have early plans for tomorrow and must take our leave now. It was a lovely dinner. Thank you so much for inviting us."

At that moment, Bessie entered, carrying a silver tray with an apple pie and small China dessert plates. "Would anyone like some pie?" she asked "It's fresh out of the oven."

"No, thank you, Bessie," Cash answered. "Our guests are leaving. You may give it to the children. And please get Colonel and Mrs. Hastings' coats."

"Yes, sir," Bessie replied, setting down the tray on a nearby table and hurrying out.

"If you'll excuse me, Colonel, I have pressing business to attend to," Cash said curtly and walked out.

Mary Jane was mortified by her husband's behavior. She said, "I'm so sorry. Please excuse me," and she hurried after Cash.

Bessie returned with the coats. As she helped Mrs. Hastings on with hers, the colonel surreptitiously took a small vial from his vest pocket and sprinkled something on the pie. He had come prepared to use this, and didn't hesitate to take advantage of this opportunity to do so.

Mary Jane found her husband in the library, where he paced furiously, trying unsuccessfully to calm down. Before she could speak, he burst out, "I knew this would happen! I told you I can't stand either one of them. Why on earth they came, I'll never understand. He didn't want to be here any more than I wanted him here."

"It would have been just fine if you hadn't upset him! Now I've lost another friend because of you and your love for your damn negras!"

She burst into tears and rushed out.

Bessie came into the nursery with the pie. Only one of the four children was awake. Cash, Jr. was reading in bed. "Here you go," she said, handing him a big piece. He took it eagerly. "But when you finish, it's bedtime."

The little boy said with a disarming smile that always reminded Bessie of his father, "Thank you, Bessie. You're my very best friend."

As Bessie left the room, she heard him trying to wake up his sleeping siblings to share the bounty. "Laura, Elisha, Green, wake up! There's pie!"

The three mumbled sleepily that they didn't want any. Cash, Jr. was happy to have it all to himself. And he was determined to eat every single bite.

The next morning, Florence, the upstairs maid, was making up the beds in the nursery. All the children were up except for Cash, Jr. "Come on, you can't sleep all day," she said impatiently. She had a lot of other work to do and needed to finish in there. She tickled him the way she did sometimes when he was being lazy. But instead of responding with his usual laughter, he lay there, unresponsive. She shook his shoulder slightly, and there was still no reaction. Then she touched his cheek. It was cold.

"Oh, my God!" Florence screamed. "Mrs. Clay! Mrs. Clay!"

An hour later, Dr. Scott came into the library where Cash waited helplessly. "I'm so very sorry, Cassius. Your little boy died in his sleep."

Cash couldn't take it in, couldn't accept it. It was impossible, unbearable. He managed a hoarse whisper. "Does Mrs. Clay know?"

The doctor nodded. "She went into shock. I gave her a sedative. She'll probably sleep until tomorrow morning."

But there was worse to come. Dr. Scott went on, "I can't tell positively yet, without running some tests, but I strongly believe he was poisoned."

That jolted Cash out of his paralysis. "What?! That can't be! Who would do such a thing?!"

"Someone who hates you and what you stand for," the doctor said bluntly. "Someone who wants to stop you, and will do anything to achieve that end. They knew this would get your attention as nothing else would."

Cash was reeling. The doctor couldn't be right, and yet, Cash knew deep inside that he was. Who could be that evil?

Dr. Scott went on, "It must've happened last night, shortly before the boy went to sleep. The poison wouldn't have taken long. I talked to the servant, Bessie, and she said the only thing he had that no one else did was a glass of milk that a servant, Emily, gave him after dinner, and later a piece of apple pie. The poison was almost certainly in one of those."

The doctor felt terrible for Cash, whose haggard expression revealed the depth of his pain. He seemed to have aged years in that moment. The doctor wanted to leave him to express his grief in private, but it was necessary to ask one final question. "I understand that all your servants, including Emily, have been with you for years. But are you certain they're all absolutely trustworthy?'

Cash nodded, unable to speak.

"Is it possible one of them might have a grudge against the family for some reason?"

Cash shook his head.

"Was anyone else here yesterday evening?"

Cash couldn't answer. His mind, which had been frozen in horror at the thought that someone might have purposefully murdered his child, raced now. He remembered Hastings' words – I'm just trying to do you and your family a favor. I've heard unpleasant rumors.

Cash shook his head slowly. Surely even someone like Hastings wouldn't hurt a child. It was unthinkable. There must be some other explanation. And yet he couldn't believe that Emily would do such a thing, either, even if someone bribed her.

But even as his mind began a torturous effort to solve this tragic mystery, his heart cried out that it didn't matter who was responsible. All that mattered was that the little boy Cash adored was gone forever.

The next morning Cash sat beside Mary Jane, waiting for her to wake. He'd sat there for an hour. Now, finally, she stirred. When her eyes fluttered open, Cash stroked her brow. "How are you feeling, sweetheart?"

For an instant, she'd forgotten what happened. But it all came back with a rush and her face drained of all color. "Is it true? Is he – gone?"

Cash nodded helplessly.

She choked back a sob, then went on unsteadily, "Dr. Scott said . . ." she could barely get the words out. "He said our son was poisoned."

Again, Cash nodded.

Mary Jane's look of agony turned to fury. She lashed out at him, "This is your fault! If you hadn't stirred up all this trouble over the negras, my son would be alive! Colonel Hastings tried to warn you, but of course you wouldn't listen! No one tells the great Cassius Clay what to do! Even if your child's life is at stake!"

"How can you say such a thing?!" he asked, mortified.

She looked at him coldly. "I'll never forgive you for this. Never."

Cash had thought it impossible to feel more devastated than he had been when the doctor gave him the terrible news. But now the profound guilt that he'd tried to push to the back of his mind from the moment he heard it might be poison, came rushing forward. He looked at his wife helplessly. Her accusation of responsibility was nothing compared to what he felt about himself.

Later that day Cash pulled himself together enough to go looking for Emily. He found her working alone in the garden, kneeling on the ground as she pulled weeds, looking as sad and confused as all the servants did. She looked up at him then rose to face him. She said nothing, waiting for him to speak.

He began without preamble, "Did you poison my son?"

Emily was horrified. "What?! How can you think such a thing, Mr. Clay? I would've died before hurting a hair on that little boy's head!"

Looking at her, Cash knew she was telling the truth. There was no way she could look him straight in the eyes and lie so convincingly. "I'm sorry, Emily," he stammered awkwardly. "I . . . I had to ask."

"Well, you asked, and I gave you my answer," she said, fighting back tears. "I can't believe you would think that of me. I thought you were different. When you set us free, I respected you and thought you respected us. Well, if I'm free, then I'm goin'."

She turned to leave, but he reached out for her, stopping her. "Emily, I'm sorry. Forgive me. It's just . . . ." His voice trembled, and he had to stop talking or risk falling apart altogether.

Looking at him, this big man who suddenly seemed shrunken in stature, she felt the enormity of his pain and loss. His apology would have been deeply affecting under any circumstances. Under these tragic circumstances, it was enormously moving. Emily whispered through her tears, "No, sir, I'm sorry."

Two days later, the graveside service was held. When the small casket was lowered into the ground, people filed past a sobbing Mary Jane and grim-faced Cash, offering their condolences. Among them were Colonel and Mrs. Hastings.

While Hortense hugged Mary Jane, the colonel played his role of sympathizer well. "I'm sorry, Clay. One hardly knows what to say at a time like this."

Cash looked at him, trying to see into his heart. Was he capable of such a thing? Before Cash could say anything, the colonel went on meaningfully, "I imagine such a terrible loss will have a profound impact on your future actions."

And with that enigmatic comment, he moved on.

Cash watched him walk away. A blind rage welled up from deep within him. He was torn between wanting to beat the truth out of Hastings, and knowing that such a rash act would only land him in jail. His family needed him too much to risk being taken away from them.

At that moment, George came up to him. "I'm awful sorry, Cash." Then he expressed the thought that had haunted him from the moment he heard about Cash, Jr.'s death. "If you hadn't made me that promise . . . helped my people the way you have . . ."

Cash stopped him, saying harshly, "Don't say that, George! Don't even think it. There's only one person responsible for my boy's death, and it isn't you or me."

As soon as the words were out of his mouth, he knew it was the ugly truth. There would always be a lingering sense of guilt, deep in his heart, but he was no longer tortured by it. Someone else was responsible and Cash felt certain he knew who it was. But he also knew that if Hastings had, indeed, somehow managed to poison Cash Jr., he hadn't acted alone. Any number of others would have at least supported such a heinous act, if not actually committed it themselves.

But Cash would die before he would let his enemies keep him from doing what he knew was right. If they thought this horrible act would deter him, they were dreadfully wrong. He was more determined now than ever that his child wouldn't have died in vain.

Cash went on slowly to George, "Sometimes God puts a person into a situation because he needs that person to help Him carry out His plan. And no matter how terrible a price must be paid, that person needs to do God's will."

"I'm afraid for you and your family," George said.

"I'm afraid for them, too, George. And I'm going to do everything I can to protect them from now on. But I'm not going to quit. I won't let my son's death be for nothing.

CHAPTER FIFTEEN

One month later, the Lincolns made their trip to Lexington. They were guests of honor at dinner at Whitehall. Cash gave her a warm hug when she first came in the entryway, and he commented on how much she'd changed from the delightful young girl he remembered. Now, he said graciously, she was a lovely woman, and her husband was a very lucky man, indeed.

Mary felt a jolt of emotion. But it wasn't the painful stab to the heart she'd half expected. It was a little prick of bittersweet curiosity about what might have been. Her husband gave her a questioning look. She smiled at him reassuringly, put her arm in his, and moved on into the house. This first moment when she saw Cash again after all these years had been what she was most nervous about. Now that it was over, she knew she would be all right.

As the two couples sat at dinner, Cash quickly turned the conversation to the reason for this get-together. He said to Lincoln, "I understand you have a strong interest in politics."

Lincoln smiled wryly. "Yes, but the political world doesn't seem too interested in me. I've failed twice in my bid to become a U.S. senator."

"But you were a state representative. And Mary informs me that you have a flourishing law practice in Springfield."

"Mary's my staunchest supporter," Lincoln said, with an affectionate glance at his wife. "Unfortunately, the voters don't seem to support me quite so enthusiastically."

"Maybe that will change. Am I right that you believe slavery is both an injustice and bad policy? Because if so, I agree wholeheartedly with your views."

"Yes, I do believe that."

Mary Jane had no interest in political conversation. She asked Lincoln, "Do you and Mary have children?"

101

Lincoln replied proudly, "Yes, we have a son who's a little over a year old now. We hope to have more children."

Mary had heard of the death of Cash, Jr. She said gently, "I heard about the loss of your son. I want you both to know how very sorry I am."

Mary Jane said with undisguised bitterness, "My son died because of my husband's political views."

The Lincolns were confused by this comment, and extremely uncomfortable at the abrupt change in the tone of the evening. Cash stared at Mary Jane in dismay. He couldn't believe she had just said that to people she hardly knew. He tried to smooth over the awkward silence. "The powers of darkness killed him."

"If that's what you want to call your negras, dear, yes, they did."

Lincoln tried to turn the conversation back to the impersonal subject of politics. "I've read your views in The True American, Mr. Clay. I must say, considering where you live, those views are most courageous."

But Mary Jane wasn't about to let go of her bitterness and anger toward her husband. "Considering where we live, those views are insane!"

Cash tried to apologize for his wife's terrible manners. "You'll have to excuse my wife, Mr. Lincoln. Neither of us have been the same since our son's death."

"His murder," Mary Jane hissed.

Cash had had enough. It was one thing for Mary Jane to blame him privately, but to do so before guests, who should have been made to feel comfortable in their home, was unforgivable. "You don't look well, Mary Jane. Perhaps you should go rest."

For a moment it looked as if she would argue, but she didn't. Murmuring, "Please excuse me," she rose and left.

There was a moment of tense silence. Cash finally broke it.

"I'd like to pursue this discussion of slavery another time, Mr. Lincoln. At the moment, my wife needs me." He turned to Bessie who was serving them. "Bessie, their coats, please."

"We understand, Cash," Mary said, and her husband nodded agreement.

As he saw them off at the door, Cash said to Lincoln, "The next time you run for Congress, let me know. Perhaps we can distribute The True American in your area. I promise you it will be a staunch supporter. We need more Congressmen like you, Mr. Lincoln, with the moral courage to speak the truth."

"Thank you, Mr. Clay. I appreciate that."

"Call me Cash. All my friends do."

"And please call me Abe."

Mary interjected, "Everyone calls him 'Honest Abe.'"

"A good name for an honest politician." He smiled warmly at Mary. "It was so good to see you again."

"It was wonderful seeing you, Cash." She meant it. She had been just a little nervous about what her reaction to him might be. But the moment she saw him, she realized that what she'd once felt for him was merely a girlish infatuation. Not the deep and abiding love she felt for her husband. She thanked God that he hadn't answered her prayers to let her marry Cash.

As the Lincolns drove off in their carriage, Mary said to her husband with feeling, "That poor, distraught woman. I hope I never know what it feels like to lose a child."

"I don't know what happened to their son, or why Mrs. Clay blames her husband for his death. But she's right about one thing. Politics has a way of killing people in the name of justice. Your friend, Cash, has a lot of courage. I can see why you think so highly of him, my dear."

Moonlight flickered across Mary's face as the carriage moved in and out of the shadows of the trees lining the long drive to the house. "I like Cash for the same reasons that I love you, dear. He stands up for what he believes in, and he doesn't care what anybody else thinks."

"I wish you hadn't mentioned that silly moniker, 'Honest Abe.' You know how much I dislike it."

"Cash is right. It appeals to voters. I wouldn't be surprised if one day that name, and our friend Cash, help you get elected to high office."

The conversation with Cash about slavery prompted Lincoln to visit Cheapside, just outside Lexington. It was the headquarters for slave trading in the U.S., and he wanted to see first hand how slaves were treated. Mary accompanied him, and the tall man and the tiny woman walked together from one side of the auction quarters to the other. They saw terrified children torn from their screaming mothers, sobbing wives taken from helpless husbands.

They stopped in front of one auctioneer's booth as a beautiful young girl named Eliza caught their eye. She was light-skinned, with fine, straight hair, and appeared to be white. The only thing that gave away the fact that she was a slave was the tormented look in her beautiful dark eyes.

"A mistress fit for a king!" the auctioneer bellowed. "Only 1/64th black, daughter of her master. This lass has actually been educated and has learned all the social graces necessary to make her a fine companion to the right gentleman. What am I bid for this beauty?"

A smartly dressed Frenchman from New Orleans raised his hand. "One thousand dollars."

A young Methodist minister, complete with backwards collar, raised his hand. "Eleven hundred."

Irritated by this unexpected competition, the Frenchman said with determination, "Twelve hundred!"

His eyes glinting with greed as he sensed that the price might be driven up much farther than he'd anticipated the auctioneer pulled the top of the young woman's dress down to reveal her breasts. "See what you'll be getting! She's worth every penny, and more!"

Mortified, the young woman covered herself and kept her eyes downcast.

The minister called out, "Thirteen hundred."

The Frenchman wanted this beauty, but he wasn't willing to spend a small fortune on her. There were plenty of other women here. He asked the minister bluntly, "How high will you go?"

"Higher than you."

"Why does a man of the cloth want such a girl?" the Frenchman demanded. The minister just looked at him silently.

Afraid that the bidding seemed to have stalled, the auctioneer lifted the young woman's dress to expose her long, slender legs. "You'll not find a finer young woman here today, gentlemen."

"Fourteen hundred!" the Frenchman called out.

"Fifteen," the minister countered.

"Fifteen twenty-five," the Frenchman blustered.

The minister didn't immediately respond. The young woman raised her eyes and the look she gave the minister was desperate, beseeching. She didn't know either of these men. But something

104

told her that the young minister would be a far gentler master than the dissolute-looking Frenchman.

The auctioneer was about to announce that the Frenchman had won, when the minister said, "Fifteen seventy-five."

The Frenchman glared at him then stalked off. The auctioneer banged his gavel. "Going once." He banged it again. "Going twice." He banged it a third time. "Sold to the young reverend there."

The auctioneer handed the young woman over to the minister. "Enjoy her, Reverend."

The reverend gave him a disgusted look. "I'm going to free her." Turning to a stunned Eliza, he said gently, "I have the papers prepared, my dear."

She couldn't believe this miracle. She'd heard of such things, of generous benefactors who bought slaves, only to set them free. But she'd never dared to hope that such a thing might happen to her. For generations, no one in her family had been free. She would be the very first.

She burst into tears, and the minister patted her lightly on the back. "There, there, my dear, it's all right. You're safe now. You'll never suffer such shameful treatment again."

Lincoln went up to him. "Pardon me, Reverend -- ?"

"Fairbanks. Calvin Fairbanks."

"I have to tell you, I was afraid you were going to stop at fifteen twenty-five."

Fairbanks smiled slightly at the implicit compliment. "I was authorized to go as high as twenty-five hundred, if necessary, by the people who provided the funds. But I was being careful with the money, because I hope to free others here today, as well."

Mary asked, "Who are these people who would do such a generous thing?"

"Several of my parishioners who believe that slavery is immoral and unjust. They're not wealthy, but whenever they can, they combine their funds and send me here to rescue some poor soul like this girl."

Fairbanks took his leave of them then, leading the girl to a waiting carriage. As the Lincolns watched them drive off, with the young woman still weeping with joy, Abraham turned to Mary and said with a catch in his voice, "I'll never forget this day and what I've witnessed in this terrible place."

"I don't think it's too strong to say that evil exists here," Mary responded. "But there is some good here, as well, as we just saw. I hope ultimately that good will prevail."

"I must believe it will," he said with fervent conviction. "But I'm afraid it won't happen without paying a very dear price."

CHAPTER SIXTEEN

One year later Cash stood in the pouring rain in a small town near Lexington, speaking with heartfelt conviction. Despite the frigid winter weather, a hundred people were there, huddled under umbrellas, listening with rapt attention. He had just read the Bill of Rights to them.

"This is a declaration of the equal rights of man, or the brotherhood of man," he intoned in his rich, deep baritone. "This quality of life makes us proud to be born Americans. In reality, we, as children, are not born equal. Some may be taller or stronger. So is this declaration of equal rights and brotherhood just so much rhetoric? No! It declares a political equality, an equality which embraces personal, civil and religious rights."

When he finished, the crowd applauded and several people shouted their enthusiastic agreement.

Later that same night, in the office of The True American, the press was churning out front page after front page. The banner headline read: SLAVERY MUST END NOW!

The next morning, at a Lexington newspaper stand, the vendor was hawking the paper, shouting, "Read all about it! Slavery must end now!"

At yet another speaking engagement, where the crowd braved falling snow, Cash said, "We broke away from a government that placed people in the position of receiving special privilege without regard to merit or qualification. From a system that made one man forever noble and another forever poor."

The appearance of most of the audience made it clear they identified with the poor, not the noble.

Cash went on, "We resolved in this new and great country that merit should make the man. That the lowest laborer in the coal mines of Pennsylvania or the lead mines of Missouri should stand on the same basis of political rights with the most petted and pampered child of wealth and fortune."

The crowd went wild, cheering the man who, in spite of his wealth, had come to be seen as a hero to the common man. He not only stood up for the rights of the black slaves, but for the rights of the white working class, as well.

Later that same night, Cash gave the same speech to a different crowd in a different town. "As the result of this declaration, men come up every day from the humble walks of life, rising up upon the wings of their own individual merits and taking rank as our great God would have them do."

His voice suddenly failed him, and he broke into a coughing fit. Trying to force himself to continue, he said hoarsely, "Andrew Jackson, in his youth, was a stable boy. My cousin, Henry Clay, started out as a mill boy and became one of the most elegant of politicians and the most refined of gentlemen. In America we are all nobles."

He began to cough again. He finished in a voice that was barely audible, "I shall never cease to admire the spirit of that southern woman, who, while in Europe was told that only ladies of queenly rank could be presented to a certain empress who she wished to see. She replied, 'Then surely I must be admitted, for I am an American queen in a land where all women are queens.' And she was right!"

The crowd, especially the women, shouted their approval.

Cash tried to go on, but his voice was completely gone now. He suddenly went deathly pale and collapsed on the platform.

The next morning Cash lay in bed, unconscious.

Dr. Scott said to Mary Jane as they stood by Cash's beside, "He's driven himself mercilessly for too long. It's definitely pneumonia. I'm afraid it's deep in his lungs, Mrs. Clay. It will be touch and go for a few days."

"Will he make it?" she asked in a flat, unemotional voice.

The doctor hesitated, taken aback by her seeming lack of concern. Then he shrugged helplessly, "I can't say."

"If he dies, it will be his damn politics that kill him," Mary Jane said tightly. "That's all he thinks about."

The doctor knew all too well where her bitter attitude came from. He said nothing.

Mary Jane was silent for a moment. Then, responding to some vestige of love, or at least loyalty, to her husband, she asked, "Is there anything I can do?"

"He needs to be kept cool. He's running an awfully high fever. Keep wiping him off with cool towels and make sure he gets plenty of liquids when he comes to. Soup, if he'll take it. Whatever you do, don't let him get out of bed until he's entirely over this, or you'll lose him for sure. I'll leave some laudanum with you. That should make him sleepy enough to stay in bed."

When the doctor left, Mary Jane turned to Bessie, who waited nearby, "Get me some towels and cool water."

"Yes, ma'am. Is Mr. Cash going to be all right?"

"Of course, he will," Mary Jane snapped. "Don't waste a moment's worry on him, Bessie. He's too damn bull-headed to die."

But for all her anger at him, she couldn't imagine a world without his towering presence.

It was a long, frightening night. More than once, Cash's breathing was so shallow and ragged, his fever so fierce, that Mary Jane thought he was about to die. Neither she nor Bessie left him. They took turns staying awake and wiping his glistening brow with cool, damp cloths. Bessie didn't give up hope. But as the long night dragged on, and Cash's strength seemed to ebb, Mary Jane was convinced that he wouldn't live to see the dawn.

She was wrong. As dawn broke, so did his fever. That morning Cash was not only alive, he had regained consciousness. More relieved than she would admit, Mary Jane spoon fed broth to him. He was exhausted, weak, barely coherent. But Mary Jane understood him perfectly when he whispered, "I love you, Mary Jane."

She had thought that after the death of their son, she could never feel a tender emotion for her husband again. But now she was caught off-guard by how touched she was by this declaration.

She replied, "You be still. You need to conserve your strength. Here, finish this broth."

In the background, Bessie couldn't contain her relief. If he was able to speak, and to take some nourishment, maybe he was going to live. She burst out, "Oh, thank the Lord!"

Hearing her, Cash tried to speak up. "Bessie – get my schedule off my desk in the library. I've got places to be."

"Forget the schedule, Bessie," Mary Jane said firmly. "Mr. Clay isn't going anywhere. Now go get some more cool cloths."

"Yes, ma'am," Bessie said happily and left.

Mary Jane gave Cash two of the pills the doctor had left. "What's this?" he asked in a tremulous voice, before swallowing them.

"Medicine that Dr. Scott says you need. He also says you have to rest for a while. You nearly died on me, Cassius. If you try to do too much too soon, that could still happen."

The bluntness of her words belied her feelings. Cash was already getting sleepy from the drug, but he whispered, "That can't be."

"You're the strongest man I've ever known, Cassius Clay, but you're not invincible. Death nearly took you last night."

Death. He couldn't believe it. He'd never given a moment's thought to his own mortality. Now the thought that he came so close to dying shook him profoundly. He'd thought he had all the time and opportunity in the world to accomplish the things that mattered most to him. Now he was forced to acknowledge that might not be the case.

As these disturbing thoughts swirled through his mind, he lost consciousness again. Looking at him, Mary Jane's expression softened, and she whispered, "God help me, I still love you, too, Cash."

The laudanum kept him in bed, where the doctor wanted him. But when he was awake, he worked on an editorial. At first his handwriting was so shaky as to be almost indecipherable. But gradually it got better as his strength slowly returned. He wrote like a man possessed, focusing the small amount of energy he had on this one task.

Early one morning, when Bessie was alone with Cash, he asked her to give what he'd written to Luther and have him take it to Whitlow, the editor at the newspaper. "Tell him I said to publish it in the next edition. And, Bessie, don't let Mrs. Clay see it."

Sitting at his desk, Whitlow looked up to see Luther coming up to him, a sheaf of papers in one hand. "Why, Luther, what brings you into town so bright and early? Mr. Clay hasn't had a setback, has he?"

"No, sir, he's doin' better an' better. He asked me to give you this." He handed over the papers and left.

Whitlow began reading, and almost immediately his expression turned to shock and dismay. He was utterly dumbfounded at the contents of the editorial. All hell would break loose when this was printed. But he knew his boss well enough not to question him. If Cash said print it, then Whitlow had no choice. He sat down at the typesetting counter and began to set the big type for the headline that would shake up readers as none other had.

The next morning, a black newspaper vendor opened his stand. Cutting the twine on a tall stack of newspapers, he read the banner headline: SLAVERY IS A SIN!

110

At Whitehall, Bessie waited outside the front door for the paper. Finally, the paperboy approached on his mule. He smiled at Bessie and handed her the paper, then went on. Bessie quickly read the headline before taking the paper inside. She put her hand over her mouth in amazement. She had mixed emotions. Finally, someone had spoken the unvarnished truth. But she was filled with fear for Cash and his family. Instead of taking the paper right in, she headed for George and Orelia's house.

In the parlor, Mary Jane came up to Florence, who was busy dusting the furniture. "Have you seen Bessie this morning? My ladies club will be arriving shortly and I want her to make something special for them."

"No, Mrs. Clay. I haven't seen her since earlier this morning."

"When you do, tell her I need to talk to her right away."

"Yes, ma'am."

George and Orelia were harvesting vegetables from their garden when Bessie came hurrying up. Without saying a word, she shoved the paper into his hands. Since Orelia had never been taught to read, he read the article out loud to her. "Unfortunately, I have been dealing with this issue in a spirit of compromise. The time has come for me, as the editor of this newspaper, to speak the truth. The Bible clearly states . . ."

George went on, reading the entire article with growing excitement. When he finished, he, Orelia and Bessie shared a look of wonder. They knew what this meant. Cash had summoned the moral authority of the Bible itself to refute slavery. He wasn't simply saying it was a bad idea for society. He was saying that anyone who engaged in it was a sinner and would go straight to hell. There was unimaginable courage in this act, and foolhardiness, as well. For it would make some people hate him even more than they already did.

Without saying a word, Bessie took the paper and hurried back to the house to give it to Cash.

As his marriage had deteriorated, Cash had moved out of the master bedroom and into another room. Now that his recuperation was moving along nicely, Mary Jane had moved him back into the master bedroom. As Bessie hurried up the stairs, she saw Mrs. Clay coming down. She'd hidden the paper in the folds of her skirt, and now she held onto it tightly, afraid what would happen if it slipped out and Mrs. Clay saw it.

"Bessie, where have you been?" Without waiting for a reply, she went on, "My ladies club will be here any minute now, and I want you to make that chocolate soufflé you do so well. It'll go real nice with our tea."

"Yes, ma'am," Bessie said nervously.

Glancing at the tall grandfather clock in the foyer, Mary Jane frowned. "It's after ten. They should be arriving by now. What on earth could be keeping them?"

Bessie didn't answer, though she understood perfectly why any proper lady in the upper reaches of Lexington society who'd read the paper that morning might have decided not to socialize with the Clays.

"Anyway, I'm sure they'll be here soon. Go make that soufflé."

"Yes, ma'am. I'll just check on Mr. Cash real quick, then I'll do that."

She started to head up the stairs, when Mary Jane asked, "Have you seen the paper this morning? I can't find it."

Bessie didn't believe in telling a lie, but this was one time when she felt it prudent to do so. "No, ma'am."

Mary Jane shook her head. "That boy is so unreliable."

She went on down the stairs to look out the front windows and see if anyone was coming. Bessie hurried into the master bedroom, the paper practically burning like a hot coal in her hand.

By noon, Mary Jane was beside herself. None of the women in her club had come. And even more surprising, none had sent their regrets. She didn't know what was going on, but she knew there was a reason for this ill-mannered behavior. And she had a dawning suspicion that it might have something to do with her husband and that newspaper that caused them nothing but trouble. There was only one thing to do. She called for the carriage to take her into town.

At Churchill Downs, the familiar sound of the bugler was heard as the thoroughbreds lined up in the wooden starting gates. The spectators were dressed to the hilt, the women wearing enormous hats, the men in top hats and ascot ties.

Morgan hurried up the aisle and sat down next to Hastings. He slapped a copy of The True American in his hand. "Read this!"

Hastings scanned the lead article quickly then looked up at Morgan. "He's gone too far this time! I want something done about this, and I want it done tonight!"

CHAPTER SEVENTEEN

The carriage carrying Mary Jane drove up to the newspaper office. A sign on the door said "Closed." A crowd had gathered in the street. They were well-dressed, clearly from the upper class. And they were furious. As Mary Jane drove up, some people recognized her. "Look! It's that damn fool's wife!"

People turned to look at her with the same hatred they felt for her husband. Someone else shouted at Mary Jane, "Where's your lunatic husband?! I'd like to give him a piece of my mind!"

A few people who were clearly not from the upper class were also there, and one of them responded to the last speaker, "I don't think you can spare even one piece of your mind! Cash has more brains than the lot of you put together!"

Frightened, Mary Jane ordered the driver to get her out of there, fast.

At that moment, Baker, Barnes and Lonsdale were sitting at a table in a secluded corner of the 12th Street Restaurant. A copy of The True American lay on the table. "This will put us right back to square one," Baker said irritably. "There's no question of compromise now. Whatever made him do such a damn fool thing?"

"It's a pity," Barnes agreed. "We've come so far using logic and reason, not trying to change things too much, too soon. This will blow up in our faces."

Lonsdale wasn't as upset as the other two. "I'm not so sure this will change how most people feel. And more importantly, how they vote."

Baker thought about that. "Maybe. Most voters will love it. The problem is Congress. Almost all congressmen own slaves, and their wives wouldn't want to do without their servants. They'll vote against anything Clay stands for now, even if it means getting run out of office in the next election."

"That wouldn't be so bad," Lonsdale said with a chuckle.

As Mary Jane's carriage drove away from the newspaper office, she saw her friend, Althea Bradford, walking down the sidewalk. "Pull over, driver," she ordered. Then she called out, "Althea!" The woman gave her a quick, angry glance, and then started to walk away. "Althea, what's wrong?" Mary Jane demanded.

"That madman husband of yours, that's what's wrong!"

"I don't understand."

"Don't you read your husband's own paper?"

"Not today."

"Well, you should. Then you'll understand why I will never set foot in your house again. And you are not welcome in mine!" She hurried away.

Mary Jane told the driver to take her to the nearest newsstand. The moment she saw the headline, she understood why no one had showed up at her house that morning.

Cash was up and dressed and about to go downstairs for the first time in two weeks, when Mary Jane came bursting into the bedroom. She threw her copy of the newspaper on the floor in front of him. "Why, Cash?! Why did you have to go so far?"

Before he could answer, she went on in a tirade, "There's a mob outside the newspaper office! Whitlow had to close up and leave, probably afraid for his life! The few friends I had left won't speak to me now! Everyone thinks you're crazy, and I think they may just be right!"

He looked at the headline. Seeing it in large type, the words practically screaming off the page, jolted him into reality. He'd been half-out of it when he wrote the editorial. Now he realized how offensive it would be to people. Including the very people whose support he needed to end slavery.

He tried to explain himself to Mary Jane. "Look, I've always held back. Always tried to compromise, because that's how everyone said I could ultimately succeed. But when I realized I came close to dying, without expressing what was in my heart, I felt I had to say what I truly believe."

"Didn't you consider how it might affect my life or our children's lives? How can you be so selfish?!"

He didn't know what to say to this. He had been too ill to think beyond the immediate goal of getting that editorial in print. But if he were honest, he'd have to admit that he would have done it, anyway. It simply had to be done. He looked at his wife, knowing there was nothing he could say that wouldn't make things even worse.

When he didn't speak, didn't apologize and beg her forgiveness, she said coldly, "I'm taking the children and going to stay with my parents."

"Mary Jane . . ."

"I can't live like this any longer, Cassius. And I won't put our children at risk. I've lost one child to your insane beliefs. I won't lose another."

Her words wounded him as deeply as she'd intended. He flinched and looked away.

Without another word, Mary Jane left.

Cash thought of going after her, but decided it would be best to let her cool down. After awhile he was certain she'd be back. It was inconceivable to him that he might actually lose his family.

But her description of the angry mob outside the newspaper office worried him. The cannons might not be enough of a defense. In spite of his weakness, he had George drive him into town. They picked up Whitlow and some others who Cash knew he could trust, and went to the office. The crowd was gone, dispersed by the authorities who were concerned it could turn dangerous and destructive.

As Cash walked up to the main entrance to the office, he found a piece of paper nailed to the door. The writing was rough, as if done in haste and anger. It read: "You are meaner than the autocrats of hell. You may think you can awe and curse the people of Kentucky to your infamous course. You will find when it is too late for life, the people are no cowards. Eternal hatred is locked up in the bosoms of braver men, your betters, for you. The hemp is ready for your neck. Your life cannot be spared. Plenty thirst for your blood – are determined to have it. It is unknown to you and your friends, if you have any, and in a way you little dream of."

It was signed, "Revengers."

If it was intended to scare off Cash, it failed miserably. When he finished reading, he simply crumpled up the note and tossed it on the ground. The ugly, naked threat infuriated him, and strengthened his resolve not to give way to the mob.

For the rest of the day and evening, Cash supervised as the others worked to shore up the newspaper's defenses. The outside doors and window shutters of the building were lined with sheet iron to prevent burning. The cannons were loaded with bullets, slugs and nails, and aimed at the front door, which was fastened with a heavy chain. Finally, a keg of powder was brought in, in case the worst happened and the office was overrun. In that event, Cash knew his life would be over, anyway. But he intended to take as many of the mob with him as possible.

Late that night a group of men, led by Hastings and Morgan, broke into the empty office of The True American. They didn't know about the cannon aimed at the door. Hastings insisted on going in first. A wire was attached to the door, and to a can filled with lead weights. The can was connected to another wire. The moment the door was opened, the wire pulled a striker across a flint, causing sparks to fall on some cotton bunting, igniting a short fuse on the cannon. Hastings only had a split second to register the fact that he was staring into a cannon, before it fired.

The others ducked for cover, as the front door and its frame were blown away. Hastings' mangled body hurtled out of the building, onto the sidewalk. Morgan gestured to two of the men. "You two get his body into the wagon! The rest of you help me get this press out of here! Hurry!"

Back at home late that night, Cash wrote an editorial intended to run in the next day's edition of The True American. Condemning "the despotic and irresponsible minority" of people who owned slaves, he wrote that slavery kept most people poor because it stunted the growth of the economy. "In Louisville, you pay about ten cents a head for killing hogs; in Cincinnati, the killer pays, on the contrary, the seller ten cents a head for the privilege of killing. Why the difference? In Cincinnati the hair is made into mattresses, the bristles into brushes, the blood into some chemical preparations, the hoofs into glue, the fat into lard and oil."

Well after midnight, Cash finally put down his pen and leaned back in his chair by the fireplace in the library. He sighed heavily. The house was so silent and empty without Mary Jane and the children. Then, exhausted from his efforts on that long, difficult day, he fell asleep right there.

When dawn came up at Whitehall, Cash was still sleeping soundly in his chair. On the table beside him were a Bible, a whisky bottle, and an empty glass.

Bessie came in and woke him. "Mr. Cash . . . wake up." He stirred and looked up at her with bloodshot eyes. "Mr. Whitlow's here and he's real upset about somethin'."

116

"Bring him on in, Bessie." He rose tiredly to face the editor.

Whitlow hurried in, looking ashen-faced. He stammered, "I'm sorry, Cash, I have terrible news. Somebody broke into the office last night."

"Did the cannons go off?"

"Yes. Judging by the blood splattered all over the floor, they did their job. But in spite of all our efforts, whoever it was still managed to clean us out. They took the press, the typesetting equipment and the type."

Cash didn't react as Whitlow expected. Thinking of Cash, Jr., he said evenly, "I know what terrible news is, and this doesn't come close. If they think this will put me out of business, they're dead wrong. I'll get new equipment in here as soon as possible. The next edition of The True American will be dedicated to the fools who thought they could beat me."

Whitlow was relieved to see Cash respond with determination. "I'll be ready to go back to work just as soon as you're ready. I hate missing out on a chance to cover all this news about the U.S. declaring war with Mexico."

Cash was startled. "War? When did this happen?"

"Yesterday. I just heard this morning. President Polk is already asking for volunteers."

Even though there had been several raids from Mexico into the Texas and California Territories, Cash knew Congress had resisted going to war. Polk must be asking for volunteers because Congress wouldn't authorize a draft. This was big news, and under normal circumstances Cash would have gone down to the newspaper office to write about it. But for a while, at least, that was impossible. In the meantime, he had something more urgent to attend to.

Whitlow left and Cash immediately called for his horse. Shortly afterwards, he was at the Warfield house. The servant who opened the door informed Cash that his wife didn't wish to see him. Cash pushed his way in.

As he entered the foyer, he heard Mary Jane's voice calling down to him from the top of the stairs. "Go home, Cash! It's over for us!"

He looked up at her. She registered the fact that from this vantage point, he actually appeared small and humbled. She'd never looked at him that way before, and it gave her courage to stand her ground.

"What about my children?!" he demanded.

"You'll be able to see them. Here. I won't let them go anywhere with you. I won't lose another one of them."

He wasn't a man to beg, but now he pleaded desperately, "Mary Jane, please . . ."

There's nothing more to say, Cash. I don't ever want to talk to you again. When you want to see the children, let my parents know in advance. I won't be around."

He wanted to tell her that he loved her, but at that moment he didn't feel it. And he knew she wouldn't care, anyway. His illness and near death had briefly rekindled a semblance of the love they'd once shared. But it was a tiny spark that quickly went out. He realized now that she was right. There was nothing more to say. He turned on his heel and left with a heavy heart.

The next day, Cash, Whitlow, Baker, Barnes and Lonsdale were seated around the conference table in the library. Cash began, "I've called you all together for a very special purpose." He turned to Whitlow. "I want you to set up a press in Cincinnati. It'll be more difficult for my enemies to attack me there."

"But what will you do, Cash?"

"I'm going away. While I'm gone, you'll print whatever my associates here tell you to do." At Whitlow's look of surprise, Cash said with a humorless smile, "I'm sure you'll find their views more moderate – and less dangerous – than mine. Something else, and this is important, there's a fellow in Springfield named Abraham Lincoln. I want you to start writing him up big. And make sure the paper gets circulated all over Illinois."

"Whatever you say, Cash. But where are you going?"

"I answered Polk's call for volunteers. Looks like I'll be spending some time in Mexico."

Whitlow was stunned. Even though the other men had already been informed of Cash's decision when he asked them to take over the paper, they still shook their heads in disapproval. Lonsdale said, "Cash, the volunteer army will be made up of misfits and neer-do-wells. Poor, white trash, frankly."

"My kind of people," Cash replied with a wry grin.

CHAPTER EIGHTEEN

1846

For some time there had been a dispute between the U.S. and Mexico over control of the Texas Territory. Cash had opposed the annexation of Texas, because he knew pro-slavery interests wanted to expand their influence there and were prepared to go to war to do it. But complex political and social pressures made war inevitable. As Cash had predicted, on May 11 the U.S. declared war against Mexico. At stake was Texas.

Despite his serious reservations about the conflict, Cash felt duty-bound to serve in the military, as his father had done in the War of 1812. Even when he had spoken against the coming war, at the same time he had said he would join in the fight if it happened. He felt it was his patriotic duty to fight for his country. He joined his father's original unit and the "Old Infantry Cavalry" set off on Kentucky thoroughbreds.

He had another reason, besides patriotism, for answering his country's call to arms. As he explained to Whitlow, "I want to prove to the people of the South that I warred not upon them, but upon slavery, that a man might hate slavery and denounce tyrants without being the enemy of his country."

The command first went to Memphis for training, where they were feted by the locals. Cash's men cheered and whistled good-naturedly when a pretty young woman gave him a flaming red ostrich plume. He stuck it in his hatband and boasted that he wanted the enemy to see him coming.

One month later Cash and a group of volunteers were on horseback somewhere in the Texas Panhandle. They'd been riding for weeks, passing great herds of wild horses, and vast stretches of empty land, without encountering the enemy. Now they were exhausted and covered with dust.

A young, tow-headed recruit, Jeff Lance, pointed to something off in the distance. "I can see the fort straight ahead, down in that valley. We should be there in half an hour or so."

"Looks more like an hour's ride to me," Cash said, amused at the boy's eagerness to get to the action.

"Who'll be in charge when we meet up with them Mexicans?"

"It's up to us to elect someone to be our commanding officer," one of the men responded.

"I nominate the old guy, Clay," one of the more mature men said.

"Old guy?" Cash replied, laughing. "I'm only thirty-six."

Grinning at Clay, the man went on, "I hear you're a mean hand with a Bowie knife. Fought more'n one man."

"In self-defense," Cash pointed out.

That was good enough for the others, none of whom had been in any kind of serious fight before. They unanimously elected Cash to be their commander.

Cash turned to Lance. "Seein' as how you're so ready to get into the action, I'm appointing you my corporal. Anything happens to me, you're in charge."

The boy was awestruck. Corporal. Wouldn't his family be proud when they heard about that?

Back in Lexington, a group of powerful men, including Morgan, were gathered in the same smoke-filled room at the Colonial House Hotel. "I think we're finally through with that devil, Clay," he said with a satisfied chuckle. "He's volunteered! Can you believe it?"

Another man jeered. "He'll be right at home with that riff-raff. And it'll keep him out of our hair for awhile."

"Maybe forever, if we're lucky," Morgan responded. "Lot of those volunteers won't be coming back. Here's hoping he's one of 'em." And he raised his glass in a toast.

At her parents' house, Mary Jane was tucking the children into bed. Young Green Clay was full of questions. "But why did Daddy have to go away?"

Mary Jane snapped, "He found another war to fight." Then, realizing she shouldn't say such things to the children, she went on in a calmer voice, "He felt that it was his duty."

"Will he be back soon?" Sally asked anxiously.

120

"I'm sure he will, honey." It was a lie, but a well-intentioned one. Mary Jane was sure of no such thing. But she didn't want the children to worry any more than they already were. Time enough to deal with that if the worst happened and their father never came back.

Cash and his men fought their first skirmish in a Texas meadow, against a small band of Mexican soldiers. They used bayonets in hand-to-hand combat. It was bloody, but quick. The surviving Mexicans were sent fleeing back to Mexico. The Americans were lucky. None of them were killed, and only two were injured, not seriously. They felt the thrill of victory – and the profound relief of surviving.

That night they rode into a small town and quickly dispersed into the bars and cantinas. The door of the Yellow Rose Cantina was wide enough so that several of them rode their horses on in. They found themselves face to face with some very drunk Mexican soldiers, and they quickly made them prisoners of war.

The next day, Cash and his men proudly rode into Fort McKenzie with their captives on a rope behind them. Most of the soldiers were standing at attention, listening to General Harold Allison. "Our orders are to make sure they do not think they can just go over on the other side of the river, wait, then attack us again, like they've been doing up to now. This time we are to follow them and drive them all the way back into Mexico itself. President Polk wants a complete victory, a total surrender. That is the only way America can make a peace agreement that will last."

The men shuffled nervously. This was a serious escalation of the conflict, and put them in even greater danger.

"Do you understand your orders, men?" the general demanded.

A few men nodded reluctantly, but no one spoke. Then finally a lone voice called out, "Yes, sir!"

It was Cash.

On the plains near Juarez, Mexico, Cash and his men, fifty in all now, chased a small band of Mexican soldiers over the top of a ridge. As Cash's group reached the crest, they brought their horses to an abrupt halt. The small band of Mexicans had joined what seemed like the entire Mexican army. The force of five hundred men, led by General Mendoza, faced the Americans.

Without hesitation, Cash raised his saber. Corporal Lance reached over to stop him. "We can't charge! It's crazy!"

121

Cash looked at his men, who were clearly terrified. "You all elected me your commanding officer. I order you to charge when I lower my saber."

"We elected you, sir; because we thought you had more experience than we did, and a little common sense to go with it. This is suicide, sir!"

Cash said tightly, "There's no way out, son. We can't outrun them. We can go down fighting, or we can be shot in the back like cowards." Lance looked at the other men desperately, as if hoping one of them would offer more hope. But they couldn't.

"This is war, Corporal," Cash reminded the young man. "This is what we volunteered for." With that, he lowered his saber and shouted, "Charge!"

The Mexican force had expected the Americans to turn and run, and they were prepared to give chase. Instead, the American soldiers were charging full tilt downhill toward them.

"Stupidos!" Mendoza muttered. Then he raised his saber and brought it down sharply. He and his men surged forward to meet the Americans.

Cash and his men fought valiantly, killing dozens of the enemy. But they were so badly outnumbered, it was no contest. In the heat of battle, Cash found himself standing over Mendoza, who'd fallen from his horse. He could easily put Mendoza away with his sword. All around Cash, his men were dying, including Corporal Lance. Cash knew that in a moment all his men would be dead if he didn't do something fast.

Instead of killing Mendoza, Cash ripped off a piece of Mendoza's white shirt, ran his sword through it, and raised it aloft, waving it frantically. Seeing the white flag of surrender, Mendoza ordered his men to stop.

The surviving American soldiers were taken prisoner. They expected to be taken to a Mexican prison. Instead, Cash was pulled aside, and his men were lined up in front of what appeared to be a firing squad.

Cash shouted at Mendoza. "What are you doing?! I surrendered!"

Mendoza didn't speak English. He gestured to one of his officers to speak to Cash. The man explained matter-of-factly, "It is customary to kill the soldiers and take the officers hostage."

"Remind the general that I could have killed him. Instead, I spared his life and surrendered in order to save the lives of my men."

The officer translated this to Mendoza. They had a brief exchange, and then the man turned back to Cash. "He says that is the custom. I am sorry."

Mendoza gave an order and the soldiers on the firing squad raised their rifles and pointed them at the line of terrified Americans. Cash grabbed the officer and shook him. "Tell him they were only following my orders! If he wants to kill someone, tell him to kill me! But spare my men!"

Angered by Cash's behavior, the officer jerked away. Tersely, he passed on the American's crazy request to the general. Hearing this, the general looked at Cash quizzically. For a moment, no one knew what would happen. Then the general shrugged, and gave another order. The soldiers in the firing squad put down their rifles. Cash and his men would be prisoners of war.

That night Cash and his men languished in a jail that was more like a dungeon. Despite the harsh circumstances, Cash fell into an exhausted sleep. A couple of the men talked in a low whisper. "Can you imagine that?" one asked. "It took a pretty brave man to do what he did."

"Unless he just wanted to die," the other responded cynically.

"No one wants to die." The soldier hesitated then asked, "Do you think they'll kill him?"

"Don't know. I hope not. I'm startin' to kinda like the old buzzard."

Cash dreamed of Mary Jane, standing at the top of the stairs in her parents' house, telling him to leave. Her bitter words, It's over for us!, were echoing in his mind when he was roughly awakened by someone shaking him.

"Wake up! Get up! Now!" It was the officer who had interpreted for Cash. "The general wants to see you!"

His men watched Cash be led away by the officer and a couple of soldiers, their rifles aimed at him. The two men, who had wondered about his fate the night before, shook their heads solemnly.

The officer and the soldiers took Cash to a cantina. Inside, several Mexican soldiers and some civilians were enjoying being entertained by a pretty young woman, who was singing and dancing to the music of a lone guitar. General Mendoza and a few of his officers sat at a table. The general gestured to Cash to sit down in an empty chair. Immediately a bottle of tequila and a plate of food were placed before him.

Cash asked the interpreter, "What is this? My last meal? I'm not hungry. Tell him to kill me and get it over with."

There was a brief exchange between the interpreter and the general, and the others at the table burst out laughing. Then the interpreter turned back to Cash. "General Mendoza says you are a very brave man. He does not wish to kill you. At least, not yet."

Cash had no idea how long this reprieve would last. But he decided he might as well take advantage of it. It wouldn't help to grow weak from hunger and thirst. He took a big slug of tequila, grimacing as it burned his throat. He said to the interpreter, "I don't imagine you have any cognac?"

This remark was translated to the others, who again roared with laughter. Taking another slug of tequila, Cash said, "Didn't think so."

Back at Whitehall, Mary Jane and the children were just finishing dinner. When Cash left, she had moved back home, feeling it would be best for the children. The moment Cash returned – if he returned – she intended to move back to her parents' house.

"Mother, is Daddy ever coming home?" Elisha asked. It had been an entire year. "Some of my friends at school say he went off to war 'cause he didn't care about us."

The other children listened intently for their mother's response.

Mary Jane couldn't bear for the children to feel their father didn't love them. Whatever Cash's faults, she knew his children meant everything to him, that's not why he left. He's a very brave man, and when there's a war, brave men don't stay home. No matter how hard it is for them to leave their families."

That answer seemed to mollify the children. Especially Elisha who now felt very proud of his father. But he still missed him terribly.

The next morning Cash woke up in a room in the cantina. Next to him in bed lay the Mexican girl who had entertained them all the night before. She stirred, opened her eyes slowly then smiled at him. Badly hung over, Cash had no idea how he had gotten here. Or why he wasn't back in the jail. The young woman didn't speak English, so Cash couldn't ask her what was going on.

He tried to think, to figure out if he'd been freed for some reason. At the very least, this could be a chance to rescue his men. Before he could form a plan, he heard shots ring out outside the cantina, and the shouts of soldiers. The amazing thing was, the shouts were in English.

124

At the jail Cash's men were liberated by the American soldiers who had overrun the town and sent Mendoza and his soldiers fleeing for their lives. An officer said to one of Cash's men, "We didn't expect to find any prisoners. They usually kill anyone they capture. Except for officers. Were there any officers?"

"Commander Clay," the man answered, shaking his head sadly. "They took him away to be shot last night."

"Would that be Cassius Clay?"

"Yes, sir."

"That's who I was looking for." He grinned. "General Scott won't be pleased that Clay's dead."

"General Winfield Scott?"

"That's him. He particularly wanted us to try to find Commander Clay."

At that moment, Cash hurried up to them. His men stared at him in shock, and then welcomed him enthusiastically. The officer watched all this with amazement. "Wait till General Scott hears about this".

On a lovely spring day in 1847, Mary Jane and the children waited anxiously at the train depot in Lexington. As the train pulled in, she bent down to them and said, "Remember, your father saved a lot of lives and you should be real proud of him."

The doors on the passenger cars opened, and people poured out. Finally, Cash appeared. His children ran toward him, yelling excitedly, "Daddy! Daddy!"

Cash swept up the children in his arms one by one and hugged them tightly. During the year he'd been gone, there'd been many times when he thought he'd never see them again. Now he didn't ever want to let them go.

When he looked up he found Mary Jane standing before him. They looked at each other without speaking. Then she threw herself into his arms and he held her close. "I love you," he whispered. "I know," she responded. Even though she couldn't say the words he longed to hear, he could tell by the way she clung to him that she still felt something for him, despite what she'd said the last time they were together.

She pulled back. "Someone else came to see you." She gestured to the waiting open carriage. Luther sat in the driver's seat. George sat beside him, a big, fat grin on his face. "Let's go home, Cash," she finished.

He hesitated. "Mary Jane, there's something I need to tell you . . ."

She said, "I'm willing to let go of the past, Cassius. And begin all over again."

The words were the sweetest he'd ever heard. She was giving him a second chance. And he was determined to make it work.

Cash and Mary Jane walked arm in arm to the carriage, the children dancing happily around them.

Cash and George hugged warmly. "Welcome home," George said with feeling.

"You have no idea how good it is to be back," Cash responded.

"We'd better be on our way," Mary Jane interjected, "or we'll be late for the ceremony."

"What ceremony?"

"Your welcome home ceremony. You're a hero."

Cash frowned. "All this fuss is a lot of foolishness. I'm no hero. It was just the way things worked out."

"That's not what your men say. The whole town's going to be there."

Cash smiled wryly. "I doubt that."

"After the article in our very own newspaper, about how you offered your life to save your men, everyone is behind you now."

He didn't believe it, but wasn't going to argue with Mary Jane so early into their reconciliation.

When the carriage arrived at the Lexington Courthouse Plaza, Cash was amazed to see that Mary Jane was right. With the exception of many of the large plantation owners, nearly the whole town was present. A band played energetically and a huge banner read "Welcome Home, Cash."

Mary Jane stood proudly at his side as they descended from the carriage, her arm linked with his.

The mayor stepped up to a podium and gestured to the band to stop. "It is with great pride that I stand here today to welcome home from that great conflict with Mexico – a war that ended in victory – Lexington's very own conquering hero. He's a man who was willing to die to save his troops. Cassius Clay!" The crowd burst into cheers and applause. Cash nodded humbly, while Mary Jane beamed with pride.

The mayor continued, "It gives me great pleasure to give to you, Cash, a token of our appreciation, this beautifully engraved sword, custom made by Tiffany's of New York, and donated by some of Fayette and Madison County's most prominent citizens."

He handed the silver ceremonial sword with its jewel-encrusted gold handle to Cash, who was absolutely astonished. He read the words engraved on the sword, "Kill the officers, spare the men. They are innocent. I only am responsible."

The crowd chanted, "Speech! Speech!" Cash moved reluctantly to the podium. This was one time he felt uncomfortable about speaking. He said sincerely, "I really do not deserve this any more than all the other volunteers. But I will accept it on behalf of the brave men who served under me. Especially those who paid the ultimate price." He smiled briefly, "Thank you very much."

The crowd roared and applauded. Mary Jane had to shout in his ear to be heard. "I'm so proud of you, Cash. The whole town loves you again, and so do I."

That night, Cash and Mary Jane shared the same bedroom for the first time in two years. At the end of a long night of passionate reconciliation, she lay in his arms and thought there was no place else in the world she wanted to be.

CHAPTER NINETEEN

1850

In Cincinnati, in the new office of The True American, Cash met with Whitlow. Also there was Cash's attorney, Barton Stevenson. "I did what you told me to do," Whitlow said. "Lincoln ran for Congress again, and we gave him all the support we could. I wasn't able to expand the newspaper into Illinois, but I printed all of his posters and flyers for his campaign committee."

"For free, I hope," Cash responded.

"Not free, but way below cost. Mr. Lincoln wouldn't take them free. He didn't want to be beholden to anyone. You know, of course, that he won by a large margin."

Cash nodded. "I have a feeling that 'Honest Abe' is going places."

"I doubt that," Whitlow said skeptically. "He looks like a giraffe in a top hat."

"Maybe so, but his moral qualities more than make up for any physical deficiency. I think he could be president some day."

Whitlow didn't agree, but he refrained from arguing with his boss.

Cash turned to Stevenson. "I'm moving the paper back to Kentucky, this time to Louisville. And I'm changing the name to 'The Louisville Examiner.' Take care of the paperwork."

This was news to Whitlow. "Why Louisville?"

"I want to build up an emancipation party in Kentucky. In order to do that, I need to broaden my base of support. You see, I plan to run for governor on the emancipation ticket next year."

Somehow neither Whitlow nor Stevenson was surprised.

Six months later, Cash stood before the assembly of Congressmen, receiving a special commendation for his heroism in Mexico. He was handed a certificate that had been mounted on a plaque. A medal hanging from a ribbon was placed around his neck.

The governor spoke. "To show Kentucky's appreciation for your heroic acts in Mexico, we want you to have this special cane with the original thirteen colonies engraved on the thirteen gold caps." The caps covered the stubs where branches had been cut off.

A well-dressed, imposing looking man stepped forward with the special cane as the governor continued, "Hamilton Rawlings will present it to you, and if you'll notice there is engraved upon the golden headpiece a very fitting description of you. 'Cassius Clay, the poor man's friend.'"

Watching proudly, Mary Jane stood with the other special guests and dignitaries. Her dress and cloak couldn't quite hide the fact that she was pregnant.

The following year, 1851, Cash made good on his promise to run for governor. Posters with Cash's likeness and the words, "Clay for Governor," were nailed to walls all over Lexington.

He was scheduled to speak at the State House in Springfield, but at the last minute he was denied the use of it. Determined to give his speech somewhere, he ended up speaking to 1,500 people from a hastily built platform near the city square.

"Would you help a runaway slave?" a man shouted from the audience.

"That depends on which way he's running," Cash shot back, to the audience's delight.

He went on to speak forcefully for over two hours, at one point saying with heartfelt conviction, "The question is whether the whole people of the South shall be free men or slaves? Or will you continue to compromise with this evil that lowers the white working man to one of being poor white trash and equally a slave to poverty. But you forget that you have no right to compromise this question; that you were not fighting your own battle; but that, like David, when he went against the giant, you are engaged in a conflict in which the Almighty himself is a party!"

The crowd roared its approval.

Sitting under nearby trees, Abraham Lincoln listened avidly to Cash's speech, as he whittled sticks. Looking at Lincoln from the platform, Cash was struck yet again by Lincoln's sad and homely, but somehow reassuring countenance.

Shortly after this speech, Cash and Lincoln found themselves traveling together on their way to New York to speak before the Young Men's Republican Union. Cash spoke at length about his views of slavery and the absolute necessity to abolish it. As was his habit, Lincoln listened politely.

When Cash finished, Lincoln said simply, "Yes, Cassius, I always thought that the man who made the corn should eat the corn."

Many people thought Lincoln's use of such common sayings made him look ill-bred and uneducated. But Cash knew this was part of Lincoln's natural, unaffected honesty. And he admired him enormously for it.

The "Committee of Sixty," a group composed mainly of plantation owners, called a meeting at the Colonial Hotel. Almost all the members were there. Morgan said bluntly, "Clay's a very wealthy man. With his new paper, he'll be hard to stop. It's going to take each and every one of us contributing both financially and through our connections in the press and other important circles to stop him. If we don't give it all we have, he's going to be our next governor."

One man spoke up. "The last fiasco cost us plenty!"

"And it got him out of the country and out of our legislature. But if you're right, this time it'll cost a lot more. We're going to have to bribe every editor of every newspaper in the state. We'll hire hundreds of people to take down his posters as fast as his volunteers put them up. Hire Pinkertons to dig up dirt on him. Spread ugly rumors. We'll sling mud like it's never been slung before!"

The mudslinging began quickly. A few days later, a headline in the Louisville newspaper that was Cash's competition, read: "CLAY DALLIES WITH DANCE HALL HUSSY." The article said, "While supposedly a hero in the Mexican-American War, Cassius Clay spent his nights drinking and carousing at the Black Cat Cantina in Toluca. He enjoyed food and drink while his soldiers were rotting in a stinking hole of a jail."

That article was soon followed by another, even more painful one. This time the headline read: "CLAY ACCUSES SLAVE OF POISONING HIS SON." The article went on to say, "According to Sheriff Jackson, Cassius Clay accused one of his former slaves of killing his son. It seems that Clay, who is running for governor, is a hypocrite who doesn't even enjoy the love of his own Negroes, as he so often claims."

At White Hall, Sheriff Jackson met with Cash in the library. "I came as soon as I could, Mr. Clay. Where is she?" As Cash lead him upstairs, he explained, "She's locked herself in her room and won't come out. She won't believe me. I need for you to tell her the truth."

When they reached the door to the master bedroom, Cash tried it, but it was still locked, as he expected. He yelled through the door, "Mary Jane! I have Sheriff Jackson here with me. He wants to talk to you."

In the bedroom, Mary Jane looked disheveled and distraught. Her hair was a mess, her eyes red from crying. She yelled back at her husband, "Who was it, Cash? Which one of them killed my little boy?!"

Sheriff Jackson responded, "Mrs. Clay, I do not believe that your servants had anything to do with the poisoning of your son. I know what the newspaper article said, but they twisted my words around. I spoke to you're your servants at the time, and I don't believe any of them would do that. You have to believe me."

After a long pause, the door finally opened, just a crack. Mary Jane peered suspiciously through the narrow opening. "He's making you say that."

"No, ma'am. No one could make me lie, especially about somethin' as serious as murder."

"But if it wasn't one of them, then who . . .?"

"I don't know, ma'am. I wish I did. I'd take great pleasure in stringin' him up, myself."

Mary Jane hesitated then said, "I need to talk to my husband alone."

Jackson nodded, then turned and left.

Mary Jane walked away from the door. Cash came into the room and they stood facing each other. "Do you swear to me, Cassius, that you're telling the truth about this?"

"I swear on our boy's life." He added, "I wouldn't lie to you, Mary Jane."

"About anything?"

"About anything."

132

"Then tell me this – is there any truth to that story about you and the cantina dancer?"

Somehow Cash had known this moment of truth would come. He couldn't lie to Mary Jane, even though he knew the truth would devastate her and perhaps end their marriage, which had been on shaky ground for several years.

He took a deep breath, then nodded slowly. "I'm afraid there's some truth to it."

Pain, then anger flashed across Mary Jane's face. "Some?! Did you sleep with her some?! I want the truth, Cassius, the whole truth!"

"The truth is, I don't know what happened. I thought I was eating my last meal. I drank too much. The next morning I woke up in . . . in bed with her. I have no memory of anything else."

She wanted, needed, him to say that nothing else happened. But he couldn't give her that reassurance. All he could do was say sincerely, "I didn't intend for anything else to happen. If I'd been sober, I wouldn't have even ended up in her bed."

"Are you using drink as an excuse?"

"No, not an excuse, just an explanation. I'm sorry, Mary Jane. More sorry than you can possibly know."

"I imagine you're most sorry about the effect this will have on your election chances," she said bitterly.

"I know the election is probably lost. I'm not happy about that. But I'm a lot more concerned with possibly losing you."

She looked at him, her mouth quivering, blinking back tears. Then, saying nothing, she threw herself into his arms, and he held her while she cried out her pain at his betrayal.

One week later a telegraph operator finished taking down a message. He handed it to a messenger. "Take this out to White Hall right away. They're waiting for it."

Looking at the message, the messenger shook his head. "Mr. Clay ain't gonna be none too happy about this."

At White Hall that night, Mary Jane and Cash had a quiet dinner alone together after the children went to sleep. Mary Jane smiled reassuringly at her husband. "You really didn't do too badly, Cassius. At least you beat the Whig candidate."

"I could have beat Taylor, too, if they hadn't spread those ugly stories about me."

"I know how disappointed you are. But maybe it's a blessing in disguise. Now we can spend more time together." An idea occurred to her and she said excitedly, "We could take a trip to New Orleans. Stay in the same hotel where we spent our honeymoon. Oh, Cassius, it would do us a world of good!"

He was too sunk in the disappointment of defeat to get excited about a trip. But he knew she was right. It would be good for them to get away for awhile, just the two of them. And hopefully finally banish the remaining tension between them because of what happened in Mexico. "All right," he agreed.

In New Orleans, Mary Jane modeled her new dresses for Cash in their hotel room. She'd been shopping for days, and there was a great deal to show off. She said blithely, "If only your darkies could vote, dear, you'd be governor and I'd have to decide which of these gowns to wear to the inaugural ball."

Cash frowned at her use of the word "darkies." He disliked it, and she knew it.

"One of these days, they will vote. We need to start educating them so they'll be ready to take on that responsibility."

Mary Jane didn't want to be drawn into another argument about a subject that she and Cash would never agree on. "Let's just forget about that for now, all right, dear?" She went to him, slipped her arms around his neck and lifted her face to his. "There are much better ways to while away our time here than talking about politics."

He bent down to kiss her and she responded with a passion that warmed his heart. She didn't share the beliefs that meant so much to him. But she still shared his bed. And she had given him the children who meant the world to him. That would have to be enough.

CHAPTER TWENTY

1854

C ash met with Whitlow in the Louisville office of The True American. Whitlow began, "We just got word Lincoln lost again." Cash shook his head in disappointment. Whitlow said bluntly, "He should've been satisfied being a congressman. He's failed twice now to get to the Senate."

"The people in his district know him and like him," Cash insisted. "The voters in the rest of the state just don't know enough about him. He'd make a good senator. And a good president, for that matter."

"I hear he used to make his living as a rail splitter. How's this for a slogan – 'Honest Abe, the rail splitter, for President'?"

Whitlow was joking, but Cash was dead serious. "I believe you may have something there. I'm going to write to him. After losing twice, he may be humble enough to take some free advice. And maybe some free flyers, next time around."

In Springfield two weeks later, Lincoln put down the letter and looked thoughtful. Watching him, Mary asked, "What is it, Abraham?"

"Our friend, Cash Clay, thinks I should run for president. He has some good ideas about how to go about it. Even says he'll back me by covering all my printing costs."

"That's wonderful!" Something about her husband's quizzical expression suggested to Mary that this wasn't all. "Is there a problem?"

Lincoln smiled. "He says he may run against me, just to keep me on my toes."

At the same time, the Reverend John Fee, a crusading abolitionist preacher, also received a letter from Cash. After reading it, he turned to his wife, Bernice. "A man named Cassius Clay read my anti-slavery pamphlet and has invited me to speak in Lexington. He says we can stay at his house while we're there."

"I hope it's nicer than the last place we stayed. We had to use half your offering to feed those poor folks."

When they arrived at Whitehall a few weeks later, both were in awe of the place. But there was no time to enjoy these luxurious surroundings that they were so unaccustomed to. Cash immediately began taking Rev. Fee to various locales to deliver his speech.

Two months later, the reverend and his wife were still at Whitehall, and he was still delivering speeches, the latest at Richmond Town Hall.

"It is God's will for all his creation to enjoy a fruitful life while still in the flesh and upon this great earth. He said, 'I was hungry and you fed me. I was naked and you clothed me. I was in prison and you visited me.' His disciples said, 'When were you naked, hungry or in prison?' And he answered them, 'That which you do unto the least of them, you do unto me.' Remember His words."

The crowd listened raptly. Fee went on, "Even those of you who consider black people little better than animals should heed the scriptures that command you to 'Go into all the world and preach the gospel to every creature.' That's right!" He pounded the podium for emphasis. "It says 'every creature.' We are told that we are to 'baptize them in the name of the Father, the Son and the Holy Spirit!' My brothers and sisters, make no mistake, this is not a suggestion from the Lord, but a commandment! He has put it in my heart to carry out this work. I have spoken before you for eight weeks now. It is time for you to listen to your heart."

Rev. Fee pointed to Cash, sitting in the front row. "Mr. Clay here has been kind enough to offer me ten acres of his finest Bluegrass land so I can build on it. First, to build a home for my wife and me. Then a church. And finally, a school to teach children of all colors. In order for my wife and me to carry out that mission, we need your help. I ask you to take a moment to pray about this with me."

Eyes closed, head bent, he went on, "Listen to that small voice in your heart, and you will know how much to give. The ushers will come among you in a minute to reap the harvest for the kingdom of God."

Ushers passed the offering baskets among the crowd. They were quickly stuffed with money. But no one gave more than Cash.

Through this young reverend, he'd found a way to make one of his promises to George come true – the education of black people.

Three years later Cash's carriage pulled up in front of the Fee's modest house. The entire family ran out to greet Cash and Mary Jane. Besides the reverend and his wife, there was a baby boy and a three-year-old girl, followed by a five-year-old black girl, Emily.

"Look!" Emily said excitedly, pointing to the beginnings of a building. "Daddy's building the school!"

George was helping the reverend with the framework. He waved to Cash, who grinned back at him.

Bernice said to Mary Jane, "It's so exciting to see the school actually becoming a reality. We can't thank you enough."

"It's been a community project," Cash said modestly.

The reverend responded, "But without you spearheading it, none of this would ever have happened – our home, the church. Bernice is right. We can never thank you enough."

"Knowing that all the children who live at Whitehall will have a school that welcomes them is thanks enough for me," Cash responded sincerely.

Several months later, the church-school that would later become Berea College was completed. Rev. Fee called it Berea after the place in the New Testament where the apostle Paul found the people "open-minded."

Cash spoke to a group of people who had contributed to the project, as well as the students. With the exception of the Fees' daughter, they were all black. "Rev. Fee has asked me to gather you all together to share with you an even bigger vision than this wonderful new school that now serves our little community. The good reverend sees the need for a small college that will also serve the needs of people of all colors."

Some people looked excited at this idea, but many seemed doubtful. The idea of starting a college was a daunting undertaking.

Cash continued, "I certainly agree that there is a need, a great need, and I felt that you all, like myself, would want to be part of building the first interracial college in America."

Looking out at the crowd, Cash knew most of them were far from convinced that such a thing could become a reality. But he didn't doubt it for a second. After all, they'd built this school. A college would just be a slightly bigger undertaking.

The college wasn't the only big dream that Cash harbored. In the summer of 1860, in the office of The True American, he looked over flyers that Whitlow had printed. They read, "Honest Abe Lincoln, the rail splitter, for President."

Smiling at Whitlow, Cash said, "You did a great job. I think he'll win."

Whitlow eyed him thoughtfully, then asked a question that had been bothering him for some time. "You're an influential member of the Republican Party. You got them to adopt a strong antislavery platform. Why don't you run for president, instead of spending your money supporting Lincoln?"

Cash admitted, "I've seriously considered it." Then he laughed. "But I couldn't even get elected governor!"

"That's different. That's just local politics. Now that you've become one of those new-fangled Republicans, you'll never be governor of Kentucky. Everybody here is a Democrat. But the presidency goes beyond the state."

"Even in Kentucky, it's the man, not the party, who gets elected," Cash argued. "If the voters like a man, it doesn't really matter much what party he's in."

Seeing Whitlow's look of silent disagreement, he went on, "Take Lincoln, for example. If his people use your pamphlets and take advantage of his humble beginnings, people will identify with him. That'll get him elected."

"Maybe," Whitlow said politely, but it was clear he disagreed. "I still say you'd make a hell of a president, Cash."

Cash didn't say anything. But a thought that he'd tried to dismiss refused to go away.

That night Cash brought up the idea with Mary Jane. "What would you think of me running for president?"

She was amazed. "Are you crazy? They kept you from becoming governor. What makes you think you could be elected president?"

"Simple mathematics. The northern states share my views, and that's where the population is centered. New York has seventy electoral votes. Kentucky only has two. They wouldn't be able to stop me, even if the state votes against me."

Mary Jane shook her head. "Cassius, I don't think I could bear to see you lose another election. It's too hard on you. And on me," she finished honestly.

Cash hesitated then said, "I could always be Lincoln's vice president."

"But how could you support him? He's pledged to keep the union together, even if it means individual states have the right to continue slavery."

"Years ago he took the position that slavery is immoral and unjust. I believe that in his heart his position has not changed. He's just trying to keep the South from seceding. And as vice president, I'd have a great deal of influence on his decisions."

"You've really given this a lot of thought, haven't you?"

Cash nodded. Then, "If he makes me his running mate, and we win, will you move to Washington with me?"

Mary Jane hesitated then smiled slowly. With a rare show of good humor about this sensitive subject, she said, "I'd have to. We'd be run out of Kentucky, for sure."

A speaker stood before a crowd in downtown Lexington. "A man of the people and for the people, that's who Honest Abe is. A man of humble beginnings, born in a log cabin. A man who has earned his living by the sweat of his very own brow."

The crowd of working class people responded enthusiastically. The speaker continued, "A rail splitter. Later, he became a surveyor, not by going to a fancy school, but by learning from books. He got his degree in law by studying and working for a judge. He made it on his own, the hard way. A working man, just like you and me."

Someone in the crowd called out, "How can we help him?"

"By putting up posters and talking to your friends and neighbors. Most of all, you can help by making a small campaign contribution and by getting your friends to do the same. Our man, 'Honest Abe,' isn't rich. He won't let the wealthy buy his loyalty. He's his own man. If he's going to get elected, he'll need your help."

A collection box was being passed around as he spoke. "Give what you can, no matter how small. Everyone who contributes one dollar will receive a piece of the very rail that our 'Honest Abe' split."

"I'll take a piece of that rail," a man shouted.

One campaign worker asked another, "Did Lincoln really split every piece of this rail?"

"It's possible. There's no way of knowing for sure."

"What would Lincoln think about this?"

"He doesn't know," the man admitted. "Look, it's not about the rail. It's the dream. That's what matters. These people want to hold a piece of his dream in their hands."

In a meeting hall on the other side of town, the governor of West Virginia was introducing his choice for president. "I'd like you to meet our current vice president, and the man who will soon be president – John Breckinridge!"

A train carrying Lincoln and his entourage was racing down the tracks to his next speaking engagement. Mary handed her husband a message from campaign headquarters just received in the telegraph car. "Senator Douglas just threw his hat in the ring for the Democratic nomination."

"Good," her husband retorted.

"Good?! He beat you twice for the senate."

"But at least half the delegates will be for Breckinridge. This will split the Democrats and give me a much better chance."

"But Cash is splitting the Republican vote, isn't he?"

"Only until the convention. Whoever has the most support at that time will get the other's backing. I can't see Douglas and Breckinridge working together like that. They're too far apart on the issues."

Mary was unconvinced. "But Cash is dead set against slavery. And it's more important for you to keep the union together."

"His message will play well in the big Northern cities. And mine will be most effective in the neutral states. He's lining up voters for the new Republican Party, and so am I."

"Are you sure he'll support you if it goes your way?"

"He gave me his word. You know him, Mary. What do you think?"

"He'll keep it," she said with conviction. "But what did you have to promise him in return?"

"He'd like to be vice president, but he knows I can't promise that."

"What if it goes his way? Could you support him as an emancipationist?"

"You know how I feel about slavery, Mary. If the country will go that way, I'm all for it. I believe in my heart that most people want to continue to live in the United, not the divided, States of America."

Cash spoke at the largest church in New York City, The Broadway Tabernacle. The huge crowd was comprised of both white and black working class people. It was the biggest crowd ever gathered under one roof in the history of New York State.

As always, Cash spoke while holding a small Bible in one hand. "There are many men professing the Christian religion who also believe slavery is a divine institution. I have never heard of a prayer offered for the holy bonds of slavery. Why not? If it is of God, then you, as a Christian, should pray for it."

The crowd hung on his every word. Unlike his speeches in Kentucky, this one had the full support of every listener.

Cash offered a sarcastic prayer. "Oh thou omnipotent and benevolent God, who has made all men of one flesh, thou father of all nations, we do devoutly beseech thee to defend and strengthen thy institution, American slavery!"

He stopped, then went on, "Have you ever heard anyone in any church pray such a prayer?" The crowd shook their heads. "No? Why not? I'll tell you why you never have heard and never will hear it. It's because it's wrong and everyone with even a little bit of Christ in their heart knows better!"

While Cash was speaking in New York, Lincoln was speaking at the University of Columbus, Ohio. The crowd was young and listened avidly. "I promise you that I will do everything in my power to keep these United States . . . united! I promise you that I will be a president of the people and for the people! I will take the time to listen to every problem, no matter how small!"

The crowd sensed that these were not just empty promises, but sincere ones. No one knew then that keeping those promises would cause Lincoln to age far more than four years during his first term as president.

After the cheers and applause died down, Lincoln went on, "The door to my White House will always be open to everyone, no matter how rich or how poor. I promise you that as a president of our new Republican party, I will always be a president of, and for, all the people of these United States of America!"

CHAPTER TWENTY-ONE

The Republican National Convention was held in Chicago in a giant wigwam built especially for the event. The noise inside was deafening, a combination of bands playing and delegates talking, shouting, clapping and whistling. Signs were raised throughout the throng. There were several different candidates' names – Bates, Cameron, Chase, Seward and Lincoln. The latter two had the most signs.

Scattered among these were several signs for Cash Clay. One read, "Our men are all for Lincoln, but their wives are all for Clay." When Mary Jane joined her husband in the Kentucky section and saw that particular sign, she frowned and looked away. It was a painful reminder of her husband's appeal to other women.

Cash's support was so strong that at least a thousand seats that were being held with signs and posters for Seward were being taken over by his supporters. As they dumped the Seward signs on the floor, a Seward supporter strenuously objected. "Hey! Those seats are reserved for our band and our marchers. You can't sit there!"

The Clay supporters ignored him, and soon they filled all the seats. These were big, tough-looking mountain men, and few delegates from Seward's home state of New York wanted to confront them. A chorus of male voices began chanting, "We want Clay! We want Clay!" They were joined by their wives, who shouted, "We want Cash!"

Outside the wigwam, a large band accompanied by hundreds of marchers dressed in red, white and blue military uniforms were chanting "Seward for President!" and making their way inside. They were stopped at the door by guards.

The head guard spoke with a heavy Kentucky accent. "You can't come in. Every seat is taken."

The head marcher spoke with a heavy New York accent. "But we already have seats! We're with the Seward delegation."

"You may have had seats," the guard responded, gesturing to the convention floor, "but someone else has them now."

At the same time the chairman of the convention was trying to quiet the crowd. "Quiet down, now! Take your seats! We now open the floor to nominations!"

The spokesman for the New York delegation stood up. "The delegation from the proud and mighty state of New York nominates our own William . . . H. . . .   Seward!" There was a rousing burst of applause from the New York section, followed by a chorus of "boo's" from the Clay supporters. Outside the convention floor, the frustrated Seward supporters who'd been denied access were yelling, "What's going on?!"

The spokesman for Illinois rose. "The great state of Illinois nominates Abraham Lincoln to be the next president of the United States!" Not only were the Illinois delegates cheering but so were many delegates from Ohio and Indiana. There were enthusiastic shouts of "We want Honest Abe!"

In the New York section, the Clay supporters who had stolen seats were shouting, "We want Abe!" One of the Clay supporters signaled to a Seward supporter who was looking in from outside. The Seward supporter assumed the noise was in support of his delegate, and he motioned to the band to start playing and to the marchers to applaud. Thus, Lincoln received the loudest, most enthusiastic response.

When the noise finally died down, the Clay supporters began chanting, "We want Clay! We want Clay!" They had diminished the response for Seward by shouting for Lincoln. Now they were shouting for their own man.

Later in the day, the delegates looked tired, frustrated and angry. A series of votes had failed to produce a clear choice. Now the latest vote took place. When the representative from Virginia rose, a hush fell over the crowd. Virginia was a border state and its vote would be critical.

"The great state of Virginia casts eight votes for William Seward and fourteen votes for Abraham Lincoln!"

The delegates from New York were shocked. They had expected Virginia to fully support Seward.

In the Indiana section, delegate Henry Lane rose to speak. Everyone knew that he supported Judge John McLean or Edward Bates, whoever could garner the most support. He spoke carefully. "In what appears to be a struggle between two candidates, William H. Seward and Abraham Lincoln, the great state of Indiana, the Hoosier State, casts all twenty-six of her votes for 'Honest Abe Lincoln'!"

If the New York delegation was shocked before, they were devastated now.

In the Kentucky section, Mary Jane turned to her husband and in a tone that revealed her disappointment, said, "It looks like your friend may make it." Cash knew she was right. He was profoundly torn. On the one hand, he'd hoped to get enough support to win the nomination outright. But if Lincoln won, there was still the possibility Cash could be his vice president.

At the end of the long, tense day the convention secretary stepped up to the podium to announce the results of the latest vote. Not a sound could be heard on the floor now as everyone held their breath. They were getting down to the wire now, and this vote or the next would almost certainly determine who the Republican nominee for president would be.

"William H. Seward of New York, one-hundred-seventy-three and one-half votes. Abraham Lincoln of Illinois one hundred and two votes. Edward Bates of Missouri, forty-eight votes. Simon Cameron of Pennsylvania, fifty and one-half votes."

Mary Jane turned to Cash. "Looks like I spoke too soon."

The secretary continued, "We are going to take a one and one-half hour break for dinner and when we return at six-thirty we'll cast a second ballot."

Back in the Kentucky section, a voice shouted, "Mr. Clay! Mr. Clay!" A young messenger was looking for Cash. He gestured to the boy, who hurried over. "Mr. Lincoln wanted me to ask you if you could speak to the Kansas delegation when they go back to their hotel for dinner. He said to tell you that they are wavering between him and Mr. Bates."

Cash said out loud, "Bates would be a big mistake."

The young messenger agreed. "Seeing as how it's really between Mr. Lincoln and Mr. Seward, Mr. Lincoln hopes you can persuade them to not waste their votes on someone who can't win."

Cash didn't hesitate. "Tell Mr. Lincoln I'll do my best."

As the Kansas delegates ate dinner, Cash stood before them and delivered an impromptu speech. "We know what your platform is, and I'm here to say that if a candidate is nominated on that platform, the South will make an attempt to dissolve the union. Your southern border extends from Maryland to Missouri, and on this side stands a determined body of men, resolute that the

145

Union shall not be destroyed except after a most desperate struggle."

The Kansans stopped eating and listened intently. "It makes a great difference to you whom you nominate. It makes a much more vital difference to all of us in the South. Our homes and all we possess are in peril. We demand of you a candidate who will inspire our courage and confidence. We call upon you to nominate Abraham Lincoln, who knows us and understands our aspirations."

The delegates began talking among themselves, some in support of Lincoln, many undecided.

Cash finished in a fierce tone, "Give us Lincoln, and we will push back your battle line from the Ohio River to the Tennessee, where it belongs. Give us Lincoln, and we will unite the strength of our union sentiment with the Union army, and bring success to your legions in the event of war. Do this for us, and we will go home and prepare for the coming conflict!"

Several delegates were on their feet, applauding Cash and shouting their support of Lincoln. Even those who weren't enthusiastic about this choice were persuaded by Cash's words.

At nine o'clock that evening the secretary read the final tally of the latest vote. "The new total for Seward is one-hundred-eighty-four and one-half votes! For Lincoln, one hundred-and-eighty-one votes!"

Cash slammed one large fist into the other in a gesture of triumph. Looking at him, Mary Jane was confused. "I don't understand. Why are you happy about this? He's still behind."

"Yes, but Pennsylvania just gave him Cameron's votes, and New Hampshire gave him their Chase and Fremont votes. When they take the next vote, most of the holdouts will have to choose between Seward and Lincoln. They don't like Seward because he's been campaigning against Chase and Fremont. Most of them won't be able to bring themselves to vote for Seward. They don't know Lincoln, so there's no reason to dislike him. I believe they'll vote for him."

By eleven o'clock, the exhausted delegates were desperate to finish this and go to bed. The secretary returned to the podium to relate the tally on what everyone knew would be the final vote. As the secretary was about to speak, Cash whispered to Mary Jane, "Lincoln has two-hundred-thirty-one and one-half votes. He needs two hundred and thirty-three to be nominated. I'm going to ask the Kentucky delegates to throw their two votes to him."

146

"But will they listen to you?"

"I'll tell them the truth – Lincoln's going to be nominated. Kentucky might as well be the first state to get on his bandwagon."

As Cash made his way to the front of his delegation, the head of the Ohio delegation, Howard Carter, saw what he was doing. In order to ensure the federal government's support for Ohio, and possibly get a coveted ambassadorship for Carter, he knew had to make a move now to tip the scales in Lincoln's favor, before someone else did.

Carter rose to speak quickly. "Mr. Secretary, the great state of Ohio desires to change four of its votes from Mr. Chase to Mr. Lincoln! The next President of the United States of America!"

The secretary flashed a questioning glance at the man in charge of the tally sheet. He nodded affirmation. Then the secretary told someone else to prepare to fire the cannons. To the delegates, he said, "Gentlemen, 'Honest Abe Lincoln' has just been nominated as the Republican candidate for President of the United States!"

Cash didn't care that Carter had beaten him to the punch. If he couldn't be president, then he wanted Lincoln to have that honor. Especially since there was the possibility that he might be vice president. He picked up Mary Jane and swung her around in celebration. She was beaming. Come the New Year, she might just be the wife of the vice president.

A huge photographic likeness of Lincoln on a banner was unfurled from the ceiling. One by one, the other states changed their votes to make the nomination unanimous. Even New York finally joined in.

In the Lincolns' suite at the Tremont Hotel, people were congratulating the nominee. He accepted their congratulations graciously, but quickly moved to have a private conversation with his closest political advisor, Alfred Hunsucker. "I'd like to seriously consider Cash Clay for vice president. He's helped me a lot in my campaign, and he has a great deal of support in the big cities."

Hunsucker frowned. "You brought me in to give you honest, objective advice. Nominating Clay for vice president would be akin to declaring war on the southern states. I saw to it that you got Ohio and Pennsylvania. In return, you have to accept Hannibal Hamlin for vice president. That was the deal."

Lincoln was surprised. "Who's Hamlin?"

"Someone who can help you get elected president. Unlike Clay, he doesn't have any enemies who'll do whatever it takes to keep him out of office."

Lincoln wasn't happy about this, but he knew Hunsucker was right. Cash Clay had very powerful enemies, and it was going to be difficult enough to get elected, without having to deal with that. He said, "What about Secretary of State?"

"Seward," Hunsucker said simply. "Without his support, you'll never get elected.

"Secretary of the Treasury?"

"Chase." Before Lincoln could argue, Hunsucker went on, "Without both of them on your side, you can't beat Douglas."

Having lost twice to Douglas for the senate, Lincoln couldn't argue. Before he could raise the issue of other posts, Hunsucker said, "Cameron for Secretary of War, Bates for Attorney General, and Welles for Secretary of the Navy. That should give you New York, Missouri and all of New England, in addition to Ohio and Pennsylvania."

Lincoln eyed his advisor thoughtfully. "You've got it all figured out, haven't you? But I won't forget about Clay. He deserves something for supporting me the way he has."

"Offer him an ambassadorship." When Lincoln frowned at this, Hunsucker said, "I'll be frank. Clay in your cabinet would be a big mistake. We can't afford to make mistakes if we're going to beat Douglas."

Lincoln knew that an ambassadorship wasn't what Cash hoped for. But he hadn't made any promises to him for a reason. He knew he might not be able to deliver. The election was far too critical to allow other considerations to jeopardize it. The Union itself was at stake.

The next day the convention hall was again full of noise as the delegates voted on the vice presidential candidate. The speaker announced the results of the first ballot: Hannibal Hamlin of Maine, one hundred-and-ninety-four votes, Cassius Clay of Kentucky one hundred-and-ten and one-half votes.

Mary Jane said optimistically, "That's how it began for Lincoln on the first ballot."

Cash was equally hopeful. "The second ballot will tell the story."

Henry Lane, an Indiana delegate, rose to speak. "Indiana moves that the nomination of Hannibal Hamlin be approved by unanimous acclimation."

Cash was completely caught off-guard. Mary Jane turned to him in confusion. "What's happening?"

Before Cash could answer, there was wild applause from the delegates who had been tipped off ahead of time about this predetermined choice. Soon others jumped on the bandwagon. In a moment, it was over. Cash would not be vice president.

Stunned at the speed with which the covert maneuver was executed, he was filled with frustration and disappointment. Mary Jane just looked at him helplessly. Before either could speak, a messenger handed Cash a message from Lincoln. It said that he would like to meet with Cash in his room that evening.

Mary Jane's optimism returned. "He'll probably offer you an important cabinet position."

Cash thought so, too.

Later that evening, Cash arrived at the Lincolns' suite in the Tremont Hotel. Lincoln took Cash's hand and shook it warmly. "I'm so glad to see you." He got straight to business. "I wanted you for my vice president, Cash. But it just couldn't work out."

"I understand." Cash waited expectantly. When Lincoln didn't say anything, but looked rather uncomfortable, Cash sensed that things were going to be even worse than he'd thought. He plunged in, "I would be honored to serve in your cabinet."

For a man as proud as Cash to raise this issue first, rather than waiting for it to be offered, was as close to begging as he had ever come.

Lincoln sighed heavily. "I'm sorry. I'm afraid that a cabinet position won't work out, either."

Cash's first angry thought was, after all I did to help him get the nomination; he won't give me anything in return!

Lincoln said hesitantly, knowing how Cash would take this, "I can offer you a position as our ambassador to Spain."

Cash's expression was grim. He said nothing. To him, this offer was worse than none at all, because it reeked of throwing leftover scraps to a dog. It took all his willpower to keep his temper in check. "If you'll excuse me, I must get back to my wife."

He turned to leave and Lincoln reached out a hand to stop him. "Cash – I'm sorry. There are political realities here that I can't change, no matter how much I'd like to. You have powerful enemies, and they're in a position to hurt not only you but my efforts to hold this country together."

Cash looked at him for a long moment. Then his anger faded and there was only acute disappointment. "I wanted the vice presidency badly. But if I could go back and undo my actions that put me in a position to have those enemies, I wouldn't do it. Because I did the right thing."

Lincoln looked at him in admiration. "That's why you can't go further in your political career. It's also why you're worth a hundred Hannibal Hamlins."

150

CHAPTER TWENTY-TWO

Cash sat in the library at Whitehall, going over the accounts. Mary Jane came in, interrupting him. "Cassius, your lunch is getting cold. The accounts can wait."

He looked at her for a moment then came to a decision. She needed to know the grim truth about their financial situation. "Mary Jane, I'm afraid I have some bad news. We're in a tight place financially."

"You mean we need to be careful for awhile?"

"It's more serious than that. We have no hard cash we can lay our hands on."

She had a difficult time taking this in. They were one of the wealthiest families in the state. How could that suddenly change? "But . . . what happened?"

"It seems I spent more than I should, supporting Lincoln's campaign, then my own. And the failure of the Cincinnati Bank has hit us hard."

It was especially difficult for Cash to admit that the bank, which he'd been strongly advised not to build, had not made it. It was his first – and he had decided it would be his last – business venture outside what he knew best, farming.

"How bad is it?" Mary Jane asked worriedly.

"We have the land and the farming equipment. We'll be all right if we can just bring in the spring crop. But we have no money to buy seed or to pay our help."

Mary Jane sat down heavily. She was torn between rage at her husband for risking their financial security, and fear of losing everything she'd taken for granted. "The Lexington Bank . . ." she whispered.

"They've already advanced money against our land. Now they're demanding to be repaid."

The thought that it was hopeless, there was nowhere to turn, immobilized her. She'd grown up in a wealthy family and had married into an equally wealthy one. It was simply inconceivable to her that money wasn't there for the taking.

Cash watched her reaction, feeling even guiltier than he'd already been feeling. He'd let down his family badly.

He went on with a heavy sigh, "I should have taken that appointment as ambassador to Spain. The salary would've kept us going."

"Maybe it's not too late!" Mary Jane cried.

"I had Whitlow check by telegraph yesterday. The appointment's been filled. I'm going to have to eat crow and write to Lincoln, asking if anything at all is available."

Mary Jane found her voice and it shook with anger. "You do that! You do whatever it takes! I've put up with a lot from you, Cassius, but I won't live in poverty with you! And I won't let our children suffer!"

With that, she stormed out. Cash sat there, feeling the sting of her words and the clear threat that she would leave him again. Bad as it was, this talk with Mary Jane was only one of the difficult things he had to do. Next, he had to talk to all their employees, the servants and the farm workers, to let them know that he wouldn't be able to pay them next month.

That night Cash and Mary Jane sat in tense silence in the dining room. Neither spoke. Suddenly, George came in, unannounced. "I'm sorry to interrupt your dinner," he began, "but I thought you'd want to know this right away. We had a meeting after you left. I told the folks how you were in this fix 'cause you spent all your money tryin' to do somethin' for 'em. We all agreed it's only right that we do somethin' for you, in return. We'll live off the land until after the spring harvest. We can get by. We've done it before and we can do it again."

Mary Jane said nothing, but her look of relief was profound. It didn't occur to her to thank George. As far as she was concerned, it was only right that their employees should be willing to do this. After all, Cash's foolish generosity toward them had created this financial mess.

Cash was overwhelmed by a sense of gratitude that brought tears to his eyes. He had to blink them back as he spoke. "I appreciate that, George. More than I can say. But I can't let you all do that."

George knew his friend well enough to have expected this response. He was prepared with a rebuttal. "So you're the only one who can give? We don't get to enjoy that privilege?"

"Of course not. But – "

"We owe you a debt of gratitude, Cash. This is our way of paying that debt."

Now Cash said what really bothered him about this. "You'd all be working for nothing. Like . . . like slaves. After all I've tried to do; I won't let you go back to that."

"When we were slaves, we had no choice. Now we do. And this is our choice."

Mary Jane saw that Cash remained unconvinced. She said tightly, "Don't let your foolish pride keep you from accepting this offer, Cassius." When he just looked at her stubbornly, she went on, "This isn't just about our family. What will happen to all those folks if we go under?"

That argument got to him. Most of those people had no place to go – at least no place where they could be free. Difficult as it was, he knew he had to swallow his pride and accept this gift of love. "All right, George. You tell everyone I said thank you. From the bottom of my heart."

George grinned. "You're welcome."

"And you tell 'em that I'll see to it their back wages are paid up just as soon as possible."

"We all know we can count on you, Cash."

George left, and for the first time that day, Mary Jane breathed a sigh of relief. "Thank God. We'll be all right now."

Cash wasn't able to take such a simplistic, self-centered view of what had just happened. He swore he'd never again let down anyone who depended on him to take care of them.

In Springfield, Illinois, Lincoln was reading the letter from Cash when Hunsacker burst in. "It couldn't have worked out better. After fifty-seven ballots, Douglas still couldn't get the necessary two-thirds majority. So they moved the convention from Charleston to Baltimore, as though that will somehow make a difference."

"What happened in Baltimore?"

153

"Oh, they finally nominated Douglas, all right. But not until the Breckinridge delegates withdrew. The delegates who favored secession then had their own convention and nominated Breckinridge. So now the Democrats have two candidates for president."

Lincoln smiled slowly. That would help his campaign enormously.

"There's more good news," Hunsucker went on. "The old Whig Party has renamed itself the 'Constitutional Union Party,' and nominated John Bell. The presidential vote will be split four ways!"

"But he'll get some of my votes," Lincoln pointed out.

"He'll get some of everybody's votes. The more informed voters will be split between Douglas, Breckinridge and Bell. The working people who bought a piece of your rail will all vote for you. We're gonna win this thing, Abe."

"Maybe. But I'm not celebrating just yet." Before Hunsucker could argue with Lincoln's cautious attitude, Lincoln went on, "It seems my old friend, Cash Clay, is in trouble. He needs an appointment that carries with it a substantial salary."

"He was quick to turn down the ambassadorship to Spain. Now he's coming begging."

"Cash Clay doesn't beg!" Lincoln snapped. "We owe him. Don't you forget it."

Hunsucker was suitably chastised. He thought for a moment then said,   "The ambassador to Russia wants to retire."

Lincoln eyed his advisor shrewdly. "You just want to get Clay as far away from me as possible."

Hunsucker didn't deny this. Clay was a firebrand who refused to play politics the way Hunsucker knew it needed to be played in order to win. And he had powerful enemies, who could easily become Lincoln's enemies. His vehement anti-slavery stance could hurt Lincoln's chances for election, if people thought Lincoln shared those views. This was a good time to get Clay out of the country.

The day after the election, the results weren't in yet. Lincoln lay on the sofa, taking a nap, while Mary sat nearby, waiting anxiously for news. Hunsucker came hurrying in, holding a telegram, and stopped when he saw his boss sound asleep.

"How can he sleep at a time like this?" he whispered to Mary. She smiled. "He said it's in God's hands, and to wake him up only if he won."

"Then we'd better wake him up," Hunsucker said with a huge grin.

Mary went to her husband and gently shook his shoulder. "Abraham, wake up!"

He stirred, then opened his eyes. Seeing Hunsucker, he said, "Well?"

"There's gonna be a rail splitter in the White House!"

He handed Lincoln the telegram. But instead of reacting with jubilation, he frowned. "Thirty-eight percent of the vote. That's not much of a victory. I'll be a lame-duck president with little power in Congress."

"That was bound to happen with so many candidates. All that matters, Abe, is that you won."

"With God's help," Lincoln said. "God put me in office for a purpose. And I believe that purpose is to hold this nation together."

"The first challenge will be South Carolina," Hunsucker said thoughtfully. "I just hope they stay in the Union, despite their threat to secede if you won."

"They've been unhappy with the Union from the very day it was formed."

"But realistically, what can they do? Form their own country?"

Lincoln responded, "That's just what I'm afraid they'll try to do. And take other states with them."

He hadn't even taken a moment to savor his victory. He'd immediately jumped forward to the very real threat that faced the country. He was terribly, terribly afraid of what the near future might hold.

CHAPTER TWENTY-THREE

1861

Cash, Mary Jane and the children were in a suite at the Willard Hotel in Washington. "As soon as I get done with my business at the White House, I'll be back to get you and the children," he said to Mary Jane. "The city's full of secessionists and traitors. The sooner we get out of here, the better. We can take the train to New York and spend a few days there before sailing to St. Petersburg."

"This is a good time to get the children out of the country," Mary Jane said soberly. "I just wish Green was with us."

Cash didn't say anything, but he shared her deep concern for their oldest son, who had just enlisted in the Union Army.

Mary Jane went on worriedly, "With all the southern states seceding, we'll probably be at war at any moment."

"So far Kentucky has remained neutral," Cash reminded her, trying to reassure her. But his words lacked conviction. He knew if there was war, no one would be able to hide behind the safety of neutrality. And their son would be in the thick of it. Because of his experiences in the Mexican-American War Cash knew too much about the horrors of battle to have any romantic illusions about it. He'd been enormously proud of Green for being courageous enough to do his duty. But he had prayed that it wouldn't come to armed conflict.

Later, at the White House, Cash was ushered in to see Lincoln's appointment secretary, Mrs. Kennedy, instead of the president himself. "I'm sorry, ambassador, but the president is tied up in urgent meetings all day. It seems the rebel forces destroyed a number of Union warships in Chesapeake Bay, and we've had numerous casualties in Baltimore."

"You mean the war has started?!" Cash was stunned. He hadn't expected this level of conflict so quickly. His first thought was of his son, Green, who might very well soon be in a battle.

"We've just learned that the South has formed the Confederacy. Virginia is the latest state to join."

"My God! That's less than five miles from here. What about Kentucky? I just left there three days ago and everything seemed calm."

"Kentucky is holding with us so far. Mr. Lincoln wanted you to know that he's grateful for all you've done in your state. He apologizes for not being able to meet with you personally, but he wants you to know that Secretary Seward has everything ready for your trip."

"Where is Seward's office?"

"Right down the hall, third door on the left." She asked carefully, "Is your family with you?"

"Yes, I'm taking them to Russia with me."

"You might want to get them out of the city as soon as possible. Rumor has it there may be an attempt to take over the capitol."

As Cash walked down the hall to Seward's office, he couldn't believe how rapidly peace had turned to war. Lincoln's election had been like lighting a fuse to a powder keg. The day after the election results were announced, South Carolina had seceded, quickly followed by other Southern states. Now there was actual armed conflict. Cash prayed that Kentucky wouldn't be drawn into it, but he knew it probably would. Mary Jane was right. This was a good time to get their children away from here.

In Seward's office, Cash accepted his credentials as ambassador to Russia. "What about expenses?" he asked, when Seward didn't raise the issue. "Isn't there an advance to cover my travel expenses?"

"Just submit a record of your expenses after you get there. We'll send you a reimbursement voucher."

"But that could take a month. There are nine people traveling in my party -- my wife, five of our children, my nephew and a nanny. I can't wait a month to be reimbursed."

"Probably more like two months, given the state of things," Seward said coolly. "Is that a problem for you, Mr. Clay?"

It was definitely a problem, but Cash wasn't about to give Seward the satisfaction of seeing that his financial situation was desperate. "Not at all," he replied then left.

Watching him leave, Seward thought, what the hell does he expect after ruining my chances for the presidency?

Outside, Cash hailed a carriage and told the driver to take him to The Willard, and to hurry. "Getting out of town?" the driver asked.

"Why do you say that?"

"Hear tell, the rebs are about to attack the city any minute now. You're my last fare. I'm leaving tonight for Philadelphia."

"That's just a rumor," Cash said.

"My cousin's one of 'em. According to him, they've infiltrated all over here, and are just waitin' for the signal."

Cash had no way of knowing if the driver's cousin knew what he was talking about or not. But he didn't want to take any chances with his family's safety. He pulled out a wad of bills. "My family's here. Can you take them to Philadelphia with you?"

The driver eyed the money greedily. "I'll be happy to accommodate 'em."

When the carriage arrived at The Willard, the driver waited while Cash ran up to his suite. When he burst in, Mary Jane looked at him in surprise. "Cash, what the –

"You've got to get everyone together and get out of here now. There's a carriage waiting to take you and the children to Philadelphia."

"Philadelphia?! But why?"

Without answering her question, Cash went on, "Check in at the William Penn Hotel. They'll extend credit to you until I get there."

"What's going on?"

"I don't have time to explain."

"But where will you be?"

"I don't know yet. But I'll get in touch with you as soon as I can."

"Cash!"

"Don't argue, Mary Jane! Please hurry."

Mary Jane gathered everyone and their luggage together, protesting all the while. Cash saw them off. His last words to her were, "I love you." He didn't know what might happen, but he was all too aware that this might be the last time he would ever see his wife and children.

Cash hurried to the Senate building, to the office of his old friend, Senator Lane. "There's no time to waste!" he insisted. "We've got to get together all the volunteers we can to stop the rebels if they do attack the city."

"I'll get together as many men as I can trust from the congressional staff," Lane responded soberly. "You can do your recruiting at the downtown military headquarters. Let's meet in the main mess hall in the Navy Yard at ten o'clock tonight."

"Tell your people to be careful who they talk to and what they say. The Willard is crawling with rebels."

"How do you know that?"

"Before I left, I checked out the guests milling around the lobby. At least half of 'em have Southern accents."

"They might have uniforms and rifles packed in their bags in their rooms," Lane said, thinking furiously.

"I checked with the bellman. He said he's never seen so many men traveling by themselves and checking in with steamer trunks."

"We'll have to check out every hotel in the city. They could be all over."

Cash said bluntly, "Don't let Colonel McGruder find out about this. I believe he'll be on their side when the time comes."

Lane didn't argue. He knew McGruder's political views. "We'll need a password to ensure that we don't get infiltrated."

"Let's use 'Green.' That's my oldest son's name."

"Green it is, then. Let's get Secretary Cameron to authorize this."

Cameron, the Secretary of War, listened intently as Cash and Senator Lane explained what they wanted to do. Cash said eagerly, "I want to offer my services as an officer to raise a regiment or even as a private in the ranks. Whatever you feel is most helpful."

Cameron was both surprised and amused at this. "I don't believe I ever heard of a foreign minister volunteering in the ranks."

"Then let's make history, Mr. Secretary."

"I don't think that'll be necessary, Major Clay. I'll issue a special order authorizing you and General Lane to enlist volunteers into your secret guard. Good luck, gentlemen!"

At military headquarters, an officer was speaking in low tones with Colonel McGruder. "I'm telling you, sir, this Major Clay has a special order from the Secretary of War, giving him and General Lane the authority to select volunteers from among our troops."

"What do they think they're gonna do with these volunteers?" McGruder asked skeptically.

"Take 'em under their command to the Naval Yard."

Now McGruder was concerned. Not only were the powers-that-be aware of a potential threat, they had taken steps to deal with it. The advantage of surprise was lost. "We've got to get word to our people to call off the attack. Get our forces out of the city!"

That night Cash and two-dozen uniformed union soldiers, with bayonets fixed to their rifles, entered the Hamilton Hotel. Cash was an imposing sight, wearing his ceremonial sword and three pistols tucked into his uniform. There was an ostrich feather, dyed red, in his hat. He didn't want to hide from the enemy. In fact, he wanted everyone to know exactly who they were dealing with.

Cash showed the hotel manager his papers authorizing him to search the hotel. Then the troops fanned out to every floor, forcing their way into room after room. In several rooms they found rebel uniforms and rifles, and they arrested the occupants.

At the same time, at the Washington Hotel, General Lane and his troops left with a dozen prisoners.

When Cash and his troops reached the Willard Hotel, the desk clerk said, "If you're lookin' for lodging, we have plenty of rooms. Half of our guests suddenly checked out."

Realizing they'd gotten here too late, Cash and his men left hurriedly to go to the next hotel.

Later that night, it was very quiet at the Naval Yard. Only the sounds of seagulls and foghorns broke the stillness. Then the sound of marching soldiers could be heard, at first barely audible, but growing louder as they came closer. Cash and his men led dozens of prisoners into the Yard, followed shortly by Lane and his men, with dozens more.

Two days later, Cash met with Lincoln in the Oval Office at the White House. The president handed him a special presentation case made out of solid oak. "I want you to have this as a token of my personal appreciation for what you have done to protect me and the capitol during these grievous times."

Opening the case, Cash found a special Colt revolver. He was enormously touched by the president's gesture. "You don't know how much this means to me, Mr. President. Thank you."

"As a result of your quick thinking and courageous action, Cash, Washington didn't fall prey to the Confederates' planned raid. I want to appoint you Major General, and I'd like you to take command of one of our largest regiments."

Cash hesitated. This was both an enormous honor and a serious responsibility that he was eager to accept. But there was an issue that had to be raised. "I cannot be a commander of troops that have a rifle in one hand and chains in another."

Lincoln frowned. "You know that I pledged to keep the Union together even if it meant protecting the southern states' right to own slaves."

"But that was before they seceded. Your efforts at compromise didn't work. There is no longer a Union to hold together at any cost." Cash hesitated. What he was about to add wasn't easy, but he felt that morally he had no choice. "When the time comes that you decide to take an official stand on slavery, then I will be happy to be recalled from Russia and assume the command you have generously offered."

Lincoln sensed how much the command meant to Cash, and what it cost him to turn it down. Very few men would have done what Cash just did. Lincoln said with genuine admiration, "I understand your position. I'll hold you to your offer when and if the time comes."

Cash saluted the president, then left.

Watching him walk away from a commission that he wanted badly, Lincoln thought what an amazing man Cash Clay was. He was all too human in many ways. He could be arrogant and stubborn and willful to a sometimes dangerous degree. He was incapable of being cautious, even when caution would have helped a situation enormously.

But he was also one of the very few men Lincoln had ever known whose commitment to his principles never wavered, no matter how high a price he had to pay.

CHAPTER TWENTY-FOUR

At New York harbor, Cash and his family walked across the gangplank onto a big steamer. Brutus was fourteen now, nearly a young man, and the two older girls, Mary Barr and Sally, were young ladies. Laura, thirteen, carried the baby, Annie.

Mary Jane was enormously excited. "I hear that Seward's good friend, Charles Adams, is sailing with us to our first stop." Adams was Lincoln's new minister to England.

After his experience with Seward, Cash wasn't thrilled by this prospect.

"What is our first stop, father?" Laura asked.

"London."

"London! I didn't realize we were stopping there. I thought we were going straight to Russia."

"I decided that as long as I was going to take this ambassadorship, we might as well take advantage of the opportunity to see some of Europe. And the president has asked me to check out how the British Parliament is reacting to the war."

A few days later, at the White House, Lincoln and his cabinet were deeply involved in a discussion of the war. Cameron was speaking. "Since Fort Sumter has fallen, it's getting increasingly difficult to protect Johnson Fort. In Baltimore we lost over a thousand men who were on their way there from Boston. And several of our ships have been sunk in Chesapeake Bay."

Lincoln shook his head sadly. "A thousand men . . . it should never have come to this."

Seward asked, "How many men and ships have the Confederates lost?"

"Far less than we have. Suffice it to say that at this point, they are winning the war."

Lincoln reached for a stack of papers and shuffled through it until he found the one he wanted. He pushed it into the middle of the conference table so everyone could take a look at it. "Some advisors have suggested this course of action. At this point, I tend to agree with them."

Cameron skimmed the paper, then looked up in surprise. "An Emancipation Proclamation? But that reneges on everything in your campaign platform."

"I was trying to keep the United States united. Things have, obviously, changed. Why should we let the Confederates use slaves to support their war effort? Wouldn't it be better for them, and for us, if they were free and fighting in Union uniforms?"

Seward responded, "This makes a lot of sense."

Lincoln was relieved to have Seward's support. Of all his cabinet members, he had worried most about Seward, who still felt he should have been president.

Seward went on, "Unfortunately, we can't put this out right now, while they're winning the war. It would look like a desperate measure on our part. And that would just embolden them to be more aggressive, and demoralize our own troops."

"Then what do you suggest?" Lincoln asked.

" If I were president," Seward said pointedly, "I'd wait until we win a battle or two, then put this out."

Lincoln considered this suggestion thoughtfully for a moment. Then he put the proclamation back in the stack of papers. "Very well. We'll wait. But not for long."

In England, Cash learned that Arkansas and Tennessee had seceded and that Jefferson Davis, the president of the Confederacy, had moved his capital to Richmond, Virginia, perilously close to Washington. At the same time that the war was going badly for the Union, Queen Victoria recognized the Confederates as belligerents, the first step in eventually recognizing their status as a separate nation.

At the House of Lords, Cash sat with John Lothrop Motley, a prominent American historian living in London. Looking around at this august gathering, Cash knew that the aristocracy would like nothing more than to see the Union dissolved. His only hope lay with the vast majority of middle-class and working-class Englishmen, who viewed the South with distaste because of Harriet Beecher Stowe's powerful novel, Uncle Tom's Cabin.

Lord Palmerston was speaking. "Finally, I have before me a petition from a number of men and women in the United States asking for aid to the Union cause."

Lord Brougham rose. "I ask the speaker's indulgence to address the House for one moment."

Lord Palmerston gestured acquiescence to Brougham and sat down.

Motley whispered to Cash. "Brougham is very liberal and an anti-slavery advocate."

Lord Brougham began, "This question of slavery in America is a delicate one. Inasmuch as this is new subject matter for our consideration, I ask that this petition be tabled without further comment until some later date."

Cash was surprised and dismayed. He whispered to Motley, "If he's anti-slavery, I'd hate to meet a pro-slavery Englishman."

"Don't worry. I've arranged a meeting with Palmerston at his home tonight."

That night Cash and Motley listened as Palmerston spoke candidly. "I'm afraid that England never allows a sentiment such as slavery to overthrow her policy of universal dominion. She is especially jealous of all rivalry on the sea."

Cash spoke with equal candor. "You're saying that England would rather see our house divided because it makes us a weaker nation, especially in terms of our navy."

"That's not what I'm saying at all, Mr. Clay," Palmerston snapped. "You're trying to put words in my mouth."

Cash had no patience for this political prevarication. "I'm afraid my government will have to take a more direct approach in our efforts to seek England's help. Good day, sir."

With that, he rose and left.

Motley hurriedly excused himself and caught up with Cash outside. "What do you intend to do?" he asked anxiously, worried about this man who was clearly a loose canon.

"You'll know when it happens. One thing is for sure, whatever I do will teach these pompous bastards a lesson."

Two days later Palmerston was enjoying lunch at a restaurant near the House of Lords, when he was joined by Brougham, who had a copy of the London Times in his hand. Brougham laid the paper down in front of Palmerston, who picked it up and saw that it was turned to an open letter from Cash.

Palmerston read aloud, "'To all the English who love freedom and everything it stands for . . .'"

Brougham interrupted. "Read the first paragraph on the next page."

Palmerston turned the page and continued reading, "The autocracy of Europe were ready to destroy the great Republic, which was ever a menace to the crowned-heads. That whilst we fought simply for empire, the people of England and France were indifferent to our success; but that, in the cause of liberty, we would have a safe check upon their rulers, who would not dare to interfere in behalf of slavery. If fall we must, let us fall with the flag of university liberty and justice nailed to the mast-head. Then, at least, we should have the help of God, and the sympathies of mankind, for a future struggle, and live in the memory of the good in all time."

Both Palmerston and Brougham were stunned. Cassius Clay had done what Lincoln couldn't do, because it would cause a diplomatic crisis between England and the U.S. Even the U.S. minister to England, Adams, was afraid to speak out, for fear of antagonizing the English aristocracy who ran the government. But Cash had characteristically ignored protocol and caution, and appealed directly to the nobler instincts of the English people.

Brougham said, "I don't think we should meet with those representatives from the Confederacy, after all. They want us to support their secession and loan them money. But the timing isn't right. Especially after the fuss this article will raise."

Palmerston agreed.

While this debate raged in England, back in the U.S. a fierce, bloody battle raged at Bunker Hill Meadow. A small contingent of Union troops were trying desperately to hold on as they waited for reinforcements and supplies.

Suddenly they were surprised by an attack from behind their own lines. Turning to defend themselves, they began firing in the opposite direction than the one they had been firing from. Confederate General Johnston raised his saber high above his head, ready to give the signal to his troops to forge ahead. Seeing that General Beauregard was ready, he dropped his saber and yelled, "Charge!"

The rebel troops began charging forward toward the Union line, screaming rebel yells as they ran. The Union soldiers were caught between bullets flying from both directions. The terrified soldiers realized they were trapped and outnumbered.

Among the Union troops was George. The deafening noise and chaos made him feel disoriented, as well as frightened. This was close-quarters combat, hand to hand. Many soldiers didn't have time to reload their muskets, so they used them like clubs on each other. Everywhere were bodies and pieces of bodies that had been blown off by musket fire or hacked off by sabers.

George fired, reloaded as quickly as possible, fired again in the opposite direction, then reloaded, turned and fired again. His aim was deadly accurate.

A rebel lieutenant shouted, "Somebody get that nigger! He's shooting us down like squirrels in a tree."

George was immediately hit in the leg, then in the shoulder. He fell to the ground, dropping his rifle, screaming in agony. He lay there, utterly helpless, while the carnage continued around him, and everyone who didn't run away became either a victim or a killer.

George saw a young rebel soldier, no older than fifteen, covered in blood that might have been his own or someone else's, or both, come rushing toward him. There was a combination of fear and blood lust as the boy raised his bayonet, preparing to shove it into George's chest.

At the last second, the boy closed his eyes. This terrified boy, determined to kill him, was the last thing George thought he would ever see.

CHAPTER TWENTY-FIVE

St. Petersburg, 1861

The beauty of the architecture and grandeur of Alexander II's palace in St. Petersburg typified the incredible opulence of the lifestyle of the tsars. Cash and Mary Jane sat at a banquet table that could easily seat fifty people. There were only about thirty there to greet the new American ambassador, but they included the most important and powerful Russians. Seated next to the emperor and empress were Prince Gortachow and his wife. On the tsar's left was Prince Gortachow's sister-in-law, the Princess Radziwill, and Princess Kotzouby, the wealthiest woman in the country.

The opulence of the surroundings and the lavish dress and jewels left Mary Jane awestruck and feeling totally out of place. But Cash had explained to her that his job was to keep the tsar on the Union side, and therefore his efforts must be focused on ingratiating himself into Russian society. He made a point of learning the special likes and dislikes of prominent people, and generously bestowed appropriate gifts on them. If someone especially liked flowers, Cash sent the most magnificent bouquets. If someone else's taste ran to fine art, he gave some of the rarest. Much of his salary actually went to pay for gifts to influential people.

Social events like this one weren't idle gatherings, Cash had told Mary Jane. They were a necessary part of his efforts to establish close ties between the United States and Russia, and thus to help save the union.

Tsar Alexander turned to Cash. "I've read many of your writings, Major Clay. Or would you prefer to be called Ambassador Clay?"

"My friends call me Cash."

But the tsar was unable to be so informal. "I was pleased to learn that you and I think very much alike, Mr. Clay. Just two months ago I freed twenty-one million serfs, or, as you call them, slaves."

Wanting to compliment the tsar, Cash turned to the empress. "Your husband is a great man, ma'am."

There was a shocked silence around them. Finally, Tsar Alexander spoke with a hint of amusement. "I find your . . . lack of pretension . . . refreshing, Mr. Clay. However, you must understand that one does not address nobility unless they speak to you first."

Cash immediately regretted his well-meant but ignorant gesture. In preparing for this post, he had been informed about the rigidity of Russian society. But in his eagerness to form a friendly relationship with the tsar, he had forgotten about this. It was so foreign to his nature to accept being treated as less than anyone's equal, or to allow others to be treated that way. He tried desperately to figure out how to properly apologize.

Before he could say anything further, the empress spoke up. "It is all right, Mr. Clay. You are free to address me when you wish. But for some of the more stodgy members of royalty, my husband's advice is wise."

Princess Radziwill, not about to be outdone by the empress, spoke up. "And you may feel free to address me, as well, Mr. Clay."

Princess Koutzouby added quickly, "When you dine with me, Mr. Clay, I hope you will feel free to open the conversation, as I often find myself at a loss for words."

Mary Jane watched this exchange in amazement. She knew perfectly well that these women were flirting with her husband, right in front of her. Even well into middle-age, his face showing the strain of a very hard life, and his dark hair streaked with gray, he was a striking figure of a man, erect and strong. He remained exceptionally handsome, and would do so until he was elderly.

While Cash and Mary Jane were being introduced to Russian royalty, back in the U.S. in a barn a rooster was crowing as dawn broke. In the hayloft, where he had managed to drag himself and take refuge, George began to stir. For an instant he forgot where he was and terror gripped him.

Then he remembered – the young rebel soldier had been shot and killed just as he was about to finish off George. He actually fell over George's prone body. It took what little strength George had left to shove the boy's body aside and crawl away from the battle, into the safety of a nearby wood.

Even though he'd avoided being bayoneted, George was still badly wounded and in excruciating pain. He tried to sit up, but couldn't. Then he heard the sound of a little girl whistling happily as she climbed the ladder to the loft. He saw the top of her head first, then her eyes. When she saw George, she froze for an instant. Then she hurried down the ladder, skipping the last few rungs and jumping to the ground

She ran screaming out of the barn. "Mama! Mama!"

Again George tried to get up. In spite of the agonizing pain, he forced himself to crawl to the ladder and somehow get down it. But when he reached the bottom, he fell to the ground and lay there, unable to move. Looking up, he saw a woman standing over him, aiming a rifle at his heart. Just before losing consciousness, he thought how strange it was to survive the fierce battle, only to be killed by a frightened farmer's wife.

But he wasn't killed. Several hours later, he lay in a bed in the farmhouse, his wounds cleaned and bandaged. Through an open door, he heard the doctor who had tended him talking to the woman and her daughter.

The woman said gratefully, "Thank you for coming, Doctor. I know you're taking a big risk by being here."

"Not as big a risk as you're taking, Miz Johnson."

"He's a human being, Doctor. As a Christian, I couldn't just let him die in our barn."

When the doctor left, Mrs. Johnson and her daughter came in to check on George. Finding him conscious again, Mrs. Johnson smiled at him. "I'm Mrs. Johnson. This is my daughter, Caroline."

"Are you . . . Union sympathizers?" George asked, assuming that was why they were helping him.

Mrs. Johnson shook her head adamantly. "I don't hold with this war. As far as I'm concerned, anyone who kills another person is wrong. Doesn't matter what excuse they use. God can't be pleased by bloodshed."

She was a pacifist, George realized. It didn't matter to him. All that mattered was that she and her daughter had saved his life.

He might still survive this war and go home to his wife and children.

At the White House, Secretary of War Cameron was speaking to the President and the rest of the cabinet. "Twenty-four thousand lives were lost at Bull Run. Almost fifteen thousand of the casualties were our own. Winfield Scott was a great general in his time, Mr. President, but his time is past. We need to replace him with someone who can get the job done. We've got to turn this thing around, and soon."

Twenty-four thousand . . . Lincoln found it hard to take in the magnitude of the horror. He didn't hesitate. "You have my permission to replace him."

"Do we have any other business before we adjourn?" asked Seward.

The President nodded. "I spoke to a man named Galen Clarke this afternoon. He came here all the way from California. He told me of a grove of giant redwood trees, each one as big around as a small house and hundreds of feet tall. He says they're all going to be cut down if we don't buy the land and set it aside for the public."

Cameron interrupted rudely. "We just lost nearly fifteen thousand of our men, Mr. President! What do a bunch of trees matter?"

Seward interjected, "Sounds like a very noble cause and well worth pursuing. The war has taken all our financial resources, and then some, but if we can scratch up a few dollars to save those trees, I'll set things in motion."

Lincoln thanked Seward then turned to Cameron. "We can't let this terrible war keep us from dealing with the rest of the country. No matter how unimportant it may seem to us, consumed as we are by this conflict, it is very important to people like Mr. Clarke. I am still President of this United States, until the day we lose to the South. And I will deal with all the business of this country."

Cameron was silent.

Soon the meeting was adjourned and everyone but Cameron and Seward left the room.

Cameron said, "I'm worried about the President. He meets with people until late at night. Seems like all anyone needs to get an appointment with him is to say they've got a problem. He needs to focus all his time and energy on this war. Not on trees!"

Seward had no fondness for Lincoln. He would always be bitterly resentful of him for taking the Presidency from him. But he'd developed a grudging respect for him over the last few months.

"He looks more sorrowful every day. That's why he keeps busy with the little problems of people. He can do something to help them. There's very little he can do to make this war go any better than it's going."

Two weeks after the doctor treated George, he was able to put his bloodstained uniform back on and prepare to leave the Johnson home. During the time he'd been recuperating there, he had learned that Mr. Johnson was away serving in the Confederate army. Knowing that made George appreciate all the more what Mrs. Johnson had done for him.

"May God go with you, George," Mrs. Johnson said warmly.

"I can't thank you enough, ma'am. Taking a risk to help a stranger."

"I'd like to think someone would do the same for my husband, if it came to that," she said simply. Then she went on, "You be careful out there. Rebel soldiers are all over. Stay in the woods, out of sight, until you cross the river. Don't cross until you come to Knight's Ferry Bridge."

After George left, Caroline turned to her mother. "He was a nice man, Mama."

"Yes, he was. But I don't want you to go tellin' your father about him when he comes home. You understand?"

Caroline looked confused. Her mother knelt down and looked her in the eye. It has to be our secret. Forever. You hear?"

Caroline didn't understand, but she nodded.

George scurried from tree to tree as he crossed a broad meadow. Suddenly he heard the sound of rifles firing. Puffs of smoke were coming from the woods on the other side of the meadow. He squinted, trying to see if the soldiers firing those rifles wore gray or blue. Finally, he broke into a huge smile of relief and began running toward the sound of gunfire. He found several Union soldiers crouched down behind a log, firing at some Confederate soldiers in the distance.

"You got an extra rifle?" he asked one of the men.

The man gestured to a dead soldier with a rifle lying beside it. George pried the rifle from the death grip of the soldier. He brought a Confederate soldier into his sights then hesitated. For all he knew, this could be the husband of the woman who had saved his life. Even if it wasn't, this soldier was someone's husband or father or brother or son. And George held his life in his hands.

173

While George hesitated, the soldier next to him was hit. Finally, George began firing. The right and the wrong of killing were beyond his understanding. All he was certain of was that he wanted to live.

In St. Petersburg, Cash quickly become enormously popular. He was considered a "true man" and a breath of fresh air in a rigid society, and a man who was friendly to all classes. He genuinely liked the Russian people. And while he never once forgot the critical purpose of his job, he enjoyed himself immensely.

Unfortunately, Mary Jane hated just about everything about Russia, especially the freezing winters and the women who were entirely too friendly to her husband. In their apartment at the embassy, she and Cash were arguing heatedly.

"I cannot spend another day in this dreadful place, Cassius! The winter is so cold, it's impossible to go outside."

"The winter isn't the only thing that's cold here," Cash said pointedly.

"What do you expect, when you're gone all the time to parties and fancy dress balls?!"

"I have a job to do, Mary Jane, and while all this socializing might seem frivolous, it's an important part of my job. I'm building a relationship between our country and this one, at a time when we need allies desperately."

"The only relationships I see you building are with the women here!"

They'd gone over this again and again. Cash repeated the words that never seemed to reassure Mary Jane. "I am expected to dance with the ladies and be polite to them. I'd much rather hold you in my arms, but every time I ask you to dance, you refuse."

"What do you expect? I refuse to put myself in a position of being compared with those women, with their Paris gowns and gaudy jewels."

Cash knew Mary Jane's insecurity was at the root of this argument. But no matter how hard he tried to make her feel better, he couldn't. She was used to being at the top of society. Here, she felt that everyone viewed her as inferior.

She said adamantly,

"You cannot change my mind, Cassius. My ship leaves for Liverpool in three weeks. I'll have to leave tomorrow with the children if I'm to catch it in time."

"Will you at least leave Mary and Sally here to keep me company until you come to your senses and return?"

"No!"

"But they are enjoying themselves here."

"I don't care. I won't have them marrying Russians and staying in this God-forsaken country."

The thought of having all his family leave him was unbearable to Cash. The large ambassadorial residence would seem like an empty mausoleum without them. But he knew from bitter experience that when Mary Jane made up her mind to walk out, nothing could stop her.

"I will miss you," he said sadly. And in spite of their differences, he meant it.

"I very much doubt that," she responded tightly. And with that, she left to pack.

In Washington, the President met with Seward in the oval office. "I believe that I have the answer to your dilemma with Secretary Cameron, Mr. President," Seward began.

"I'm glad someone has some answers. The war is still going badly, and now Cameron refuses to face that fact."

"You need to get him out of the country and appoint Stanton as your new Secretary of War. Stanton won't oppose your effort to retire General McClelland, as Cameron does. Maybe then we can turn this war around."

"Where could I send Cameron?"

"Ambassador Clay could return and take up that Major General commission you offered him. And Cameron could be ambassador to Russia. Clay's a proven military leader. He's shrewd and he doesn't like to lose. Maybe he's the kind of man we need to help turn things around."

Lincoln considered this plan. It was a good one. There was just one problem. Would Clay change his mind about what he'd said to Lincoln when he was originally offered the commission? There was only one way to find out.

Lincoln said to Seward, "Get a message to Clay that he's being temporarily recalled."

A few weeks later, Cash arrived in Washington just in time to hear of the Confederate general, Jeb Stuart, a black plume waving from his hat, and his cavalry, run roughshod over the Union's Army of the Potomac. An invasion of the North seemed imminent and even Washington itself was at risk of being overrun. If that happened, President Lincoln himself might very well be killed.

Cash was having a brandy in the oval office while the president drank water. Lincoln concluded, "So that's why I brought you back. I need you here, Cash."

The thought of coming home, being able to see his family at least occasionally, and doing his military duty was enormously appealing to Cash. He'd give anything to be able to say yes to Lincoln. But . . .

"Remember what I said before, Mr. President. I will not take a command until you declare all the slaves free men."

Lincoln hesitated, and Cash went on persuasively, "I know the Union may fall. But if we do, let us fall with the flag of universal liberty and justice nailed to the masthead."

Lincoln said slowly, "I've thought very seriously about issuing an Emancipation Proclamation, freeing the slaves in the Confederate states. Perhaps the time has come for me to do just that. But I'm afraid it would cause neutral states, like your own Kentucky, to side with the Confederacy. After all, your fellow Kentuckian and our former vice president, John Breckinridge, is now a Confederate general."

"I'm aware of that. But Kentuckians have heard me and others discuss the issue of slavery for a quarter of a century. They've made up their minds about it. Those who stand with slavery are already with the Confederate army. Those who intend to stand by the union will not change their minds. And they represent the majority."

"The Kentucky legislature is in session. Will you go down there and see how they stand on this issue and report back to me?"

"Of course, Mr. President."

As Cash left he felt excited about the fact that he would soon see his family again.

Cash was on horseback, accompanied by half a dozen seasoned Union soldiers assigned to protect the new general. He had arrived in Lexington by train, but had to make the rest of the way to White Hall by horse. He was only about thirty miles from home when he heard artillery booming in the near distance. Automatically, Cash spurred his horse toward the action.

It was the same area where George was fighting. The lieutenant in charge shouted to his men, "We have to fall back!" The men, including George, began retreating through the woods, firing blindly behind them as they went. Wallace, the general in charge, was frustrated. These mostly young, raw recruits were scared out of their wits, but doing the best they could to be men. Still, they were badly outnumbered.

Suddenly General Wallace couldn't believe his eyes. Riding toward him was an amazing sight. Cash wore a new uniform, complete with ceremonial sword and the Colt pistol given to him by Lincoln. He had the red-dyed ostrich feather tucked into his hat, which was cocked jauntily to one side and over his left eye. .

"You're a sight for sore eyes!" Wallace said jubilantly when Cash reached him. "I've been asking for reinforcements for two weeks. Kirby and his rebs outnumber us three to one."

"I'm afraid I'm not your reinforcements. I'm General Clay on a special assignment for the president. But I'm happy to be of service to you."

"My men have had little training and they're young and inexperienced. We're losing on every front. There's not much you can do on your own."

"This is where I grew up. If you drop back to one of the narrow passes like Windy Gap, you'll have no problem standing your ground. Do you know how to get there?"

"We haven't even been given accurate maps. They were in such a hurry to get us here, they forgot about that little detail."

"I can show you the way." Cash shouted to the bugler to sound the retreat.

As they made their way to Windy Gap, Cash rode beside the column of men, checking their condition. He noticed one barefoot soldier who was limping, one foot covered with a bloody bandage. "Go back to the cannons and get up on the carriage," Cash ordered him. The man – hardly more than a boy, really – looked up at Cash in gratitude.

As he continued riding down the column, he saw one soldier who looked awfully familiar from the back. "George!"

George turned at the sound of his name. His forlorn expression turned to a beaming smile. Cash jumped down from his horse and hugged his old friend. "Are you all right?" he asked anxiously.

"As all right as any of us can be."

"Here, ride with me." And he helped George up on his horse.

Soon they arrived at a narrow gorge and pass. Cash turned to General Wallace, who was riding beside him. "This is Windy Gap. There's only one way in and one way out. A half-dozen men and a light cannon can protect the pass and keep Kirby and his troops from coming any farther."

"You may not have been what I was hoping for," Wallace said gratefully, "but you're sure what I needed. If I can ever do anything for you, General Clay, just ask."

"There is something." Cash gestured to George, riding behind him. "I'd like to take this soldier with me, if that's all right with you."

"Of course. He's yours."

"No, he's his own man. But he'll come with me."

As Cash and George left Wallace and his men, Cash said, "We're going to Frankfort."

"We're not goin' home?"

"Not yet. Windy Pass is blocked. Besides, I've gotta get to the legislature and give a speech first."

George grinned. "Just like old times."

The next day Cash was just finishing his speech before the legislature. "For those states, like our great Kentucky, who have stood with the Union, they will be able to continue to have slaves as long as their laws allow it. For those rebel states who do not surrender from this tragic war and come back into the Union by the first of January, their slaves will be declared free and their former owners will not be compensated."

Sitting in the front row, listening to this, George felt like he could burst with pride in his friend. Cash was now proclaiming what he had promised George so long ago.

Cash continued, "Why should these slaves be allowed to continue to serve the needs of those rebels who are raining rifle balls on our brothers, uncles, fathers and neighbors, when instead, as free men they can serve in a blue uniform like my good friend, George, here."

Cash motioned to George to stand. He did so reluctantly, feeling self-conscious, but also very proud of the uniform he wore. "I have been sent here as a special emissary to the President. He wants to have your support in this. What do I tell him? If you approve, let me know now so I can let President Lincoln know that you are for a United States of America!"

The majority of representatives burst into thunderous applause, leaving no doubt where Kentucky stood.

George was still standing and he looked around in amazement at this support that Cash had managed to rally. At long last many of his people would be free. All that was left was for Cash to inform the President so he could sign the document that would begin to change the course of the nation.

As the tumult continued, Cash shouted into the ear of the young lieutenant who had accompanied him. "Please let my wife know that I've gone back to Washington to give the president this news. It can't wait."

Cash couldn't believe he was so close to home, and yet wouldn't be able to enjoy the homecoming and reunion with his family that he'd yearned for. But he had a responsibility that outweighed his longing to see his family.

A week later he was once more sitting with the President in the Oval Office. "You can count on Kentucky, Mr. President."

"Thank you, Cash. I know how hard it must've been for you to come back here instead of going straight home. But you take some time for your family now. You've earned it. Now I must go to another meeting."

Cash wanted to talk to Lincoln about freeing all the slaves, even those in the states that were loyal to the Union. He wanted to talk about education for the former slaves. But the President was already gone.

CHAPTER TWENTY-SIX

One week later, Cash, accompanied by George, finally made it home. He found Mary Jane supervising major reconstruction on the house. Their financial situation had gradually improved, helped enormously by Cash's salary as ambassador, and Mary Jane was eager to spend the extra money they now had. Instead of welcoming him, she was cool and distant.

When he tried to embrace her, she pulled away. "What's wrong?" he asked.

"I heard you were in Frankfort over two weeks ago, and you couldn't be bothered to come see your family."

George was anxious to get away from the tension between these two. "I'd best be gettin' home to Orelia," he said, and hurried away.

"I was on a critical mission for the president," Cash tried to explain. "I came home as soon as I could."

"And how long have you been back in the States?"

"Six weeks." He tried to embrace her again, but she jerked away with even greater vehemence, as if she couldn't bear for him to touch her.

"What's wrong with you?" Cash demanded. He was profoundly hurt by her rejection. He'd hoped that she missed him as much as he missed her, and that this reunion might also be a reconciliation.

"I've lost a cousin and a brother to this war! Obviously, I've lost my husband to it, as well. You've always cared more about your 'cause' than you did for me. You had wealth and social position. What did you do with them? Lost most of your wealth to that 'cause' and forfeited your position in society because of it. You say you love your family, but you're always gone. You love that damned 'cause' more than you love us!"

He knew he should tell her she was wrong, that he loved her over and above anything or anyone else. But he couldn't. She was right.

The next morning, Bessie's daughter, Young Bessie, was serving breakfast to Cash in the dining room when Mary Jane entered. He said politely, "Good morning. Sleep well?"

"Very well," she responded coolly.

"I want you to know that I wrote a letter to the president, resigning my commission."

Mary Jane was silent. He went on doggedly, "Halleck wouldn't give me my own command and Stanton backed him up. You know they hate anyone who's anti-slavery. They wanted me to serve under General Butler in New Orleans. Half the men in that area haven't died in battle, but from the plague."

Mary Jane still didn't say a word.

"I asked Lincoln to return me to St. Petersburg, where I can be of some value to the country. I'm sure he'll honor my request."

At the mention of St. Petersburg, Mary Jane finally reacted. "If you go back to Russia, you go alone, Cassius. I won't spend any more time in that cold, dreadful place, and the children feel the same."

"Would you rather I keep my commission, go to New Orleans, and take my chances with the plague?" he asked tightly. When she didn't respond, he said, "I went over the accounts on this reconstruction. We need my ambassador's salary to complete the work."

"I don't care what you do," Mary Jane said evenly. Then she got up and left, without touching her food.

Cash sat there, feeling helpless. There was no way he could reach Mary Jane. The sooner he left here and got back to his post in Russia, the better.

Just then George came in, holding a newspaper. Without saying a word, he handed it to Cash. The banner headline of the Lexington Herald read: "EMANCIPATION PROCLAMATION ISSUED!"

Cash hurriedly read the article.

"On the first day of January, in the year of our Lord one thousand eight hundred and sixty-three, all persons held as slaves within any State, or designated part of a State, the people whereof shall then be in rebellion against the United States, including the military and naval authority thereof, will recognize and maintain

182

the freedom of such persons, and will do no act or acts to repress such persons, or any of them, in any efforts they may make for their actual freedom."

It went on to read, "I, Abraham Lincoln, hereby enjoin upon the people so declared to be free to abstain from all violence, unless in necessary self-defense; and I recommend to them that, in all cases where allowed, they labor faithfully for reasonable wages. And upon this act, sincerely believed to be an act of justice, warranted by the Constitution upon military necessity, I invoke the considerate judgment of mankind and the gracious favor of Almighty God."

Finally, Cash thought. Finally, Lincoln had done the right thing. He looked up at George who stood there, with tears of joy in his eyes. "It's just the beginning, George," Cash said proudly.

"You were part of this," George said in an unsteady voice. "And I know how much it cost you."

"God made it happen. Not me, or even President Lincoln. And whatever price I paid to do God's work I have to believe was worth it."

CHAPTER TWENTY-SEVEN

At New York Harbor a huge passenger steamer was preparing to leave. The gangplank was lifted and the order to "Cast off!" was given. The crew unfurled the huge, multi-strand rope from its tie-down post on deck. As they threw it toward the dock, the sound of the steam engines could be heard and the loud horn blew its warning that the ship was pulling out of the harbor.

Hundreds of people were on deck, waving to those at the dock who they were leaving behind. Some were throwing kisses, others weeping. In the crowd, one tall figure stood rigidly still. His hands gripped the railing as he looked out at the crowd on the dock. There was a sad, haunted look in his eyes. Neither Mary Jane nor any of his children had bothered to travel to New York to see him off, even though it might be years before he was able to see them again.

He had a rare reflective moment as he stood there. He had started out life as a member of a wealthy, socially prominent family. He could have simply enjoyed that wealth and position and focused his energies on maintaining them. If he'd done so, he would have probably enjoyed the warm, close family life he craved. Instead, he'd sacrificed nearly everything to the great cause of his life that he viewed as a sacred purpose. Despite the high price he paid, he believed it was worth it. Lincoln's Emancipation Proclamation was the culminating act of his life's aspirations.

In spite of everything, he felt that his good star stood high in the heavens.

At Camp Nelson in Kentucky, where thousands of former slaves came to enlist in the Union army, a drill sergeant was speaking to a group of mainly new recruits, with a few seasoned African-American soldiers among them. "My name is Sergeant White. There are nearly three hundred thousand of us in the Union army now. Two hundred thousand have

185

escaped from the South and joined with us free men from the North. At first the army didn't want us. They thought we couldn't be good soldiers. Time came when they got desperate and they needed us. Then they found out that we could fight better than any white soldiers who ever put on a blue uniform."

Among the soldiers listening to this speech was George. He felt a surge of pride as the sergeant continued, "'Why do we fight better? Because we have something to fight for that they don't. The freedom of every slave in America depends on us. If we lose this war, then we might as well shoot ourselves for we will be severely punished by the victors. We will be punished for having the courage to step over the line that they drew for us."

He finished grimly, "If there are any among you who are not willing to fight to the death for this cause, then let him step aside while he has the chance.

Not one soldier moved.

Days later George was back in battle. The black battalion that he was part of was rapidly advancing through an open meadow, firing and reloading with grim determination. Confederate soldiers fell before them. George didn't hesitate this time.

Cash descended the gangway at St. Petersburg after a long, lonely journey. A young man hurried to greet him. "Ambassador Clay, I'm your new assistant, William Jones. I have a carriage waiting to take you to your apartment."

"Good," Cash said tiredly. "It was a difficult trip and I could use some rest."

"I'm afraid that's not possible, sir. The prince has a big dinner and welcome back party for you. You barely have time to change your clothes." Jones looked around, as if searching for someone. "Where's your family, sir?"

"I'm afraid they couldn't make it."

This was unusual, but Jones could tell by his boss's expression that it would be best not to ask questions.

At the capitol building in Washington, the floor of the Senate was packed. President Lincoln spoke. "Whereas, the Senate of the United States, devoutly recognizing the supreme authority and just government of Almighty God in all the affairs of men

186

and nations, has, by a resolution, requested the president to designate and set apart a day for national prayer and humiliation. And whereas it is the duty of nations, as well as of men, to owe their dependence upon the overruling power of God, to confess their sins and transgressions, in humble sorrow, yet with assured hope that genuine repentance will lead to mercy and pardon, and to recognize the sublime truth announced in the Holy Scriptures and proven by all history, that those nations only are blessed whose God is the Lord."

Senators and cabinet members nodded their heads in agreement.

"And, inasmuch as we know that by His Divine law, nations, like individuals, are subjected to punishments and chastisement in this world, may we not justly fear that the awful calamity of civil war, which now desolates the land, may be a punishment inflicted upon us for our presumptuous sins, to the needful end of our national reformation as a whole people."

Flash powder exploded from the bank of photographers below the president. The photographers and reporters covering this historic speech could hardly believe what they were hearing.

Lincoln continued, "We have been the recipients of the choicest bounties of heaven. We have been preserved these many years in peace and prosperity. We have grown in numbers, wealth, and power as no other nation has ever grown, but we have forgotten God!"

It was so quiet now you could hear a pin drop. "We have forgotten the gracious hand which preserved us in peace, and multiplied and enriched and strengthened us; and we have vainly imagined in the deceitfulness of our hearts that all these blessings were produced by some superior wisdom of our own. Intoxicated with unbroken success, we have become too self-sufficient to feel the necessity of redeeming and preserving grace, too proud to pray to the God that made us! It behooves us, then, to humble ourselves before the offended power, to confess our national sins, and to pray to the God that made us!"

Now the president came to the proclamation itself. "Now, therefore, in compliance with the request, and fully concurring in the views of the Senate, I do, by this my proclamation, designate and set apart Thursday, the 30th day of April, 1863, as a day of National Humiliation, Fasting and Prayer. And I do hereby request all the people to abstain on that day from their ordinary secular pursuits, and to unite, at their several places of public worship and their respective homes, in keeping the day holy to the Lord, and devoted to the humble discharge of the religious duties proper to the solemn occasion."

One reporter whispered to another, "Looks like we get the day off." The second reporter grinned cynically. "Politicians will do anything to get re-elected."

Despite the tone of their words, they sensed, as did everyone else in the chamber, that the president was utterly serious. Lincoln went on, "All this being done in sincerity and truth, let us humbly in the hope authorized by Divine teachings, that the united cry of the nation will be heard on high, and answered with blessings, no less the pardon of our national sins, and restoration of our now divided and suffering country to its former happy condition of unity and peace."

Applause and cheers filled the chamber, as nearly everyone rose to their feet to give their president a standing ovation.

After a moment, President Lincoln motioned to them to sit down. It took a moment for everyone to take their seats once again and for the noise to die down.

Then he finished, "In witness whereof, I have hereto set my hand, and caused the seal of the United States to be affixed. Done at the city of Washington, the 30th day of March, in the year of our Lord 1863."

At Whitehall, Mary Jane sat at the big, roll-top desk in the library and read a letter from her husband. It had taken weeks to arrive. "My dearest Mary Jane. I am writing this letter from my hotel room in New York. Words cannot describe how much I miss you. It was so lonely during the journey here, and the nights seemed to last forever without you. Please join me, and if none of the older children want to come with you, will you at least bring Annie? I miss her hugs so much. I have enclosed my first month's salary advance to meet your needs. Yours forever, Cassius."

Mary Jane sat there for a long moment, lost in thought. Then she took out a sheet of paper, dipped a quill into the inkbottle, and wrote her response. "Dear Cassius, I received your letter of April 26th today, and I must say your check arrived just in time to pay some urgent bills. Brutus has joined his brother and enlisted in the war that you helped to start. I alone must shoulder the responsibility of the work on the house. Therefore, I am unable to leave. You are in a situation of your own choosing. I am sure you will not remain lonely for long. I will give Annie a hug from her father."

188

She signed it simply, "Mary Jane."

The Union force of over one hundred black soldiers that George was part of were doing surprisingly well against a larger, better armed rebel force. The Confederate soldiers were in desperate retreat when suddenly they heard the sound of bugles blowing. In the distance they saw a cloud of dust created by an entire Confederate regiment. With the Confederate flag flying, this regiment of fresh troops passed their compatriots.

Now it was the Union soldiers who were forced to retreat.

George and his comrades ran from the withering fire of the enemy. They paused briefly every few minutes to turn and touch off a volley, then continued running. It was a bitter cold winter day, and many of the black soldiers were barefoot. They slid and fell on the frozen mud, their home-made uniforms getting black and torn. The Confederates, in their factory-made uniforms and sturdy boots, pressed on, leaning forward, shoulders hunched, closing the gap ominously.

George heard the sound of musket balls tearing into flesh, and the screams of his compatriots as they fell, writhing on the ground, mortally wounded. He smelled the almost unbearable odor of death, nauseating and overwhelming.

His arm ached from working the ramrod in his musket. His gun was so hot now that he could barely stand to touch it. Still, he paused as often as he could in his pell-mell race to safety to return fire. He had a job to do, he repeated over and over to himself. He must do it.

George's thoughts were a jumble of terror and determination. He didn't want to let down his fellow soldiers. He didn't want to die and leave Orelia alone. But more than anything, he desperately wanted to go home, to get away from this savagery.

A Confederate soldier on horseback took aim at George and fired. His shot hit its mark. George felt the familiar sensation of a musket ball tearing through his body in an explosion of agony. He stumbled and fell, dead before he hit the ground. As he lay there, the expression on his face was oddly peaceful. He was no longer part of this horrific conflict. His prayer had been answered. He was home, safe at last in the arms of his Lord.

CHAPTER TWENTY-EIGHT

St. Petersburg, 1863

C ash attended the renowned Russian ballet. The theater was magnificent, with large balconies, golden chandeliers, elegant drapes and hand-carved cornices filled with classic statuary. There was nothing like it in the United States. Going to the ballet had been one of the few things Mary Jane enjoyed about living in St. Petersburg. On this night, as Cash sat alone, he missed her companionship more than ever.

The dancers onstage were all lovely and graceful, but the prima ballerina, Anna Marie Petroff, stood out. The longer Cash watched her, the more enchanting she seemed. When the ballet was over, Cash made a point of going backstage to meet her.

"Miss Petroff, I am the United States ambassador to Russia, Cassius Clay. But please call me Cash." Taking her hand, he kissed it in the continental manner common there. At five feet, ten inches tall, Anna was unusually tall for a ballerina and used to looking down on most men. But she had to look up at the big, handsome Kentuckian. She was immediately as intrigued with him as he was with her.

Her light blue eyes had a spark in them as she said, "Ah, America. I hope to go there one day. By the way, I prefer to be called Marie – Cash."

"You're even more beautiful up close," he said.

She was used to compliments from men, but they weren't usually offered so quickly or so directly. Instead of being put off by what most people would consider impudence, she was charmed by it.

He went on, "I'd like to see you again, Marie. And not onstage."

She hesitated. Not because she had any intention of saying no, but because it didn't do to appear too eager. Finally, she said slowly, "I am free Friday night."

191

"Friday night it is, then." He bowed and left.

When he turned off the kerosene lamp next to his bed that night, he thought of Marie. He told himself that if only Mary Jane were lying beside him, Marie would have been forgotten. But despite his letters to her, begging her to return, she hadn't come. And now he couldn't put the image of Marie's face from his thoughts.

It was a typically cold, blustery day. Fall leaves blew across the plaza in front of the large building that housed the American embassy. In his office, Cash sat in an oversized burgundy leather chair, going over papers that covered the carved mahogany desk. His assistant, Jones, came in.

Cash said, "Get me a ticket to the ballet for tonight."

Jones was confused. He'd just gotten a ticket for the ballet only days earlier. Perhaps his boss hadn't been able to attend and wanted to make up for that now. "Certainly, sir. I take it you were not able to use the other ticket?"

"On the contrary. I enjoyed it so much, I want to go again."

Jones hadn't thought of his boss as an avid ballet aficionado, but he knew better than to question him. He handed Cash a letter. "This just came for you, sir, from your wife."

Jones left and Cash quickly opened the letter. "Cassius, I hate to be the bearer of bad news, but I think you'd want to know as soon as possible that George was killed last week. I feel so sorry for Orelia and the children. The money you have been sending is just barely enough for us to get by and to do a little work on the addition. If there is any way for you to send more, it would enable me to get the addition completed." It was signed simply, "Mary Jane."

Cash sat there, immobile, for a long moment. George dead? It was agonizingly hard to accept. From as far back as he could remember, George had been part of his life. They had shared adventures as boys, gone through the rite of passage as young men, experienced love and parenthood at the same time. Cash blindly assumed that they would grow old and one day reminisce together about the tragedies and triumphs of their lives.

No one had ever been a better friend. No one knew Cash as George had. The cause that had consumed Cash's adult life was inspired by his friendship with George. Looking at George, Cash had seen not a slave, not even a black man, but simply a human being, who felt the same emotions, shared the same hopes and

192

dreams, struggled with the same fears, as any other human being.

The thought of living in a world that George was no longer a part of was acutely painful.

With Mary Jane his wife in name only now, and with George gone, Cash felt more painfully alone than he ever could have imagined.

In spite of his depression, or perhaps because of it, he went ahead with his plan to attend the ballet. But during intermission he had far too much to drink. The second half of the performance was a drunken blur to him. When it was over, he made his way backstage, staggering as he went. When Marie opened her dressing room door to him, she saw a man who could barely stand up.

"What is wrong? You look as if you've lost your best friend."

"I have."

Seeing the utterly lost look in his eyes touched her heart. "You need to lie down. Come in."

He stumbled in and practically fell onto the sofa. The moment he lay down, his eyes closed, and he fell into a deep, drunken sleep. Marie looked at him laying there, his long legs hanging over the end of the sofa that was wide but short. There was something about such a big, strong man revealing vulnerability that drew her to him even more than before. She covered him with a blanket. Then she lay down next to him and fell asleep beside him.

In the conference room at the White House, Lincoln met with his cabinet. "As you know, the Confederates want to surrender and put an end to this devastating war. It's just a matter of finding a reconstruction plan that they can accept. Then we can put this country back on course."

After a brief stint replacing Cash as ambassador to Russia, Cameron had returned to once again become Secretary of War when Lincoln granted Cash's request to be sent back to Russia. Cameron said, "I'm more concerned about what our intelligence has reported about France trying to get the rest of Europe, and Russia, to come over on the side of the confederacy. Not just with financial help, but with their naval forces."

Lincoln responded, "I'm confident that Ambassador Clay will keep the Russians on our side."

"I hope so," Cameron said grimly. "If the Russian navy gets into this on the side of the confederacy, we're in serious trouble. We could still lose this war."

In St. Petersburg, Cash diligently performed his duties, which involved a great deal of socializing with important members of the government and society. But even when he was frequenting fashionable clubs or entertaining lavishly at his residence, he was lonely. And he actually preferred to visit the freedmen of the countryside in their rustic cottages, participating in the Russian ceremony of hospitality, the khleb-sol', the taking of bread and salt with the family.

One day he received an urgent wire from the White House. His orders were clear – at all costs, persuade the Russian government to stay out of the war. It wouldn't be easy. Apparently, there were Confederate representatives in the city, meeting with sympathetic members of the government and military. It was even rumored that they'd met with the tsar himself. Cash was scheduled to attend a party given by Tsar Alexander that night. It would be an opportunity to try to find out which way the tsar was leaning.

At the Imperial Palace that night, an orchestra played while guests enjoyed a sumptuous buffet with delicacies imported from around the world. The tsar, his wife, foreign minister Prince Gortchacow and his wife were seated at the head table, along with other aristocrats. At the tsar's invitation, Cash, accompanied by Jones, joined the tsar at the head table.

Cash exchanged polite small talk with Tsar Alexander for a few minutes then decided to boldly confront the critical issue. "I understand that agents of the Confederacy have met with you."

The tsar smiled enigmatically. "That concerns you, doesn't it?"

"Yes. Very much, sir."

"Don't worry, my friend. I told them that in spite of France, Spain and England's willingness to side with the Confederacy, Russia will stay out of the conflict."

Cash tried to appear more blasé than he felt. But inwardly he breathed a huge sigh of relief. "On behalf of President Lincoln, I want to express the gratitude of my country, sir."

"How deep is that gratitude?" the tsar asked pointedly.

Cash realized immediately that the tsar's support for the union would be part of a quid pro quo. The only question was whether the price of Russia's support would be too high for the beleaguered U.S. to be able to pay.

He answered guardedly, "Why don't you tell me exactly what you want in return for your support, sir."

"A mere pittance, my friend. A few pennies an acre for some territory that we have no use for."

Cash knew what Tsar Alexander was referring to – Alaska, an endless expanse of supposedly worthless land. Cash had been aware that Russia might be interested in selling Alaska, because of the difficulty of administering such a far-off region, and fears that England might try to seize it. He'd made a point to gain knowledge about the region's resources – furs, timber, mineral potential, and the immensely valuable fishing grounds. In fact, he had sent this information to Secretary Seward and other influential politicians.

Cash said carefully, "At nearly four hundred million acres, those pennies add up, sir."

The tsar smiled. "Yes, they do."

Cash hadn't expected Russia to give their support without demanding something in return. But buying Alaska wasn't something the U.S. government would easily agree to do. The money simply wasn't there. But Cash knew that if the tsar said this was the price, he meant it. If the U.S. couldn't meet that price, Russia might very well support the confederacy. And a war that had already taken an unimaginable toll on the U.S. would continue indefinitely.

Cash thought furiously. He wasn't from Bluegrass Country, the home of the finest thoroughbreds, for nothing. He knew a thing or two about horse trading. That's all this was – a competition to see who could get the better end of the deal.

Finally he said, "As you know, the war has cost my country dearly, both in loss of life and in financial resources. The price for Alaska is simply too high for us to pay – at this time."

"What are you suggesting?"

"Suppose we do purchase this land, at the price you set, but on terms that allow us to pay in full at some point in the future when the United States is stronger financially?"

Tsar Alexander considered this offer. There were advantages and disadvantages to it. Russia would have to wait for the money. On the other hand, being able to unload that worthless tract of land for any price, under any terms, was a good thing. Like all good negotiators, he didn't want to appear to be too eager to make the deal.

He said slowly, "Perhaps we could consider such an arrangement. I would have to think about it, of course."

"Of course," Cash replied, knowing full well that the tsar would ultimately agree to these terms. He went on, "But I must also ask you, sir, to go one step further than simply not joining France, Spain and England. I ask you to anchor your navy in both San Francisco and New York harbors as a warning to other nations to not interfere in my country's private conflict."

The tsar considered this escalation in the deal. His first impulse was to refuse. Who was this American to dictate terms to him? After all, he was emperor of all the Russia, heir to Peter the Great.

Sensing Tsar Alexander's reservations, Cash went on quickly, "Of course, that wouldn't simply be to the benefit of my country, sir. It would force those other countries, who might not always give Russia the respect it is due, to acknowledge the superiority of the Russian navy."

The tsar was an intelligent man, but he was as susceptible as anyone to flattery. He hesitated then smiled slowly at Cash. "You ask much, Ambassador Clay." As Clay held his breath, the tsar went on, "And you will receive much in return. Our ships will begin to steam there as soon as we agree on a price for Alaska."

"I think I can assure you, sir, that we will be able to reach such an agreement."

Little did Cash know that the sale of this seemingly "worthless land" would become known as "Seward's Folly," simply because Secretary of State Seward signed the papers that sold Alaska to the United States.

Later that night, Cash and Jones were in his office at the embassy, sending a telegraph under code to President Lincoln. It concluded, "So as you can see, for only a few million dollars we can buy the assurance of non-intervention, as well as the symbolic support of the Russian navy, and at the same time, acquire some land that has great potential value."

Cash said to Jones, "Get this off immediately, then destroy the original."

Exhausted, Cash went to bed. He knew he'd accomplished something critical to the war effort that night. He felt good about it. Anything that he could do to help end the war that had cost so many lives, including that of his best friend, was a good thing. But he wasn't thinking about this triumph as he fell asleep. He was thinking about Marie . . .

196

CHAPTER TWENTY-NINE

1864

It was late in the afternoon in Washington, and the sun cast a warm yellow glow over the White House. In the oval office, the president was in one of the meetings with "the people" that he had promised to represent.

"I understand that the embargo is hurting your cotton business. And I appreciate your loyalty to the union. But I'm afraid that until we end this war, it will have to remain in effect."

The cotton fabric spinner, Jensen, wasn't consoled by this hard truth. But the fact that the president was presenting it to him directly made it more acceptable.

At that moment the president's secretary came in and handed him a message. "This just came from St. Petersburg. It's been decoded and is marked 'extremely urgent,' sir."

Without waiting for Jensen to leave, Lincoln quickly read the message. He knew the fate of the Union might very well hang on it. When he finished reading, his expression relaxed visibly. Looking up at Jensen, he said, "Mr. Jensen, you may only have to put up with the embargo for a short time longer."

Jensen was immensely relieved. "I'll hold out a bit longer then, Mr. President." And he left.

Lincoln turned to his secretary. "Get hold of Seward and tell him to immediately start the process of funding this acquisition. Without outside interference, I believe we can soon end this war."

In one of the private offices in the House of Lords, members of the British elite, including Lord Palmerston, were meeting with representatives from the confederacy. One of the representatives said, "On behalf of President Davis and the entire confederacy, I assure you that you are making the right move. We appreciate this loan and the naval support you have promised us."

At that moment, Palmerston's secretary hurried in with an important message. He whispered something to him, handed him the message, then left. As Palmerston read it, his expression hardened. There was utter silence for a moment, and then Palmerston looked up. "I am afraid, gentlemen, that we will have to call off our loan. And we will not be able to follow through with the other plans we discussed."

The Confederate representatives were stunned and furious. One barely kept his temper in check, as he demanded, "Why?! What would cause you to go back on your word?!"

"Russia has just warned us to let the American war sort itself out without any involvement on our part."

"But . . ." the representative started to argue.

"Russian ships are already on their way to U.S. ports. Confronting a United States torn by civil war is one thing. Risking war with Russia is quite another."

Palmerston turned to his secretary. "Send a message to the emperor of France. Say that his plan is foolhardy and England wants no part of it."

The Confederate representatives abruptly took their leave. They knew that the Confederacy had just fallen. All that remained were details.

In Washington Lincoln was preparing for the re-election campaign. He was talking to several prominent people in his party, and the discussion was heated. Thaddeus Stevens spoke angrily, "Can't we find a candidate for vice-president without going down to one of those rebel provinces to pick one up?"

Lincoln tried to be diplomatic. "Your suggestion, Congressman Stevens, to change the party name from the Republicans to the National Union Party, was a good one.

And the more I considered it, the more I felt that if we could have a Southern Democrat on the ticket, we could not only win, but could help pull the country back together again when the war is over."

Stevens' expression hardened. Johnson was a staunch abolitionist, and unpopular with many people for that reason.

Seward joined in the debate. "I agree, Mr. President. And Andrew Johnson's the toughest war Democrat of them all. He's just the man we need to strengthen the administration in these times."

Lincoln responded, "Johnson has demonstrated unquestioned loyalty to the Union. And he has submitted a comprehensive plan for the reconstruction of his state, Tennessee. With his help, Tennessee is about ready to come back into the Union. He's just the man we need."

Stevens had lost the argument, and he knew it.

Seward said, "We need someone like Johnson to act as a buffer between the various interests of North and South."

Lincoln was thoughtful. "I just hope," he said slowly, "that the buffer doesn't get destroyed in the process."

In Nashville, Tennessee, Johnson was arguing with one of his aides. The aide said, "Many people are saying that the Negroes are not fit to be free, that they have been slaves for so long that they are not qualified to be freemen. It's proposed that we keep slavery for another twenty years, and during that time we prepare them for freedom."

Johnson was steadfast in his convictions. "I have no such fears. The Negroes will be thrown upon society and governed by the same laws that govern any community. They will be compelled to fall back upon their own resources, as all other people are. Political freedom means liberty to work, and at the same time to enjoy the products of one's labor. If the black man can rise by his own energies, in the name of God, let him rise!"

In Baltimore, a huge wigwam was set up for the national convention. Thaddeus Stevens was addressing the convention from the floor. "I move that Tennessee and the other southern states that stood against the Union not be allowed to be represented in this convention."

Parson Brownlow, a friend of Johnson's, spoke up. "I warn my fellow delegates that to shut these states out would be tantamount to recognizing secession, which is contrary to the reason why we fought the war."

Another delegate interrupted Brownlow. "I move that we allow the delegates from Tennessee, Arkansas and Louisiana to be admitted, and the delegates from Virginia to be seated without the right to vote at this time."

The motion was approved by a nearly unanimous vote.

Immediately following the election, Lincoln met again with his cabinet. The mood was lighter than it had been in years.

"Congratulations on winning a second term, Mr. President," Seward said.

Lincoln knew what it cost Seward to offer such congratulations. "Thank you, Mr. Secretary. I have deeply appreciated your support during this difficult time."

"It is due to your leadership that the nation has weathered this period as well as it has."

"I share any credit for that with many people, Mr. Seward. Including you." And including Cash Clay, Lincoln thought. If Cash were there, Lincoln would tell him that the Alaska deal had very likely saved the Union.

At the American embassy in St. Petersburg, the British Consul, Lumley, was talking with Cash. "Congratulations on your president's re-election. I suppose this means you're here for another four years."

"I haven't thought that far ahead," Cash replied evasively.

The truth was he was terribly torn. He had kept in regular communication with his children through letters, advising them about the books they read, their educational plans and religious affiliations. He sent gifts of jewelry to the girls and obtained an interest in some Russian oil wells for his son, Green. But it had been years since he had seen them. He was terribly homesick for his family and for White Hall.

But there was something that made the thought of leaving Russia very painful to contemplate. His attraction to Marie had developed into a feeling of real love unlike anything he had experienced in many long, lonely years. They went sledding together on artificially constructed "mountains," rode in troikas with fur lap robes keeping them warm and danced together in the Hermitage, under artistic masterpieces.

They were careful to appear to be merely friends when out in society. But when they were alone in Cash's beach house by the Neva, he told her how much he loved her. And she clearly felt the same.

One day in 1865 Cash was going through his mail. There was a message from President Lincoln. General Lee had just surrendered at Appomattox. The war was over. Cash felt the exhilaration of victory wash over him. The horror of the last five years was over. The country could now begin to heal from its

200

painful divisions. There was no reason to be anything but optimistic about the future.

In Washington, the president and his first lady went for a leisurely drive. It was a beautiful spring day. "I can't remember the last time we did this," Mary said happily.

Lincoln looked relaxed and at peace for the first time in nearly five years. "I haven't been able to spend time with you like this in a long while, Molly. But now that the war is over, we'll be able to enjoy many more days like this."

Their driver smiled to himself. He hadn't seen Mr. and Mrs. Lincoln look so happy since their little boy, Willie, had died.

Mary's lighthearted expression turned serious. "If the amendment that your party proposed is passed, what will you do with the freed blacks? Do you still think they should be colonized back into Africa?"

"No, I do not. They've had a poor existence here, but now they have the possibility of bettering their lot. It's our responsibility to help them."

He paused, then went on, "But let's not talk politics on this beautiful day, Molly. That business can wait. Today is just for you and I."

The day that Lincoln had set aside to spend with his wife concluded with an evening at the theater, something he hadn't been able to do for some time. He and Mary, along with a few friends, sat in their private box at Ford's Theater, enjoying the play, a comedy. He laughed heartily at the funny lines. Looking at him, Mary thought she hadn't seen him this happy in years.

In the corridor outside the box, a tall, dark-haired man took a pistol out of his waistband and went to the door leading into the box. He opened the door quietly and slipped in, unnoticed by anyone. Everyone's attention was focused on the stage. Moving behind the president, he fired the pistol at nearly point blank range. Before anyone could react, he jumped to the floor below, breaking his leg.

The audience sitting in the main floor heard the shot and saw the man drop to the floor. They thought this must all be part of the play.

The man somehow managed to drag himself out a side door. In the alley there, a man waited on horseback, holding the reins to another horse. The assassin, in great pain, pulled himself onto the horse and they raced away.

Inside the theater, the audience finally realized that something terrible had just happened. The play came to an abrupt halt.

In the president's box, his wife bent over his body, crumpled on the floor. The president's two bodyguards, who had been on the first floor, came rushing in. "Did you see who did this?!" one of them demanded.

One of Lincoln's friends said in a ragged voice, "John Wilkes Booth, the actor! He did it! He shot the president!"

A doctor, who'd been in the audience on the first floor, came rushing in. Shoving everyone except Mrs. Lincoln aside, he quickly examined the president then said, "Let's get him next door to the Kirkwood house."

Later that night, Lincoln's lifeless body lay on a bed in the Kirkwood house. "I'm terribly sorry, Mrs. Lincoln," the doctor said gently. "I'm afraid he's gone."

Mary knelt beside her husband's body. After all the agonizing years of watching their little boy slowly die . . . and suffering with the country through the war . . . why did it have to end like this? The tears she had fought back so far finally came in a torrent that felt as if it would never end.

It was three o'clock in the morning in St. Petersburg. Cash awoke to the sound of someone knocking loudly on the door to his apartment. Throwing on a robe, he opened the door to find Jones standing there in his pajamas, a coat hastily thrown over them. Before Cash could ask what this was about, Jones burst out shakily, "It's the president, sir! He's been assassinated!"

Cash stood utterly still. It was impossible. No one would kill a president of the United States. But Jones' distraught expression made it clear this was no mistake. President Lincoln was dead. Even as he tried to take it in, Cash's thoughts went back to his little boy, Cassius Jr., murdered by ruthless, Godless people who hated his abolitionist stance. Somehow he suspected that Lincoln had probably been murdered by pro-slavery interests, also.

He was torn between grief and rage. He said slowly, his voice breaking with intense emotion, "The powers of darkness killed our president and my son. People filled with bitterness and hate did this."

Jones just stood there, saying nothing. He had heard that his boss's son had been murdered long ago. But Cash had never spoken of it, and Jones knew better than to raise such a painful topic. Now the assassination of the president had reopened that old wound. Looking at Cash, Jones thought he had never seen a man look more haunted by tragedy.

PART TWO

The Price of Victory

CHAPTER THIRTY

Fall had arrived at the White House, and those leaves that hadn't already fallen were vivid yellow, orange and red. In the Oval Office, Andrew Johnson sat behind the President's desk.

His secretary entered. "It's official! Alabama just became the twenty-sixth state to ratify the 13th Amendment. Slavery is now abolished in America."

President Johnson was disappointed. "I was hoping Kentucky would get on the bandwagon. Now I suppose they'll never ratify it."

"Do they have to?"

"All we need is a two-thirds majority to have it become the law of the land. I just hoped they would join in the spirit of unity."

"I hear they're bitter about what Cassius Clay promised them when he talked the Kentucky legislators into supporting the Emancipation Proclamation."

"That's nonsense. Clay had no way of knowing at that time that the 13th Amendment was coming. Lincoln's assassination made getting the amendment ratified a lot easier."

"It's what he wanted," the secretary said sadly. "It's too bad he couldn't live to see this day."

She suddenly realized what she had said.

"Not that you're not going to make a great President. I meant . . ."

The President put his hand on her shoulder. "It's all right. I am not certain, though, if he would have ever seen this day had he lived."

"The country just didn't appreciate his greatness until they no longer had him with them. It seems that he accomplished as much in his death as he did when he was living."

205

She went on carefully, "It's awful, though, about Mrs. Lincoln. I hear she's gone nearly insane with grief."

Johnson stiffened, and his secretary remembered that he disliked gossip. She changed the subject quickly. "Speaking of Clay, Secretary Seward asked me to inform you that the bargain price for Russian America has turned into nearly ten million dollars!"

President Johnson looked at her in disbelief. He didn't need a ten-million-dollar problem added to those already facing him.

It was a bright sunny day in downtown Lexington and Mary Jane was walking down Main Street with some of her purchases in hand. As she passed people she knew, she tried to greet them, but no one would speak to her.

"Good morning, Mrs. Terwilliger. How is Jack getting along?" Mrs. Terwilliger looked right past her, as if not seeing her, and hurried on.

Mary Jane nodded to another couple passing by. "Mr. Burch, Mary." Again she was ignored.

She got into her carriage and tearfully told the driver to take her home.

At the Warfield mansion, Dr. Warfield had his arms around his wife, who was crying. "Don't worry," he said, "I'll get you some new servants."

"But who? I can't believe they all left."

"It's my fault," said the doctor. "I should have offered them some extra money."

"Well, it's too late now. They've all gone north."

Dr. Warfield shook his head in anger and disgust. "If it wasn't for that son-in-law of ours, none of this would have happened. I tried to tell Mary Jane she was making a mistake when she agreed to marry a Clay, but she wouldn't listen."

Mrs. Warfield was quick to agree. "Cassius caused all these problems, then he left the country. Left Mary Jane to deal with running the household and hardly any money to do it with."

Congressmen Bowes was standing on the floor of the Kentucky state capitol building, addressing the entire house. "Inasmuch as the 13th Amendment has become law, whether we ratified it or not, I move that Kentucky should join in with the rest of the country and ratify it too."

House Speaker Pruitt looked at Bowes with disgust, but he forced himself to go through the ritual. "The 13th Amendment was not what the great State of Kentucky was promised by our supposed friend, Cassius Clay, when we stayed with the Union and agreed to go along with the Emancipation Proclamation. But we do have a motion. Do I have a second?"

There was a deafening silence, as no one wanted to second Bowes' Motion. Shouts of "That Clay was a traitor!" could be heard from the gallery.

"Yeah! He said we'd be able to keep our slaves if we stayed in the Union. He lied!"

"Sold us down the river!"

"Sold us a bill of goods!"

Speaker Pruitt looked around. Everyone was silent now.

The motion died for lack of a second.

In St. Petersburg, fifty carriages were gathered together in the huge circular driveway in front of a grand mansion. The drivers stood in a group, talking, while inside the mansion a grand party was in progress. The wealthy elite who were strongly opposed to the tsar's efforts to free the serfs, thus drastically changing Russian society, were drinking wine, eating hors d'oeuvres and dancing to a classical Russian musical piece.

The host sitting at the head table stood and motioned to the musicians to stop playing. They did so immediately. The hushed crowd turned to hear what he had to say. "We will soon have great cause to celebrate. At this very moment, all over the city of St. Petersburg, our agents are setting fire to the homes of those who support the Empire."

The crowd nodded in agreement.

The host continued, "When the tsar is no more and we are in power, these fires will remind those who would free our servants that they will pay dearly if they resist us!"

The aristocratic crowd was excited by the prospect of regaining their slaves, along with control of the government.

The host concluded his fiery speech. "By this time tomorrow, we will once more be in control. We will immediately begin rounding up the twenty-three million serfs that rightfully are our property!"

Out in the streets, rough-looking men threw incendiary materials into the front windows of several mansions, igniting the drapes.

The overstuffed furniture quickly caught fire, and the homes were turned into blazing infernos.

At firehouses throughout the city, men opened the wide doors so the horse-drawn equipment could rush out. Teams of sturdy white horses flashed by with their nostrils snorting as they were whipped into a frenzy by the drivers. The firemen rode on top of the apparatus and were busy buttoning, up their uniforms as they went.

At each fiery scene, fire wagons pulled up and began spraying the infernos. But there were too many fires and they were too large for the inadequate equipment.

At the Neva River, men cut through the thin ice with huge fire axes, and dropped hoses into the water. At the pumper wagon, four men, two on each teeter-totter-type pump, worked desperately, pushing and pulling the device.

At the scenes of the fires, men in robes and women in negligees and fur coats stood in the street, watching their homes burn.

One woman clutched priceless jewelry to her chest, while her terrified children stood beside her. Everywhere, the victims wondered who could have done this and why.

The next day at the American Embassy, Jones and Cash were seated at a conference table, along with the embassy secretary, who was feverishly taking notes. Cash had been torn between grief and rage at the assassination of his friend and president, Abraham Lincoln. This threat to the tsar re-opened that wound. The forces of violence and destruction were everywhere.

He said now, "Thank God the tsar had gotten word in advance of this planned insurrection. The city was on guard, and they were able to get the fires out before all of St. Petersburg burnt to the ground. The attempted revolution was planned by a group calling themselves 'nihilists'."

An American soldier stationed outside as a precaution against any violence knocked on the door.

"Come in!"

The soldier entered, holding a message. He handed it to Cash, then returned to his post. Cash quickly skimmed it then jumped to his feet. "There's been an attempt to assassinate the tsar! Get out my dress uniform," he ordered Jones, "along with my sword and pistols. I must get to the palace."

Outside the palace, a light snow, the harbinger of coming winter, fell in wispy flakes that dusted the ground with white.

Inside, Cash, dressed and armed for battle, wearing the hat with the red ostrich feather, was brought into Tsar Alexander's private office. The Tsar greeted him in a heavy voice, his expression worn.

"Are you all right, sir?" Cash asked in genuine concern.

"I am fine and so is the tsarina."

"What happened?"

"We got word through our intelligence sources that an attack was planned. That allowed us to be prepared enough to catch the men who set the fires and the man who tried to kill me."

"Nihilists?" asked Cash.

The tsar slowly shook his head. "No. That is what is so sad. The people who actually started the fires were former serfs, people who I set free from bondage not so very long ago. They were paid large sums of money by the Nihilists to burn down the city."

Cash said thoughtfully, "This is the same problem that I fear will happen in my country. The former slaves have been freed. But they have almost nothing. Their situation is desperate. They aren't allowed to participate in government, and aren't prepared for such participation, anyway. Until we see that they are educated, they will be blown about by the winds of any change that promises them prosperity or power."

The Tsar listened intently as Cash continued. "We must educate them and help bring them to a point where they can take on the responsibility of civil leadership, rather than to engage in blind violence in order to accomplish their needs."

The tsar nodded in agreement. Then, looking at Cash's uniform, he said with a wry smile, "I see you came prepared for battle."

"I didn't know if you needed my services as a special guard, but I can make myself available to you, day and night, if necessary."

Alexander was very touched by this gesture of friendship and support. "I appreciate your concern, Cash, but I believe that we have things under control at this point."

Cash knew that the tsar might not be entirely out of danger. There could be further attempts on his life and his government. He thought hard for a moment, then said, "This might be a good opportunity for our government to return the favor you so kindly did for us recently. A statement of total support for your monarchy by our president could be helpful. And a visit to your country by some vessels of our new navy could be just the show of strength that will intimidate your enemies. You know, we now

209

have great battleships covered with iron plating. I am sure that your detractors would be most impressed.

The tsar was even more touched now. "Thank you, my friend," he said simply but with feeling. "Your gestures of support, both personally and on behalf of your country, are most appreciated. I will consider your generous offer."

Then his warm expression changed to a more businesslike one. "I must raise a critical issue with you. I have received no answer regarding your purchase of our Russian-American territory."

Cash felt it was best to be completely frank. "My country is hard-pressed to come up with that much money right now. No one had any idea that we were talking abut 360 million acres when we agreed to pennies an acre."

Alexander appreciated the predicament. He wanted this deal badly, and tried to come up with a solution. "When I said 'pennies an acre,' that meant it cannot be less than two cents to be 'pennies' plural. That would make the price seven point two million. That is my final offer."

"I will convey this to Seward," said Cash. "And I'll try my best to convince him to go forward with the purchase."

The tsar poured two large glasses of cognac. "Let us toast to a continued long friendship between our two countries. We have so much in common – both good and bad."

They both lifted their glasses high.

Cash said soberly, "You may not have heard yet that the assassin of our great President has been caught, along with all of his co-conspirators. He burned to death in the barn that he hid in. A fitting end for such a despicable person."

The tsar replied grimly, "My own would-be assassin has been hung. I'm afraid, however, that this is not the end of the troubles for either of our countries. I believe the struggle to change the entrenched social order is just beginning."

"The most important thing I learned from studying history", said Cash, "is that no nation stands still in the course of time. Our founding fathers had great ideas that have stood the test of time. But they operated under different standards that no longer apply to contemporary society."

The Tsar responded enthusiastically, "Exactly! Look what happened to Rome and the Greeks."

210

"And the Mongols", Cash replied, "Did you know that they were once a great, kind nation that gave their surplus to other countries? It will take vigilance on the part of both our nations to ensure we do not end up a debauched society living in the ruins of our once great cities."

Alexander raised his glass. "I join you in that hope, my friend."

Days later, St. Petersburg was again peaceful and it was safe to go out and about. Cash and Marie climbed into an ice-sled on a wooden platform some forty feet above ground level. A wooden chute went from the platform to the ground. They were dressed warmly, in beautiful furs, with Cash wearing a black fur hat, and Marie enveloped in a beautiful silver hat and cloak.

As they started down the chute, they began to pick up speed, going faster and faster down the one-hundred-and-fifty-yard run. They bounced up and down and back and forth as they hit dips and the sides of the wooden chute. Marie was smiling in exhilaration and holding Cash tight.

They came to the end of the ride, a deep, soft snow bank created for this purpose. They both broke into laughter, then kissed like two young lovers who had just discovered each other.

That night they were both at a lavish party at the American embassy, though not together. Marie came with Jones, who had become Cash's accomplice in providing a cover for the illicit relationship. Late in the evening, Cash found an opportunity to dance with her.

As he whirled her around the room, he whispered in her ear, "Let's go outside." She nodded, and he led her out onto the veranda, where they could be alone.

He started to kiss her, but she pulled back and said with uncharacteristic seriousness, "Cash, there is something I must tell you." He looked at her anxiously, hoping she wasn't about to end their relationship. He'd fallen deeply in love with her and couldn't imagine life without her. She said simply, "I am with child."

His first, instinctive reaction was joy. Their love had created a child. Could anything be more wonderful? Then reality set in. There were serious complications for both of them, and most importantly, for their child. Suddenly he noticed that Marie was looking at him with undisguised concern, and he realized what she must be thinking.

"It will be all right," he assured her, taking her in his arms and holding her tight. "I'll take care of both of you, always. And I'll love our child as deeply as I love you."

It was a promise he would keep, no matter what it cost him.

Back in Lexington, Kentucky, Cash's fiercest detractors, the plantation owners, were once more gathered in the smoke-filled room where they had hatched various plans to try to defeat him.

They were now "former slave-owners" and filled with a bitter hatred for the man who helped bring about that drastic change. They took turns looking at a copy of the New York Gazette, which featured a very clever cartoon showing a corpulent-looking Cassius Clay, wearing his full dress uniform and hosting a party. Two caricatures of painted-up women with exaggerated bodies were at either side of him. The caption read "RUSSIAN AMBASSADOR LIVES IT UP ON OUR MONEY."

"Where did you get this?" asked a tall, red-haired man.

"From someone who went to New York on business," one of the other plantation owners answered.

"See to it that his wife gets this, along with those other articles. That bastard is going to pay for what he's done to all of us."

The leaves had all fallen at White Hall, and the trees were bare. Puffs of smoke came from the chimneys. Mary Jane sat at the large dining table with her two older daughters. The table was piled high with a veritable feast. This was a homecoming celebration.

"It's so good to have you both home from school," Mary Jane said with a catch in her voice. "It's been very lonely around here with your father being gone for so long. I thought he'd return for President Lincoln's funeral, but he said in his last letter that important business keeps him at his post."

A loud banging noise at the front door caught their attention. "Now who can that be?" Mary Jane called out to her maid, "Bessie!"

Mary jumped up from the table. "It's all right, Mother. I'll see who it is."

Mary opened the door and found a package lying there. Picking it up, she saw that there was no name on it. She decided that must mean that it was all right to open it. She did so as she headed back to the dining room, where her mother was asking her sister, "So how do you like college, Laura?"

Laura was eager to share her new purpose in life. "I heard someone speak on women's right to vote. She really made sense. I'm helping her in our area. Her name is Susan Anthony, and I've invited her to come and spend a few days with us here. I hope you don't mind."

"Why, no," said Mary Jane, "I think that would be very nice." She added tightly, "It's a good thing your father isn't home. You know how he feels about such things."

"I didn't know he had an opinion on the subject."

"He feels that the wife should have input, but that the man should make the final decision and cast the vote. He would have the black man vote, but not white women like us."

Laura was surprised at this attitude – if it was true. She was old enough to have realized that the estrangement between her parents often colored what her mother said about her father. "Still, I can't believe that all men feel women are not competent to vote."

Mary handed her mother the open package. Mary Jane looked at the contents, then quickly wrapped them up again and excused herself, saying she'd be right back. When she was gone, Laura asked curiously, "What was in the package?"

"Hate mail! A bunch of articles and cartoons about Father that weren't very nice. This is all so hard on mother. I don't understand why he doesn't come home."

"It was her choice not to go with him," Laura reminded Mary. "We could have all been together like we were the first time he went to St. Petersburg, but mother refused."

Despite his long separation from his children, Cash had been diligent in remaining in frequent communication with each of them. He tried to be a father to them, advising them on their choice of books to read, educational plans and religious affiliations. He sent generous gifts – a beautiful, ornate gold bracelet for Laura for her seventeenth birthday; an interest in some Russian oil wells for his eldest surviving son, Green, who had made it through the war unharmed.

Laura missed their father, but had no bitterness toward him as Mary did. She changed the sensitive subject. "Mother says the black men will get to vote before we will. Isn't that ridiculous?" (Laura couldn't know that it would take over thirty years after black males were given the right to vote before women -- black or white -- had the same right.)

In a meadow near Irwinsville, Georgia, a group of former Confederate soldiers were encamped in several small tents. The President of the Confederacy, Jefferson Davis, was also there. He sat over a cup of what was supposed to be coffee but was really mostly chicory and burned corn grits, with only a hint of coffee flavor. He was anxiously awaiting his wife's arrival. She finally got there after midnight and they had a tearful reunion.

Early the next morning, Davis and his wife huddled together under a blanket. Through a gap in the tent flap, he watched the sun coming up over the horizon. It was time to leave. He whispered to his wife, "We best start moving into the woods."

Mrs. Davis got up and handed her husband a heavy shawl. "Put this on, dear. It's freezing outside."

He reluctantly put on the long sleeveless shawl, worried how he would look in it. His dignity was still important to him, even though the confederacy had fallen and he was a hunted man. They stepped out of the tent, and he started toward the tent of his bodyguards. Then something caught his attention out of the corner of his eye.

A half-dozen Union soldiers were quickly advancing on him. Davis grabbed his wife's arm and started to run. She resisted, screaming for him to stand his ground. It was hopeless, and she knew the Union soldiers needed little excuse to kill her husband. Davis stopped and held his terrified wife in his arms. She sobbed.

Looking at his captors, Davis murmured in a resigned tone, "God's will be done."

As the soldiers grabbed him, pulling him from the arms of his hysterical wife, Davis did not resist. But when they attempted to drag him to the Commander of the 4th Michigan Cavalry, waiting nearby, he brushed off their arms and walked beside them. He intended to surrender with dignity.

President Johnson was in the White House conference room surrounded by his cabinet at the huge mahogany table. Secretary of War Stanton, who had replaced Cameron, sat on one side of him and Secretary of State Seward was on the other.

The President spoke in a voice devoid of any sense of triumph. All he felt was relief. "My $100,000 reward for the capture of Jefferson Davis proved to be effective. I just got word that he was captured yesterday."

Stanton grinned. "I heard he was disguised in a dress."

The cabinet members all laughed, except Secretary Seward. He rebuked them. "I know Davis, and I don't believe that."

Johnson stopped the budding argument. "That's not why I called you here this morning. As you know, President Lincoln was adamant that we allow the Southern States that seceded to return to the Union without oppressive conditions. I agreed with his position. The document before you is my proposal."

Everyone read the document carefully. The reaction was uniformly negative.

Stanton demanded clarification. "You're proposing that for purposes of representation in Congress, the blacks be counted as a full person instead of three-fifths of a person?"

Johnson met the disapproving looks of his cabinet. "Do any of you suggest that because one is black that he is not a whole person?"

No one spoke, except Stanton. "That will give the southern states more members in Congress than the north will have."

Johnson smiled grimly. "The catch is that they have to ratify the 13th Amendment in order to join Congress."

"Sounds like a good trade off," Seward said slowly.

"But what about pardons?" asked Stanton?

The president had that covered. "Everyone is pardoned by Presidential Proclamation, except for high ranking officers and owners of over $20,000 in property. These people will have to apply to me personally for a pardon."

The cabinet members exchanged quizzical looks. They knew this proclamation put President Johnson in a position of having a lot of power over his Southern brothers and fellow Democrats.

He continued before anyone could object further, "The proclamation gives white voters who are loyal to the Union the exclusive right to attend any constitutional convention in any state. It also gives white voters the right to determine the qualifications of voters within each state."

That elicited the strongest response of all. Everyone knew this was hardly what Lincoln would have done. Johnson was showing absolutely no loyalty to the man who had made him vice president.

Stanton was sarcastic. "Your Southern Democrat friends are gong to love you. This gives them a South that will be guaranteed to be ruled by whites."

Johnson reacted angrily. "President Lincoln knew that I was both a Southerner and a Democrat when he chose me as his running mate. These concessions are what it is going to take to bring our great country back together."

At the Willard Hotel in Washington D.C., a group of well-dressed politicians were seated in a corner table in the Grand Salon, an ornate hotel bar which was finished in elegant mahogany paneled walls. They had gathered here out of profound concern for the state of the Union under President Johnson.

Speaking was Senator Summer, a towering figure of a man. "Our new president waited until the Senate was in recess before he put out his absurd proclamation. This Republic cannot be lost, but it appears that Andrew Johnson has done much to try and lose it."

Thaddeus Stevens was a gaunt, grim faced, craggy-browed yet somewhat handsome man of seventy-three. He didn't look his age because of an expensive, dark brown toupee. "He's certainly no Abraham Lincoln," agreed Stevens. "Is there no way to arrest the insane course of this president?"

Senator Lyman Trumbull responded in a cold, unsympathetic tone, "We have to find a way. Without some kind of protective legislation, the freed slaves will be tyrannized all over again. They certainly will be abused, and if nothing is done, virtually re-enslaved. Have you seen the new 'Black Codes' they've come up with down there?"

"As a matter of fact," said Stevens, "I brought a list to go over with you. "He pulled out a list and read from it in a disgusted tone, "In Opelousas, Louisiana, they passed a law that Negroes cannot live within the town limits unless they work for a white person. They cannot even enter the town without written permission from their employer, and in no instance can they be on the town streets after ten o'clock at night."

"In Florida," Trumbull interjected, "blacks cannot own any kind of weapon, and they need special permission to engage in any kind of commerce, or even to preach. The penalty is thirty-nine lashes on the bare back."

Sumner went on, "Most jurisdictions have passed what they call 'vagrancy' laws that put the Negroes in prison and subject them to forced 'free labor' if they have no visible means of support.

216

Out of fear, former slaves are moving back to their shanties on the plantations and working under almost the same conditions as before."

"For all practical purposes, slavery is almost back to where it was before," Trumbull said. "But what can we do about it?"

Stevens handed out a proposal. "I've put together a comprehensive plan which we will need to support in both the House and the Senate. The biggest defense for the Negro is the right to vote, thus balancing the power of the Southern whites."

"That makes a lot of sense, Thaddeus," Sumner said in approval. "Andy Johnson gave the South the power to count the Negroes and now we give them the power to vote."

Stevens wasn't finished. "In addition, we set up a Freedmen's Bureau to protect their rights."

Trumbull read Stevens' proposal carefully. "I see here where you propose that this new bureau establish nearly one-thousand new schools for the blacks."

"And several new colleges," said Thaddeus.

Stevens finished, "Finally, I propose that anyone who supported the Confederacy during the war not be allowed to vote or to set voting requirements."

Sumner gave him a direct look. "It certainly is a daring plan. Do you think there's any possibility of getting it passed?"

"Only if we act now. If we wait for the former slave-owners to put their puppet governments back into place, we'll never be able to bring justice to the freed salves."

A few days after this momentous meeting, Cash was busy at the embassy going through his stack of mail. By now he got quite a bit of correspondence, much of it caused by the critical cartoons and articles being printed in the Washington area newspapers. He found it easy to dismiss most of it. But he couldn't dismiss the cartoons that suggested he was spending all his time in St. Petersburg partying and womanizing.

He worried about what Mary Jane might think if she saw these cartoons. When he opened a letter from Mary Jane and read it with growing consternation, he realized the cartoons were the least of his problems. Someone had told her specifically about his relationship with Marie.

You think you're getting away with what you're doing because you're so far away, but I know what has been going on between you and that woman.

Cash knew that one of his many enemies had made certain that Mary Jane found out about his affair. It didn't matter who had done it. What mattered was Mary Jane's response, which was unequivocal. "Don't try to convince me that what I am saying is not true, for I have irrefutable proof, and I will not listen to your lies. However, I will not tell our children. I want to spare them the misery and humiliation that I feel. You need not bother to write, but we certainly could use some financial support from time to time. You seem to forget that."

Guilt and anger warred within him. Mary Jane was right. He was being unfaithful. He wasn't proud of it. But when she left him and kept refusing his repeated pleas to come back to St. Petersburg, he had finally accepted that there was no attachment left between them. The marriage was over in everything but name only. His religious beliefs told him it was still wrong to have an affair. But his lonely heart couldn't resist the love and companionship Marie offered.

His anger stemmed from her financial demands. He sent her as much money as he possibly could, and it should have been more than enough to provide for his family. But Mary Jane had decided to embark on an extremely expensive remodel of White Hall. That was the reason for her insistence that she needed more money.

All of those issues were disturbing, but his greatest concern was for his children. He was enormously relieved that Mary Jane hadn't told them of his actions. He had managed to remain in regular communication with each of them, despite the distance separating them. He couldn't bear to think of losing Laura, Mary, Green, and little Annie. And he knew that was precisely what would happen if he didn't return home at some point in the near future.

But if he returned home, he would not only be leaving Marie, probably forever, but the child they were about to have.

Suddenly, the reality of his illicit affair hit him where it hurt, and he knew that whatever course of action he chose, other innocent people would be hurt, as well.

CHAPTER THIRTY-ONE

Congress reconvened at the capital building in Washington. Representatives from eight southern states that had met President Johnson's conditions for readmission to the Union demanded to be seated. Among the newly elected representatives were many Confederate war heroes.

The Speaker of the House was introduced. He began, "Mr. Chairman, I move that the first order of business today is to put the president's reconstruction program in limbo until we can appoint a committee to come up with a more permanent alternative. I further move that this committee be made up of myself... ....."

Over at the Senate, it was much the same story, with the former vice-president of the Confederacy now the newly elected senator from Georgia. Alexander H. Stephens had declared that for the black man, "slavery or subordination to the superior race is his natural and normal condition." Chants of "Good Ol' Andrew Johnson, one of our own!" were heard along with rebel yells.

The Majority Leader interrupted them. "I have just received a letter from the House of Representatives stating they have formed a committee to draft a new reconstruction program, and I move that we not take any further action until the program is adopted into law. I call for a vote of all senators representing states already acknowledged as members of our senate, and that no senators from states waiting to be admitted shall be allowed to vote."

"Roll call vote," responded the chairman.

The chairman started down the line, calling for the votes of only those senators from states already admitted and a part of the Senate. Johnson's allies from the eight southern states were ignored, and the former vice-president of the Confederacy was not allowed to vote. Over the vociferous objections of the furious southerners, the voice of the chairman could be heard, but only after he hammered his gavel several times. "Motion carries. We are dismissed until further notice."

In the Oval Office, President Johnson was fuming as Alexander Stephens went on an emotional tirade about what had just happened in the senate. About that time, Secretary Stanton walked in. Seeing the former Confederate Vice President he started to turn and walk out. Johnson stopped him.

"What do they think they're doing in the Senate?!" he demanded.

Stanton replied boldly, "They have formed a committee to draft a reconstruction plan, and they intend to vote on it and make it a law. I believe that is the proper way to do things."

"But Lincoln did many things by Presidential Proclamations!"

Stanton looked pointedly at Stephens as he responded, "We were at war then. Now we are not. Therefore, it is no longer appropriate, nor is it legal."

"If they try to change anything, I'll veto it. That, too, is legal," Johnson retorted.

Stanton was disgusted. "And if they have enough votes, they will override your veto. Good day, Mr. President."

Johnson stopped him again. "Whose side are you on, Stanton?"

Stanton met the president's look. "The side of the nation, Mr. President, and what is right."

Stanton left as Secretary Seward entered. "He certainly left in a huff. Best you replace him right away," said Seward.

Johnson smiled. At least Seward was loyal. "It's too soon after the assassination. It would look bad. But it will be done if he doesn't come around."

It was late at night in Washington, and Senators Sumner and Trumbull, and Congressman Stevens were at a back table in a private room, along with Secretary of War Stanton. A whiskey bottle was passed around and Stevens adamantly refused to take some.

"We missed overriding his veto by just one vote," said Stevens bitterly. "One lousy vote."

Senator Trumbull asked, "What can we do to turn things around? We barely missed the opportunity to change the moral fiber of the nation."

Summer was a realist. "They say a miss is as good as a mile. Maybe Johnson's right. Maybe the country's not ready for such a drastic change."

"Nonsense!" Stevens retorted hotly. "If we're going to get the Negro the right to vote and to be educated, we cannot give up at the first hurdle. We must persevere. That one vote could change or even die!"

Stanton was appalled. "You're not suggesting . . ."

Stevens was equally appalled that Stanton would even think such a thing. "Of course not. I'm just saying that one vote can change. People do get sick, they do die, they do retire, and they are replaced in office every day. We must not give up. One or two votes can also change the next time around."

"I hope so," said Trumbull. "The President's veto amounts to giving into the worst racial elements in the South."

The Southern Democrats were elated by Johnson's veto. Three days later, it was celebrated by over 6,000 participants at a Democratic rally. They marched to the White House to "serenade" the president.

"What is all that ruckus?" the President demanded of the head of his Presidential Guard.

"A bunch of your supporters, sir. They're here to celebrate your veto."

Johnson went to the window and looked out. There was a huge crowd outside. Going to the front door of the White House, he welcomed the celebrants, then delivered a rambling, disjointed speech that lasted over an hour.

Referring to the Republicans, he said, "These traitors are no better than Judas Iscariot, who also helped the attackers of the most just man of them all, Jesus."

Someone in the crowd cried out, "Who are these traitors?" Another demanded, "Give us their names!"

Johnson had had a little too much to drink, which wasn't unusual, and he pulled no punches. "I say Thaddeus Stevens of Pennsylvania! I say Charles Sumner of Massachusetts! And I can name countless others of the same stripe!"

The crowd erupted in enthusiastic applause.

At a Washington hotel, a large number of politicians were seated in the hotel's restaurant. Senator Fessenden sat with

Congressman Dawes of Massachusetts. They had both been strong supporters of President Johnson, at least until now.

Dawes handed Fessenden his copy of the newspaper. "Did you read here about the speech the President made at the White House last night?"

"Yes. It was shameful. Andy has broken the faith and now he must sink from detestation to utter contempt." Everyone nodded in agreement.

"I was telling my wife this morning," said Dawes, "that our friend has deprived us of the least bit of ground to stand upon and defend him. I am afraid that this latest outburst is the end for me."

"Why he would stoop to such personal levels, naming names. It's disgusting."

Fessenden said soberly, "I understand that a new version of the same bill that was vetoed is going to be proposed in the house today."

"I heard the same thing," said Dawes. "I doubt we'll be able to sustain his veto this time."

"We?" asked Fessenden. "I no longer feel I can stand with him any longer."

The anti-Johnson momentum was growing. "I understand," agreed Dawes. "I'm beginning to feel the same way."

President Johnson addressed the House of Representatives. "By giving blacks immediate citizenship, we discriminate against foreigners. They are required to wait five years to even apply. And they are required to learn important facts about our great country. This law gives a degree of protection to blacks that even whites do not enjoy and is therefore discriminatory to the white race."

The Southern Democrats cheered the president.

Thaddeus Stevens jumped to his feet, even though it was painful for him to put any weight on his bad foot. He steadied himself with his cane and spoke with the authority of a great orator. "There are those here today who say the freed black men do not need protection, and that they are not fit to testify as witnesses, nor should they ever serve on a jury. My office sent one of my aides down through the deep South to investigate and bring back a report."

He turned to a young man sitting beside him. "Tell everyone, Johnny, what you heard."

The young man stood up and nervously shared with the congress his experiences down South. "One redneck, a former rebel soldier, said, 'If you take away the military, the buzzards won't be able to eat the niggers as fast as we can kill 'em!' Others agreed with him."

There were murmurs of dismay at this shocking statement.

Stevens jumped back in. "There are men here today who would say that all blacks are illiterate and incapable of learning. I would like for you to hear from a former slave who fled the South and received some education here in the North. I introduce to you Mr. William H. Garnett, and I'll let you be the judge."

A well-dressed black man stood, and with a deep, resonant voice, he spoke loud and clear. "We are engaged in the stubborn war with unrelenting forces, which we mean to fight to the end on our native soil, aiming to complete the establishment of our rights and liberties. Our weapons are the spelling book, the Bible, the press and the implements of industry; our impregnable fortifications are schoolhouses and the church."

The republican side of the house voiced its support through cheers and applause.

One entire side of the house had come to its feet, and soon even a few from the democratic side joined in. Stevens continued before the enthusiasm died down, "There are those here today who will say that we don't need a civil rights act that guarantees that all Americans receive an education. We don't need a civil rights act that guarantees them the protection of their very lives, along with freedom and the pursuit of happiness. I say men like William H. Garnett are people just like you and I, and they need this act passed to guarantee that others like Mr. Garnett will have their lives protected and will receive an education so they will be able to perform in life."

Thaddeus looked proudly at Garnett. "As Mr. Garnett here just proved he can do."

Stevens now had the crowd completely in his hands, and he took advantage of the moment. "I move that we override the President's veto and pass this bill today!"

The cheers and applause were deafening. There was no longer any doubt the bill would pass.

The following day the headline of the Washington newspaper read "SENATE ENDORSES CONGRESSIONAL BILL – CIVIL RIGHTS ACT PASSES."

CHAPTER THIRTY-TWO

1867

A Log schoolhouse was under construction. Black parents joined in and helped, as happy and excited black children watched the new school go up. Troops composed of a mixture of black and white soldiers marched through the South, while shocked white folks looked at the black men carrying rifles, with bayonets affixed to them, walking down the main street of their town. Soon 985 new schools were built in the South.

At a registration booth, a long line of blacks were waiting to be registered to vote. Soldiers, both black and white, stood by to protect them.

A white schoolmarm stood at the door of one of the newly completed schoolhouses, greeting children as young as three and four years old. Adults of all ages were also in the line, waiting to learn what they'd been forbidden to do under slavery – read and write.

A crowd of rednecks watched disdainfully as the blacks entered their new school. "Where they gettin' all these white women to be nigger teachers?" asked one.

"They're missionary women!" He shook his head. "What's the church comin' to?"

On a road leading in and out of town, black freedmen and women could be seen going in both directions. White onlookers were standing on their porches watching this unceasing procession.

"Where are they all goin'?" asked one onlooker.

"Hear tell they're tryin' to find their kinfolk," answered another. "Sons tryin' to find their mother or father, and women tryin' to find their mate."

A third onlooker spit a wad of tobacco at them in disgust. Part of it stuck in his scraggly beard. "They're sure a sorry lookin' bunch."

Freedman Bureau workers and volunteers passed out food and provisions to a line of both blacks and whites. As one old white former confederate soldier got his goods, he commented politely, "There is much that you kind people are doing that takes away the bitter sting of what's happened to us."

In another part of town, a black couple was dressed in clean but plain clothes that had been lent to them by the volunteer white minister and his wife. The minister spoke solemnly. "These two are gathered here today with their friends and family to make their vows permanent before the Lord. Something that they always wanted to do, but were not allowed to do until now."

A survey team was busy surveying some farmland. The soil had recently produced corn that was rotting on its stalks as the former black slaves were too occupied with getting married, finding lost loved ones and getting their 40 acres and a mule to even think about picking it.

A carriage drove up and the plantation owner, dressed in a Prince Albert suit, got out and approached the surveying team. "And just what do you think you're doing?"

The team kept on surveying as their manager introduced himself. "I'm William A. Kenton with the Freedmen's Bureau of Reconstruction and Abandoned Lands Act."

"This land isn't abandoned! I own it."

"I'm sorry, but it's been declared abandoned, as it isn't being worked. We're just doing our job, sir."

"It was being worked until your government declared all my workers free!"

"What about you, sir? Couldn't you have picked the corn?"

"Why, you insolent young upstart!" stammered the plantation owner. "What do you intend to do with my land?"

"Redistribute it, sir."

"Redistribute it? To whom?"

"To freed blacks and poor whites who don't have any land."

"Who do you think you are?! Don't you know that English Kings were beheaded for doing this very kind of thing! You'll hear from my lawyer!" The plantation owner climbed into his carriage. With

226

his whip, he spun the horses and the carriage around, and went off in a cloud of dust.

Near Lexington, a young black woman plowed her new field with a homemade wooden plow that barely cut through the soil. She held the reins, which were attached to her husband, pulling the plow in place of a mule. Their 40-acre parcel that they got from the government had stacks of tree trunks they had cut down to serve as fences.

"When are we gonna get our new house built, Abraham?"

"First we got to bring our crop in, Orelia," said her new husband. "And prove up the land so we don't lose it. Then we can start buildin' a house."

"I wish that George's friend, Cash, would come back. That wife of his ran all the women off that didn't have a husband to work in the fields. Cash would help us. He'd let us borrow a real plow and some horses."

Mary Jane pulled up in front of her parents' house. Her carriage was somewhat in disrepair, and the horses looked gaunt.

Inside the mansion, Mrs. Warfield was looking out the window. "It's Mary Jane," she announced to her husband. "She's by herself. You know she had to let her driver go."

Doctor Warfield was not all that sympathetic. "She's probably here to beg for money again."

Mrs. Warfield opened the door to her daughter. Mary Jane took one look at her father's stubborn expression and burst into tears. Mrs. Warfield gave her husband a reproachful look and put her arm around her daughter to comfort her. "There, there, dear, sit down and rest." She glared at her husband. "Everything's going to be all right."

Mary Jane took a hanky from her mother and collapsed on the divan. "I haven't heard from Cassius in over three months, Mother." She started to cry again. "And then it was just a little bit of money and no letter. Oh, Mother, I just don't know what I'm going to do."

Her fathered answered firmly, "You'll just have to sell the stock, like I suggested you do the last time you came here for money."

"I sold all the livestock two months ago. It just made things worse. Now we have to pay for beef and milk. We can't afford butter or cheese. The only thing I haven't sold is his saddle horse and what's in the wine cellar."

"Well, what are you waiting for?"

Mrs. Warfield turned on her husband. "Elisha, don't be so cruel to your own daughter."

"I am not being cruel to my daughter. She doesn't ride his horse and she doesn't even like wine."

Mrs. Warfield put her hand on her daughter's shoulder. "How much do you need, dear?"

Mary Jane brightened, and the words she had so carefully rehearsed came tumbling out. "To pay Mary and Laura's tuition and what I owe the few remaining servants, I'll need two thousand dollars."

"Father will instruct the bank to credit your account with twenty-five hundred today." She gave her husband a fierce look that brooked no disagreement. "Now, you are staying for dinner, aren't you?"

"I can't. I have to get back and pay the servants. And if I don't take care of the tuition, they're liable to send my girls home."

As soon as she left, her father said in frustration, "Fifty years old, and we still have to pay her bills! If that no good, nigger-lovin' husband of hers doesn't come home pretty soon and take on his responsibility, we'll be broke, too!"

Fort Monroe was in a beautiful area of southwest Virginia. The facility stood out against a background of pine-covered mountains, and the U.S. flag flew proudly against the blue skies that were filled with big, puffy white clouds. It was Christmas Day and the soldiers had decorated a large pine tree that stood directly in front of the fort.

Jefferson Davis was sitting in a chair reading the Bible. He was guarded by two armed soldiers who stood at attention, watching his every move but not saying a word to him. There was the clanking sound of a cell door being closed, then Mrs. Davis entered the cell, along with their attorney. Davis embraced his wife for a long time before finally pulling back and smiling at her warmly.

"This is the best Christmas present that I could ever receive," Davis said to his wife. "You don't know how good it is to see you. I have no privacy, yet it's like being in solitary confinement. No one will talk with me. I have no idea of what is going on in the rest of the world. If it wasn't for the strength that I receive from His word, I would go crazy."

The attorney, who had been waiting patiently, finally spoke. "I've notified the president's office of your desire for an immediate trial.

I do not believe that their charges can hold under the Constitution. It's obvious to me they're afraid to go to trial, and they're just stalling."

"But they can't just keep me in here without trying me!"

"They've indicted you for treason," explained the attorney. "But the government claims they're not ready to go to trial."

"It's been over two years. How much time do they need?"

"I've filed a Writ of Mandate with the High Court. I'm certain that arrangements will be made before Easter to release you on bail."

Davis breathed a heartfelt sigh of relief. "Thank God. I don't think I could stand much more of this."

Mrs. Davis pulled a wrapped present out from under her coat. "I brought you something from a very special friend who wanted you to know that he is praying for you and your release."

As he unwrapped the gift, he said, "I can't believe they let you bring anything in here."

"I think they were afraid to say no. When you see it, you'll understand why."

Davis stared at the contents of the package -- a crown of thorns.

"It's from the Pope," his wife said, fighting back tears. "He's praying for you, and he wove the crown from real thorns with his own hands, just for you."

At the White House the spring flowers were in full bloom, and the cherry trees were beginning to blossom. In the conference room, the cabinet sat in a meeting with the President. The Chief Justice of the Supreme Court addressed them. "I'm afraid you have no choice. If you go to trial, he will probably prevail, as the Constitution is on his side. I shouldn't even be here telling you this, but we can't afford the embarrassment that such a decision would cause."

No one spoke. There was nothing to say.

Later, Stanton, Trumbull, Sumner and Stevens met privately. There was a shared sense of frustration. Stanton said, "If we don't do something, he's going to be released on bail."

"Maybe the time has come to put a throttle on that court," said Stevens. "We can pass legislation . . ."

Trumbull interrupted, "We best be cautious about taking such a drastic step or we may lose all the ground we've gained."

"But that traitor deserves to hang!" Stanton insisted. "You know how many people died because of the rebel government he led."

"I agree with you," said Sumner. "But he's just one man, and we have over three million freedmen who need our help in order to start new lives."

Stevens said slowly, with great reluctance, "Sumner's right. We have to stay with our priorities. And let Jefferson Davis go on to whatever sort of life is left to him."

Log home communities of freed blacks were going up all over the South. Each community had a log school within easy walking distance. The children didn't have to be forced to attend school. They knew what a precious gift it was to be able to learn. That gift had been denied their parents and grandparents.

Howard University had just been finished. It was named after General Howard, who joined the Freedman's Council to make a difference. He used thirty thousand dollars of the fund to purchase the land and to start construction of what would one day turn out to be one of the finest black colleges in America. The memorial plaque read: "Dedicated to the Freedmen of America," Major General Oliver O. Howard, Chairman and Chief Administrator, Freedmen's Bureau and Abandoned Lands Act.

Hundreds of men lined up for a photograph of the first freshman class at the University. Among the black students were white teachers and General "Bible" Howard, himself. The white general delivered the dedication speech. "Today is significant in the course of the history of our great country. As these young men of all colors and circumstances take their place in this house of learning, they will begin to form a new generation of people, black and white, that slowly will learn to accept one another. It is hoped that one day the graduates of this university, and others like it, will prove what the Constitution and the Bible guarantee us. That all men are created equal in the eyes of God and the purview of the law."

Hampton University had also been completed, and a large group sat and stood in front of a brick university posing for a photograph. The men ranged in age from what looked like thirteen or fourteen to other men who were in their late thirties or early forties. The majority, however, were in their early twenties. Of the group of about fifty, ten were teachers, seven black and three white. The white principal and the school's treasurer were also in the picture.

Two black students were talking while the cameraman fired rounds of flash powder and snapped photographs. "Four years

230

from now we'll be the first graduates. What do you plan to do then, Booker T.?"

"I'm going to be a teacher," said young Mr. Washington. "A great teacher, I hope. Right now, our whole race is trying to go to school. It seems like few feel they're too young, and none are too old to learn. There just aren't enough teachers, especially black teachers like we have here."

"You're going to be a great teacher, " his friend said confidently. "I bet you'll be principal one day."

"It was the middle of the afternoon at the Capitol Building in Washington, and the House was still in session. A particularly dignified black man addressed the other members. Robert Brown Elliot, South Carolina's second black U.S. Congressman, had attended Eaton College in England and spoke several languages fluently. He had an Eaton accent, and his resonant voice was filled with confidence.

"This bill will provide transportation for the poor, hospitals that are so badly needed, institutions for the orphaned and insane so they no longer have to roam the street or rot in prison. One day you will look back on what we accomplished here today with great national pride."

There was a roar of approval. Thaddeus Stevens pushed himself to a standing position with his cane. It was extremely difficult for him, but he didn't want to lose this moment to someone else. "I heartily second Congressman Elliot's bill. It is time for the dawning of a new nation, one that is compassionate and cares about all of its people. I ask you to support this legislation, not as a Republican, as I am, or a Democrat, as many of you are, but rather as a fellow human being whom God made, just like he made Congressman Elliot here."

The Republican side stood in applause. Soon the whole house was on its feet, some reluctantly, but even many of the Democrats had caught this progressive vision.

In the gallery, Stevens' mulatto "housekeeper," Lydia, could be seen applauding enthusiastically. Her pride in Thaddeus was apparent. Although the times would not allow them to marry, in their hearts they were husband and wife, bound to each other for life.

That night in Georgia, near one of the new log cabin communities built for the freed slaves, a rider, wearing a white hood, held a burning torch as he raced toward the community. His eyes were illuminated by the torch through the jagged holes cut in the hood. It was a grotesque sight. He was soon joined by many more men on horseback, all wearing white hoods.

They rode to the center of the cluster of cabins, dragging something behind them. Then they lifted up the wooden cross they had been dragging and began to set it on fire with their torches.

Black families started to pour out of their homes. They were shocked and terrified by what they saw. The Klan leader was dressed in red. He shouted, "We are the ghosts of dead rebel soldiers! If you vote tomorrow, we will burn your houses down with you in them!"

Frightened children clung to their mothers and fathers. But their parents were too frightened, themselves, to give them much comfort.

CHAPTER THIRTY-THREE

St. Petersburg - 1868

In his office at the embassy, Cash was working at his desk, when Jones came in with a priority message. It was brief and to the point.

Ulysses S. Grant had defeated Johnson for the Presidency. This was no surprise. Johnson had been so unpopular that he'd barely survived impeachment only months before the election. The election had a very personal significance for Cash. He was being called back.

"That's great news, as far as I'm concerned," said a jubilant Jones. "I don't think I could bear another Russian winter. What are your future plans?"

"I can't leave just yet. You're free to go, but I will not leave my post until my replacement steps through that door. I'll send a letter to Seward to that effect."

Jones was puzzled. Surely Cash couldn't believe that Grant would keep him on. He must know that a new ambassador would be arriving in the near future. What could make him want to spend every last moment here? Then he realized what the answer must be. Marie. And their young son, Launey.

Most people weren't aware that she had a child. She had gone away for an extended "rest," then returned a few months later and taken up her ballet career again. No one but Jones knew that the father of her child was Cash. And he knew that Cash had quietly adopted the boy. When Cash left Russia, he would leave behind the woman he loved and his three-year-old son.

It was Christmas morning at Cash's apartment, and his son was happily riding his new rocking horse. The floor was littered with wrapping paper and presents. Cash had been especially generous to both Launey and Marie. He knew this was at least partly out of guilt. He hadn't yet told Marie that he would have to leave soon.

Marie gazed lovingly at Cash, the man who had swept her off her feet and inspired her to risk the career that mattered so much to her. He was, in the French vernacular used by Russian high society, un homme qu cet homme-la. A true man. He was nothing like the rigid Russian men she had been used to. He was entirely unique and completely irresistible.

Cash caught Marie looking at him, the light of love in her eyes, and he knew that he could no longer put off telling her what was about to happen to him.

He said quietly to Marie, "I've been told that my replacement will arrive in February. I'm afraid . . . I'll have no choice but to return to America then."

Marie looked stunned. On some level she'd always known this day would have to come, since ambassadors came and went, and few remained as long as Cash had. But as time went by, she'd found it easy to ignore that painful eventuality. And when she gave birth to their son, it was even more difficult for her to contemplate that he could ever leave them. They were a family, in her eyes, even if not in the eyes of the law or the church.

Cash hurried on awkwardly, "I'll take care of both of you."

"We don't need your money!" Marie said bitterly. "We need you here, with us, being a father to your child."

"I can't stay, Marie. I won't have my ambassador's salary. Any money I could spare has gone to my family. There's nothing left."

"We're your family, too! Launey and I!"

He sat there in abject silence. There was no good resolution to this painful problem. And he knew he had no one to blame but himself and his very human weaknesses.

It was evening at Fort Monroe, and a small pine tree out front was covered with handmade decorations and candles. The sounds of the soldiers singing Christmas carols floated through the still night air.

In his cell, Jefferson Davis read his Bible. His two guards stood in silent watch, as always. In the distance, Davis could just make out the song the soldiers were singing -- "Joy to the World."

The jail door clanged as it was thrown open and Davis heard footsteps approaching on the cold stone floor. Looking up, he was overjoyed to see his wife, his two children and his lawyer.

"I had given up on you," Davis said to his wife, embracing her first, then the children.

"We're late because we had important business to finish. I have a most wonderful surprise for you, darling."

The lawyer handed Davis an official document. Davis read it quickly, then looked up in confusion. "I don't understand. Johnson offered a $100,000 reward for me, dead or alive. Now he pardons me?"

"You don't have to understand," Mrs. Davis said happily. "All that matters is that you can come home now."

He looked at his lawyer. "You mean I'm free to go immediately?"

The lawyer nodded. "You don't have to spend one more minute here. You can gather up your things and we can walk right out of here."

Davis looked around his Spartan cell. Picking up his Bible, he said, "This is all I want to take. Let's go home."

It was a bitter cold February day, and smoke was billowing out of all four chimneys of White Hall. In the dining room, Mary Jane, Mary and Laura were sitting at the big table, along with little Annie, who was now nearly eight years old.

Mary Jane began, "I've called you all together to explain my circumstances. It seems that we're going to have to make some changes in order to pay our bills."

Mary Jane was interrupted by the sudden entrance of Young Bessie, who was bringing in the mail.

"I'm sorry to interrupt, Miss Mary Jane, but there's a big ol' fat letter from Mr. Cash an' I thought you'd want to see it right .   . ."

Mary Jane grabbed the letter from Young Bess, interrupting her, and tore it open. This was the first letter she had received from her husband since she wrote to him seven months earlier, telling him not to write. She finished the brief letter quickly, then carefully examined the two warrants on the Federal Bank that were enclosed. Her eyes widened as she read the amounts.

"What is it, mother? asked Mary. "Is everything all right with father?"

"It seems that after six long years, your father has finally decided to come home," said Mary Jane sarcastically. "He's arriving in New York on the 17th of March."

The girls reacted with excitement. Mary and Laura remembered their father well and even young Mary, who harbored a deep resentment toward him, had missed him terribly. All his letters hadn't made up for his absence. It would be a big day for Annie, too. She couldn't remember what her "daddy" looked like.

"Will everything be all right with you and your circumstances?" Mary asked, "Now that father's coming home?"

"Yes, everything will be just fine now," Mary Jane said slowly. At least financially, she thought.

In St. Petersburg, Cash had turned over the embassy to the new ambassador and said his good-byes to the friends he'd made there over the years. He knew he'd miss so much about Russia, especially the white summer nights that were an extended twilight. There was something utterly poetic about those nights. Some of the most romantic moments he'd shared with Marie were at those times, as they sat in his beach house by the Neva, watched boats filled with lovers go by and listened to the distant strains of the unutterably sad Russian music.

He'd repeatedly tried to see Marie and Launey, but she adamantly refused. Her door was locked to him, and she wouldn't accept his letters. Her anger toward him was so profound that she wouldn't even let him say goodbye to his son. He dragged out his leave taking, hoping she would change her mind. But she didn't. And finally he had no choice but to go. He left the woman and child he loved deeply in Russia, but he took something with him that would last for the rest of his life – a guilt that could never be assuaged and a longing that could never be satisfied.

A big steamship pulled up to the dock at New York Harbor. The sound of the anchor chain being lowered was heard as huge ropes were thrown onto the dock to be tied down. It was March, and the docks were covered with a thick blanket of snow. Passengers crowded the ship's rail, looking out at the crowd below for their loved ones. Cash looked down anxiously. At first it looked as though there was no one here for him. Then he noticed a young woman waving at him.

Young Mary Clay had seen her father, but he didn't recognize this lovely young lady who was so different from the girl he'd last seen. Mary cupped her hands to her mouth so she could be heard above the din of other voices and yelled as loud as she could. "Father!"

Now he recognized her. He made his way quickly towards the gangway. At the same time, Mary Clay pushed her way through the crowd towards the gangway, which was being lowered to the dock.

Cash had made his way closer to the gangway, and only a dozen or so people were ahead of him. He said to the quartermaster, "Excuse me. "I'm the American Ambassador to Russia, and I must disembark immediately. I have an important message for the president that can't wait." It was a lie, but Cash couldn't wait to greet his daughter.

The Quartermaster shouted to the crowd, "Let the ambassador through!"

Cash pushed his way to the front of the line just as the gangway settled on the dock. He unhooked the chain himself and hurried down the steps to meet his daughter. Mary had pushed her way though the crowd and met him at the bottom of the gangway. They embraced warmly, her anger toward him forgotten in the sheer joy of seeing him again.

When they finally pulled apart, Cash looked down at his lovely daughter and asked tentatively, "Your mother – ?"

Mary couldn't quite look her father in the eye as she said uncomfortably, "She couldn't make it. There was so much to do. So many things to take care of, with the renovation. You understand, father."

Cash just nodded soberly. He understood perfectly.

CHAPTER THIRTY-FOUR

1870

Daylight was turning to dusk, and a cold wind howled through the leafless magnolia trees when Cash and Mary drove up to White Hall in a carriage. Young Bessie stood in the open front door, calling behind her for her mistress. "Miss Mary Jane! He's home, Miss Mary Jane!"

Cash was about to walk through the front door when Mary Jane appeared. She stared at her husband, and for a moment he felt an illogical hope that she might actually embrace him. Instead, she stood rigidly in the open doorway, as if blocking his entrance.

"May I come in?" Cash asked his wife.

For a moment she hesitated, and he wondered if she was actually going to bar him from his own home. Then, with obvious reluctance, she stepped aside. "Of course. It's your house."

He walked into the magnificent new foyer. He had drawn up the plans for the renovation before going to Russia and Mary Jane had overseen the construction entirely on her own.

Looking around in approval, he said, "You've done a wonderful job." In an effort at conciliation, he refrained from adding that she'd moved more quickly, and spent far more money, than he'd planned for.

She replied tersely, "I could have done more if you'd sent more money." The unspoken accusation was clear. He had taken money that should have been spent on his home and instead squandered it on an affair or affairs. If he'd hoped for some kind of reconciliation between them, or at least an effort at a friendly relationship, he was clearly doomed to be disappointed. Her manner was colder than the Russian winter he'd just left. He realized he shouldn't assume he would be sharing the master bedroom with her.

"I'm tired from the journey. If you'll show me to my room . . ."

Without saying another word, she led the way upstairs to a new room that was minimally furnished. It wasn't quite finished. The fireplace didn't even work. In this cold weather Cash knew he'd freeze in here. But he also knew it would do no good to protest, unless he wanted an emotional confrontation with Mary Jane. And he definitely didn't want that.

For several months they shared a marriage of convenience, living under the same roof but interacting very little. Meal times were silent and tense. Cash spent as much time as possible outdoors, supervising the estate. When he was indoors, he mainly stayed in the library and his uncomfortable bedroom. He ceded the rest of the house to Mary Jane. The only times they appeared together socially were when they visited friends or entertained Lexington society.

One of the most glittering of these evenings at White Hall would turn out to be the final nail in the coffin of this dead marriage.

Laura Clay was twenty-one now, not nearly as pretty as her mother, but as bright and headstrong as her father. Just as her father had found his life's purpose in fighting to free the slaves, Laura found hers in the women's suffrage movement. She met Susan B. Anthony, who, along with Elizabeth Cady Stanton, had formed the National Women Suffrage Association the previous year. Laura had become passionately involved in the movement and quickly became one of the leaders. She developed a close friendship with Miss Anthony, and called the older woman "Auntie Susan."

When Laura asked her parents if they would have a party in "Auntie Susan's" honor when she came to Lexington to speak, Cash was happy to do so. Miss Anthony had been a staunch abolitionist and loyal supporter of President Lincoln. On that score, she and Cash were in agreement. But he didn't agree with her views on women's suffrage. For all his efforts to help black men get the right to vote, he saw no need to extend that right to women.

Despite his lack of support for the cause, it was a pleasant evening. The cream of Lexington society was there, the house was ablaze with candlelight and looked magnificent, and Cash and Mary Jane appeared to their guests to be a perfectly happy couple. Cash liked Miss Anthony and enjoyed their spirited but friendly debate about the cause that meant so much to her and to his daughter.

"Having worked so long to help free the slaves, I don't understand how you can oppose giving them the right to vote," Cash challenged her.

"It isn't so much that I oppose granting them that right, Mr. Clay. I simply believe women should be granted the same right," she retorted. "All just governments derive their power from the consent of the governed. That consent is given through the vote. It is an insult to women's intelligence and good judgment to deny us the opportunity to participate in our so-called democracy."

"Women exercise that opportunity through their influence on their husbands, brothers and fathers. This is no insult to them."

"Oh, really?" she asked dryly. "Then why does the law specifically prohibit 'lunatics, idiots, felons and women' from voting?"

Laura had been listening to her father's statements with increasing irritation. Now she jumped into the conversation. "The laws of Kentucky, like the laws of every other state, deny equal protection to women. A father can deny the mother of his children the right to custody of them. Women are not allowed to be jurors and are therefore denied the right to trial by a jury of our peers."

Miss Anthony nodded approval of Laura's argument, and added, "The laws are particularly unfair when it comes to property. A husband gets a life-interest in all land owned by his wife. But the wife only gets a life-interest in one-third of the lands owned by the husband. Indeed, a married woman cannot even make a will."

Cash responded stubbornly, "But it isn't necessary for a married woman to concern herself with such matters. It is her husband's responsibility to take care of her and to provide for her."

Laura and Miss Anthony exchanged a look of commiseration. "You'll never change Father's mind," Laura said with a sigh of frustration. "He's as stubborn as. . ." She searched in vain for a strong enough comparison.

"As stubborn as I am," Miss Anthony interjected with a wry smile. "We'll see whose stubbornness stands the test of time."

As Cash continued his stimulating argument with his daughter and Miss Anthony, and Bluegrass society enjoyed the lavish spread laid out for them, a coach drove up to the house. A heavily veiled woman stepped out then turned to help a little boy from the coach. They were met at the door by a servant who led them into the foyer. The servant asked them to wait as he went to get Mr. Clay.

A moment later, Cash hurried out to meet them. Seeing the boy, his face lit up. "Launey!"

The boy shouted, "Father!" and threw himself into his arms.

Now the woman drew back her veil, revealing her identity – Marie. Seeing her again after all these months was a bittersweet joy for Cash. He hadn't stopped loving her and had missed her terribly. But even now, as she stood before him, and he wanted to take her in his arms, he knew he couldn't have her. He'd lost her forever when he left Russia.

She gave Cash a cool, level look. "I did some very serious thinking after you left, Cassius. I considered various courses of action. It pained me to think of Launey being raised by servants while I devote myself to a demanding career. Finally I reached a difficult but inevitable decision. The best thing for our son is to be raised by his father."

Cash was completely caught off-guard. He'd never considered such a possibility. It didn't occur to him that Marie would give up their child. Part of him was grateful to her for being so selfless. And part of him wondered how she could bear to do it.

"Marie . . . are you certain -- ?"

"A boy needs a father. And Launey is utterly devoted to you. He's been distraught since you abandoned us."

Cash flinched at her choice of words, but knew they weren't unfair.

Marie went on, "There is only one question to be answered. Do you want him?"

Cash knew what this would mean to his marriage and to his place in Lexington society. But he didn't hesitate. Looking lovingly at his son, he answered firmly, "Of course I do."

Marie gave a heavy sigh of either relief or regret. Cash couldn't tell which it was. She bent down to kiss her son goodbye and whisper a few final words to him that Cash couldn't hear. But Cash could see his son's expression go from excitement at this reunion to one of heartbreaking loss. Tears ran down Launey's cheeks and he clutched tightly at his mother for a moment. Then she pried loose his little hands, and hurried out to the carriage, without looking back.

Cash took Launey's hand and the two of them watched the woman they loved disappear from their lives forever.

When the carriage was out of sight, Cash turned back to Launey. But they were no longer alone in the foyer. Mary Jane had come out to see what was keeping her husband from their guests. She had witnessed the brief, emotional, all-too-revealing exchange. Her expression was both devastated and enraged.

Either forgetting about their guests, or too angry to care if they heard, she shouted, "You allow your mistress to come into my home! Bringing this -- !"

"Mary Jane!" Cash snapped, his powerful voice stopping her before she could attack Launey.

She glared at him, breathing hard and clenching her fists.

He went on in a quieter tone, "I'm taking the boy upstairs to my room. After I get him settled, I'll meet you in the library to deal with this."

Then he quickly led a wide-eyed and scared Launey up the stairs.

Cash was only gone for a few minutes. But when he came back downstairs, the guests were gone. He had no idea what Mary Jane had said to them to explain the abrupt end of the party. But he was certain she had laid the blame on him.

As soon as he walked into the library, where she waited impatiently, she exploded. "Do you actually expect me to allow your bastard child to live here?!"

"Launey is my adopted son," Cash began, but he was cut off.

"Your adopted son! What kind of fool do you take me for, Cassius?!"

He said quietly, "I'm sorry, Mary Jane. I mean that sincerely. I know this is difficult for you, but . . . "

He got no further. Years of pent-up jealousy, anger and pain came spewing out in a torrent of bitter, near-hysterical recriminations. "After all I've done . . . all I've put up with! While you were with that woman in Russia, I took care of this family! You weren't here to see to the children's education or help them get settled into marriages."

But Cash had his own feelings about what had gone wrong in their relationship. "You took my children away from me. I begged you to stay by my side in Russia, as a loyal wife should. I needed you, Mary Jane. I needed your love and support. At the very least, I needed your companionship. When you refused that, I asked you to at least let one of the children stay with me, so I wouldn't be completely alone. But you didn't care about me. You only cared about the money I sent to finance your lavish improvements on this house and to allow you to live in style with your socialite friends."

"You didn't have to stay in Russia!" she protested. "You could have come back here!"

"I was doing work that was critical to the survival of this country. I helped end a terrible war. But that meant nothing to you." He shook his head slowly. "I shouldn't have been surprised. You've never cared about anything I've tried to do, no matter how important it was to me."

"You could have served your country here."

"You would have been happier if I'd stayed under the command of General Butler in New Orleans, even if I died from the plague! That way you would have been left a well-off widow and enjoyed the sympathy of the society that means so much more to you than I ever did. It's been a long, long time since you saw me as anything more than a source of financial support."

The bitter truth of his words only made her even more shrill in her anger. "I wasn't unfaithful! You were!"

He was silent for a moment, unable to deny the accusation. Finally, he spoke in a voice heavy with conflicting feelings. "Yes, I did wrong. I hurt people I cared about. I'm not proud of that. But unlike you, I couldn't bear to live without love. The superficial trappings of a comfortable life weren't enough. I needed someone to actually care about me." He finished defensively, "If you'd just stayed with me, none of this would have happened."

But Mary Jane wasn't about to share the responsibility for the breakdown of their marriage. She said coldly, "You've humiliated me for the last time. The tenants are out of our house in Lexington. It will suit the girls and me just fine. We'll move in tomorrow."

"Despite everything, Mary Jane, I don't want you and the girls to leave. Not again."

"You should've thought of that before your mistress and your bastard invaded my home." She turned her back on him and ran up the stairs to her room.

A few days later, he received a letter from a lawyer informing him that Mary Jane had done the unthinkable for a couple of their social standing. She had filed for divorce.

CHAPTER THIRTY-FIVE

1880

Cash took up giving speeches again, traveling far and wide to express his strong views on what was happening to the country during the violent period of Reconstruction. On one Fourth of July he delivered an especially strong oration to a huge crowd of both whites and blacks in Lexington. He advocated universal suffrage, which would have pleased Laura if she'd been speaking to him, universal amnesty for Southerners who had fought in the war, and a presidential candidate who could bring a deeply divided country together.

His first priority – freedom for the slaves – had been accomplished. His second was restoring the states to their original sovereignty in such a way that the nation would forever remain one and indivisible. He still wielded a great deal of clout in political circles, and could draw an eager crowd to his speeches.

But despite his energetic efforts, the country was not coming together. North and South remained bitterly at odds, even though not formally at war.

And many of the gains that blacks had made in the years immediately after the war, were lost to corrupt and evil men who were determined to keep them being truly free.

When it became obvious that blacks were going to be prevented from voting in an election in which his son, Brutus, was running for the House of Representatives, Cash typically took action. He gathered dozens of black men together, led by Tom Peyton, filled a carriage with arms, and marched with the men to the polls.

A guard stood watch over the carriage while Cash went alone to the judges at the polling location and asked this these men be allowed to vote. Glancing worriedly at the carriage filled with weapons, the judges briefly conferred, then agreed to allow them to come to the polls.

Despite this, and the fact that he won more legitimate votes than his adversary, Brutus was defeated by fraud. His opponent's supports simply had their people vote more than once.

Ever since he had come back from Russia, Cash had been harassed by pro-slavery forces. His barns were burned, his outbuildings filled with grain destroyed. The Ku Klux Klan had declared a vendetta against him.

Late one night Cash and Launey sat together in the library at White Hall. At fourteen, Launey was very tall, like his father. He sat strumming a guitar and singing a song in Russian. His father sat nearby, listening with quiet pride.

At seventy, Cash's bearded face was beginning to show his advanced age, and his dark hair was streaked with gray. He and Launey lived quietly at White Hall, cut off from the rest of the family. None of Launey's half-siblings had been willing to meet him, let alone accept him.

Three black servants took care of them – the cook/housekeeper, Sarah White, her son, Perry, who Cash didn't like but employed for Sarah's sake, and Alma Jones, Launey's nurse.

Suddenly the windows were bright with the reflection of dancing flames. Without saying a word, both Launey and Cash ran outside. They found a huge cross burning on the front lawn. Fifty yards away a dozen men on horses were visible in the light of the fire. They were dressed in white robes, with hoods covering their faces, and held torches. One of them rode toward Cash.

"Get my Lincoln revolver and my sword off the wall in the library!" Cash shouted to Launey. "Be quick!" As Launey raced back into the house, one hooded rider came up to Cash and threw something at him.

Cash caught it adroitly as the man rode back to join the others. Then they raced off together, their torches blazing against the night sky.

Launey ran up to his father with the pistol and sword in hand. Cash unrolled the message that had been tied with heavy string. "What is it, father?" Launey asked, frightened.

"Nothing worth repeating, son," Cash snapped. "If they think they can intimidate me, they don't know who they're dealing with!" He didn't want to scare the boy further by revealing the truth – the Klan had a bitter, longstanding vendetta against him. They would stop at nothing to make him pay dearly for past and present actions supporting blacks.

The next morning Cash called his black foreman, Tom Peyton, into the library. While Launey listened intently, his father explained, "They threaten to kill you if I don't replace you with a white foreman."

Tom was stunned. "But why? I've done a good job for you."

"Of course, you have. And I don't want to replace you. But I needed to warn you."

"What will you do, Mister Cash?"

"I don't want your blood on my hands, Tom. If you want, I'll keep paying you a foreman's wages and you can continue working. But I'll bring in someone else to be foreman."

Tom's expression hardened. "I'm much obliged, sir, but I can't let you do that."

"But you're in danger, Tom."

"I know that. But what would you do if you were me?"

Cash didn't hesitate. "Stand up to 'em."

"Then if you'll defend me, sir, I will stand up to these people."

Cash thought hard for a moment. He was impressed by Tom's courage, but very concerned for his safety. He said, "I don't know if I can save you. Or even myself. But I will stand by you, to the death."

He went on, "Here's what we'll do. Have the men get the cannons that are in the barn, next to the presses. Set 'em up by the front door. I want everyone equipped with a gun and a lance."

He handed Tom the Lincoln revolver. "Carry this with you at all times."

Looking at the engraved Colt pistol, Tom said, "I can't take this, sir. It was a gift to you from President Lincoln."

"I believe it will do more good hanging on your belt than on the wall," Cash said with a grim smile.

When Tom left, Launey asked, "Who were those men last night, father?"

"They call themselves the 'Klan.' But they're just a bunch of cowards who can only get up their courage when they run in a pack. There's not a man among them brave enough to face me alone, man to man."

"They scared me."

"I know, son." He smiled reassuringly. "We'll have to change the name from White Hall to Fort Green Clay." He asked wryly, "Have you ever fired a cannon?"

Launey's eyes grew wide. "No, sir."

"Then you'll have your first lesson tomorrow."

The next morning the silence was pierced by the thundering sound of cannon fire and the flash that accompanied it. The cannon ball sailed over the target, bales of hay with the crude outline of a person drawn on them. Cash and Launey stood behind the cannon. Cash stuffed the primer into the barrel with a huge padded plunger on the end of a long wooden pole. Then he reloaded the cannon with a heavy ball.

"I'm still aiming too high," Launey said dispiritedly.

"It's all right, son, you'll get the hang of it. Lower the ratchet a notch."

Launey adjusted the tilt of the cannon. Then he stepped aside as Cash lit the fuse. The big gun belched flame and smoke once more, and the ball spurted out like a big iron marble. This time the ball hit the figure on the hay, blowing it away.

Cash and Launey whooped in excitement.

That evening Tom was riding toward the little house he shared with his wife and children, when he sensed danger. He glanced around nervously. Then he saw them – a group of hooded Klansmen waiting behind a clump of trees. They moved quickly onto the road, blocking his way. The torches lighting their hooded faces created an eerie, frightening sight. One of them – the "Grand Dragon," wore a red robe and hood.

Tom's first instinct was to try to go around them and get to his house. But he didn't want his wife and children to see what he knew with sickening certainty was going to happen. He spun his horse around and raced away. The Klansmen gave chase.

The lynching of Tom Peyton left Cash feeling both heartbroken and enraged. He immediately arranged for Tom's distraught widow and terrified children to leave the county. Then he went looking for a new foreman. Instead of caving in to the Klan, he was determined to hire another black man. And this time he would make damn sure nothing happened to him.

He went to see Orelia's husband, Abraham. It was hard to see her with someone other than George, but he knew Abraham was a good man. He came straight to the point. "I need a foreman. Would you be interested?"

Abraham was touched by this gesture of trust. "I surely would, Mr. Clay."

"Call me Cash. Everyone does." He hesitated then said slowly, "You know it could be dangerous."

Abraham nodded. "I know."

"Technically, Launey will be in charge, so you won't have the foreman's title."

Abraham looked disappointed.

"But you'll have the foreman's salary and responsibilities."

Abraham's face lit up.

Cash went on, "I've been reading about a variety of Southdown sheep that average close to two hundred pounds per head. Most of the land could be used for their natural grazing. And we could cover our costs with the sale of the wool."

"Sounds like a mighty fine idea . . . Cash. I'd be proud to help out with that."

A few weeks later, two rough-looking men sat on horseback some distance from where Cash's new herd of sheep grazed. Launey leaned against a fence, eyeing the sheep with approval. He didn't see the men watching him.

"He left the kid in charge while he went to town," one man said.

"Looks like he might do okay with those sheep. They're gettin' bigger by the day."

"Yeah."

"Getting' rid of Peyton didn't do no good."

"Then we'll have to hit a little closer to home." He gestured to Launey. "That should get to Clay."

"How we gonna do that?"

"I've already taken care of it. His new housekeeper, Sarah White, has a no account son, Perry. He'll do it for a hundred bucks."

"What's he gonna do?"

"Poison. It'll take a little time, but this way no one will know what happened."

Alma shook Launey as he lay in bed. "Come on, you've gotta help your father with the shearin'."

Launey just turned his back to her. "I don't feel good. I'm sick to my stomach and I have a real bad headache."

"You're not eatin' enough. You're gettin' downright skinny. How about if I bring you some of Sarah's chicken soup?"

Launey just groaned in response.

"That soup makes me throw up. When is my father gonna be back?"

"Today, child. He'll be back today."

Later that day Cash returned. He went straight up to Launey's room to check on him. He was concerned about how listless the boy was getting, and he didn't seem to have much appetite. Cash found Launey sleeping soundly – far too soundly for the middle of the day. Alma sat next to the boy, gazing at him in concern. Cash knew something was very wrong.

He went downstairs and headed to the kitchen. He wanted to talk to Sarah about what Launey was eating. Maybe there was something that didn't agree with him. As he reached the partially open door to the kitchen, he heard Sarah talking to Perry, and he stopped. Cash didn't like the shiftless Perry and had told Sarah he wasn't allowed in the house. He was trying to decide if he should go in and give Sarah her notice, or just tell Perry to leave, when he heard something that made his blood run cold.

Perry was saying, "They want to know how much longer it'll be 'till the boy's done for."

"He's gettin' sicker by the day. He can't even get outta bed now. Another couple of bowls of my soup should do it."

Cash burst in. His expression of murderous fury was terrifying. "Get out! Both of you! Now! If I see either of you anywhere near here again, you'll be dead!"

Perry ran out without waiting to see if his mother was behind him. She was so frightened, for a moment she couldn't move. "Mister Cash . . ." she mumbled. "You got it wrong – "

"If you weren't a woman, you'd be dead right now," Cash said in a voice that made Sarah tremble. She turned and stumbled out of the house.

Cash stood there for a moment, shaking with rage. Pulling himself together, he hurried back to his son's room. Throwing off the covers, he picked up Launey as if he weighed no more than a feather and carried him downstairs, bellowing for his carriage to be brought around.

An hour later Doctor Pritchard had finished examining the boy and had given him some medicine. "You're a very lucky man, Mr. Clay. I don't know what that woman was giving him. Rat poison, or something like it, is my guess. But he couldn't have taken much more of it."

Cash said worriedly, "But he'll be okay now?"

"Should be. Just let him get plenty of rest and keep giving him this medicine." The doctor shook his head. "I wonder why . . ."

He didn't finish the thought, but Cash knew what he was getting at. "I think I know. Someone was paying her. Someone who hates me."

He was certain he knew what group that person belonged to, even if he didn't know the person's name.

Back at White Hall, Cash put Launey to bed, then went downstairs to the library and poured a stiff drink. It had been the second worst day of his life. If he'd lost a second son to the blind hatred of bigots, he didn't know how he could've gone on living.

Perry was holed up in an abandoned cabin with Alma, who had left White Hall with him and his mother. When Alma learned what he and Sarah did to Launey, she was badly shaken. But she loved him too much to leave him or turn him in. Now she begged him to go away with her. "We have to get out of here, Perry. If we don't leave, he'll kill you for sure!"

"I'm not gonna run from that old man!"

"Perry, what're you gonna do?"

"You'll see. They'll pay me for killin' Clay, same as for killin' his boy."

"No, please, don't . . ."

She clutched at him but he shook her off. When she tried to grab him again, he slapped her so hard, she fell to the floor. She lay there, crying, as he stormed out.

One week later, Launey was feeling well enough to ask if he could go for a ride. He was tired of being cooped up in his room. Cash didn't think he was strong enough to ride by himself, so he took him up on his horse with him. They rode out to the pasture where the sheep were grazing peacefully. It was a beautiful, clear day, and Cash felt better than he'd felt in a long time. Launey was going to be his old self again soon. The sheep were going to bring in enough income to keep the estate going. Everything was going to be all right.

Behind a nearby tree, Perry took careful aim with a rifle and fired.

The bullet whizzed past Cash's head, barely missing him and Launey. Cash's horse shied at the sharp sound. Cash looked in the direction the bullet had come from and saw Perry getting ready to fire again. Instead of trying to run away, he urged his horse forward and yelled to Launey to hold on tight.

As he galloped straight for Perry, Cash pulled out the revolver that he always carried with him and aimed it. Perry was desperately trying to reload his rifle when there was the flash of exploding gunpowder and his body jerked in agony. He crumpled to the ground.

When Cash reached Perry's body, he brought his horse up sharp and jumped off. He stood over the still body, glaring down at it, his gun pointing at Perry's head. But there was no need for a second shot. The first had killed him.

One month later Cash was called before a grand jury that had been convened to look into the killing of Perry White. He sat at the defendant's table while the county prosecutor, who despised him, spoke to the all-white jury. "You have been convened to determine whether the defendant, Cassius Marcellus Clay, should be indicted and brought to trial for the murder of one Perry White."

One of the Klansmen who had killed Tom Peyton, and paid Perry White to kill Launey, whispered to the man sitting next to him, "The old man's a goner for sure, this time. Look who's foreman."

The foreman, Johnson, who was the Grand Dragon of the Klan, sat at the head of the jury.

The prosecutor continued, "The state isn't going to call any witnesses, because the only witness is dead. Clay had admitted he killed White, and that should be enough for an indictment. Your job here isn't to find Clay guilty. That comes later at a trial. All you have to determine is that there is enough evidence to show that it is possible that Clay killed White then let the trial jury do the rest."

Cash stared at the jury foreman. He focused on the foreman's hate-filled eyes. They were uncomfortably familiar, but he couldn't quite remember where . . . then it came to him. He remembered the night the cross had burned on his lawn – and the Grand Dragon was there.

The judge didn't want to waste time on this hearing, since he was sure the case was going to trial. He also knew that a lot of people in Lexington wanted to see Clay hang, even if it was for killing a black man. He asked Cash, "Do you want to make a statement, Mr. Clay?"

"I stand on the eternal laws of self-defense of me and mine. That is all."

The judge turned to the jury. "There seems to be no one here on behalf of the defendant. So I will ask the Grand Jury to vote, unless, of course, there is some defense."

Launey, who sat right behind his father, shouted, "That Perry White and his mother tried to kill me!"

The judge banged his gavel. "There will be plenty of opportunity for you to testify at the trial, young man. But if that's true, then there was plenty of motive for your father to want to kill White." He turned to the jury. "You may retire to the jury room and vote."

Just then Alma, who was sitting in the gallery, stood up and said in a shaky but determined voice, "Wait!"

The judge banged his gavel again. "I will have order in this court. You are not allowed to testify in a court of law, girl."

Alma wasn't about to be silenced, even by a judge. "The boy's right. Perry and his mama tried to kill him. When Mr. Clay sent them packing, Perry laid in wait to kill him. I loved Perry, but what he did was wrong."

The judge pounded his gavel on his desk. But it was too late. The jury knew what it must have taken for a black woman to come there, to speak on Cash's behalf. She wouldn't have done so if she was lying. There would be no trial.

That night Johnson and some other members of the Klan were drinking heavily. "We almost had him. 'Till that nigger bitch spilt her guts." He was silent for a moment then he said slowly, "If we can't kill him, we can still destroy him. From now on, instead of bein' Cash Clay, the friend of the black man, he'll be Cash Clay, nigger killer."

CHAPTER THIRTY-SIX

Reverend James Fee was at the front entrance of the Berea Church he had founded, shaking hands with the members of his black congregation as they left.

A young man was out among the buggies and wagons, passing out flyers to everyone as they came out of the church. An older couple received one of the flyers, and they handed it over to one of their young sons so he could read it to them. "Well, what does it say?" asked the father.

"It says that Cash Clay kilt the young son of one of his black servants and an all-white jury let him off."

The couple looked at one another in dismay. "I can't believe it. He was always such a good man."

His wife said sharply, "I heard he took up with some other woman, and his wife left him. Maybe he isn't so good anymore."

At the old slave shack that was now the general store for the local black community, the owner put some money into his cash box, an old cigar box that was filled with coins, some folding money and mostly I.O.U.'s. Then he picked up the flyer his elderly customer had brought in and read it aloud. "Says here that Cassius Clay murdered the son of one of his servants, and he got off Scott free!"

Throughout the county, the flyer was circulated. And people talked.

Cash was in the library at White Hall when Reverend Fee came to see him. "What brings you here, Reverend?"

"We've disagreed at times, Cash, but we've always traveled down the same road."

"Get to the point, Jim. You didn't come all the way up here to philosophize."

"I'll give it to you straight. The black folks are saying that you killed one of their own in cold blood. They're having a meeting tomorrow night to talk about what they can do about it."

Cash was taken aback. How could they believe such a thing of him? Whatever else he'd done in his life, whatever shortcomings he'd surely had, there was one thing of which he could be consistently proud – his efforts to help black people.

Cash said in a profoundly hurt tone, "I have sacrificed so much, including a son, for these people. I've shed my own blood. Now they turn against me?"

"I think they're being stirred up by your enemies. I just wanted you to know. And there's more. I think the carpetbaggers are trying to stir up the people for some reason I can't understand."

"Where's the meeting being held?"

"In the church. But I don't think you should go, Cash. Feeling is running high. Anything could happen."

The next night at the little church in Berea, the lights were on and the muffled sounds of a speaker could be heard as Cash approached.

Inside, a northern "carpetbagger," secretly paid by Johnson, was addressing the congregation. "We've given you the vote and have taken it away from any white rebel who supported the confederacy. You have the ability to change your fate on your own. You don't need white heroes who say they're on your side one day, and murder your people the next. I ask you, do you judge Cassius Clay by what he may once have been, or by what he is today, a cold blooded murderer?"

Cash's old driver, Luther, stood up. "Cash is the same man now he always was." He tried to look every person there in the eye. "The question is, who was your best friend when you most needed one? Cash Clay, that's who!"

Cash stood in the doorway of the church, listening to Luther defend him. His eyes glistened with tears of gratitude.

"I'll ask another question," Luther went on. "Who risked his own life in our cause while men like this one joined with our enemies to destroy him? He says his kind freed us and gave us the vote. Well, long before he came here, Cash Clay freed me, and a bunch of other people! And he did it before any law told him he had to!"

Suddenly, there was a murmur amongst the crowd as they realized that the man they were talking about was here and walking up the aisle of the church. Cash walked up to Luther and gave him a warm hug of affection and gratitude. Then he turned to face the crowd.

"I am as much the friend of the black man as I ever was." He flashed a hard look at the carpetbagger. "I want no quarrel with you, or any other man. But as long as you abuse and plunder these people, you and your friends can consider me your enemy!"

Looking at each person in the room, he went on. "We are now, thank God, equal politically. We don't want a white man's party nor a black man's party; but a party of the people, for the people, and the good of all. You must be careful when you listen to these carpetbaggers who've come from the north to seek revenge and take advantage of us. For the moment you're in the majority here as eligible voters. But the reality is that in the whole South, white people are still very much in the majority."

Cash pointed at the carpetbagger. "Is this man really being your friend when he tries to arouse your feelings against white people like me? I tell you as a friend, it is not just, nor to your interest, to bring on a quarrel with white people when the numbers are, on the whole, against you. You are likely to be yourselves the sufferers. These men, who come down here to make money off you, are ever ready to embroil you in conflicts with white people. You were stirred up by them to get into riots at Vicksburg and Friar's Point. And you lost."

There were murmurs of agreement among the crowd. Cash went on in a voice that grew more passionate. "Now I ask you -- who was killed? Whose houses were burned down? If this man can tell me of one carpetbagger who was ever killed or who ever had his house burned down in one of these riots, then I will come down from this platform right now and forever be silent!"

The carpetbagger squirmed uncomfortably in his seat. He couldn't meet Cash's fierce stare. And he didn't say a word.

Luther had sat down when Cash began speaking. Now he stood up and started clapping loudly. In a moment, others stood up and began clapping, until finally the entire crowd was on its feet, applauding Cash.

Looking out at them, Cash felt relief wash over him. If these people had believed the worst of him, and turned on him, he would have felt like worse than a total failure. He would have felt like all the sacrifices he'd made in his life – including the unintentional sacrifice of his son – would have been for nothing.

PART THREE

The Lion in Winter

CHAPTER THIRTY-SEVEN

1888

Cash continued to write and lecture on a wide range of subjects. He delivered the address for the reunion of the Class of 1832 at Yale, and spoke to the Mexican War veterans. Reporters, historians and students sought him out. They found a man almost as strong, intellectually and physically, as he had been when he made his first abolition speech at Yale sixty years earlier.

But none of this made up for the fact that he was profoundly lonely. Many of his oldest friends were dead. Launey was away at school in Boston. His other children rarely spoke to him. And White Hall seemed like a huge, empty mausoleum.

One day he decided to visit one of his few remaining long-time friends. He took a steam locomotive to the small station in Peru, Indiana. With its wheels braking, it shuddered to a screeching halt. Cash disembarked and looked around expectantly, then smiled when he saw a white-haired man, using a cane, coming toward him. "Sam McClure, you're a sight for sore eyes!"

The two old friends exchanged a warm handshake. "I'm glad you could stop by on your way back to Kentucky, Cash. I've heard you're doing a wonderful job for Blaine, now that you've become a Republican again."

"The party let me down for awhile, Sam," Cash said frankly. "But I decided it's worth trying to fix what's wrong with it."

Then a lovely, dark-haired young woman in her mid-twenties joined them. Sam said proudly, "Let me introduce my granddaughter, Minnie Louise Ellis. Minnie, meet one of my best friends, Cash Clay."

Minnie looked up at the tall, distinguished-looking man who still showed vestiges of his once handsome appearance. His eyes were

261

still as clear and blue as a summer sky. And his magnetic presence made all the young men she knew pale in comparison. To Cash, she was a beautiful girl who was far too young for him. But to her, he was unlike any man she'd ever met.

As they walked to a waiting carriage, Sam asked Cash, "How long will you be staying?"

"Just one night. I need to get back to White Hall. I have a reliable overseer, but I still like to keep an eye on things."

Minnie Louise was disappointed and it showed. "Oh, but surely you could stay a bit longer, Mr. Clay? We have a beautiful lake just a few miles from Grandfather's house. Do you like to fish?"

"Yes. But I haven't had much time to do it for quite awhile."

"Then that settles it. You must take some time to enjoy what this town has to offer."

Sam couldn't believe his eyes. His young granddaughter was flirting with his old friend. And even though Cash was being circumspect, Sam knew him well enough to see that he was attracted to her, as well. He only hoped that common sense would keep Cash from encouraging the girl's interest.

A few days later, Cash sat in a boat with Minnie Louise, idly fishing. It was a beautiful day. The water was a deep blue. Billowy white clouds drifted across the azure blue sky. Thick woods surrounded the lake. Cash looked at Minnie Louise. Her exquisite white lace dress and matching parasol set off her dark hair and natural beauty. She was enchanting. And he was utterly smitten. He couldn't believe that she felt the same way about him. But her every word, every glance, suggested as much.

"I'm sorry you haven't caught a single fish today, Cash."

"There's nothing to be sorry about. This has been one of the nicest mornings I've spent in a long time."

"I packed a picnic lunch for us. There's a cove not far from here where we can put in. There's a pretty little meadow with shade trees. It'll be perfect."

Cash reached for the oars and put them in their locks. "Just point the way."

A few minutes later they were sitting on a blanket, eating cold fried chicken and sipping wine. Smiling impudently at Cash, Minnie Louise said, "Don't you like me, Cash?"

"Of course I like you. Why would you think I don't?"

"Because we've been together for several days now, and you haven't once so much as tried to hold my hand."

He shook his head. "You know nothing about me, Minnie Louise."

"But I do! Grandfather told me how you were a great hero in the war with Mexico. And you single-handedly saved the capitol from a coup. And President Lincoln honored you with a special Colt revolver. See, I know all about you!"

Cash chuckled. "Your grandfather gives me far too much credit. I was no hero. I just did what I had to do. And I didn't 'save' the capitol by myself. I was one of many men who acted when we realized there was a threat."

Cash's humble attitude just made him all the more appealing to Minnie Louise. "Grandfather said you're not one for boasting."

"Did he also tell you about . . ." He hesitated.

"About your ex-wife? Yes." She looked at him with tremendous compassion. "Living in a big house, all by yourself, must be very lonely."

She was right, he thought. Now that Launey was away at school, White Hall was a big, empty mausoleum that he rattled around in all by himself. He was more desperately lonely than he would have wanted to admit.

The look Minnie Louise gave him was so unabashed in its admiration for him that he felt emotions stirring deep within him that he hadn't experienced in a long, long time. She was utterly irresistible, lovely and charming and sweet. And he knew that if he kissed her, she wouldn't pull away. They looked at each other for a moment that seemed an eternity, then he broke the contact.

"We'd better be getting back," he said with clear regret in his voice.

She was enormously disappointed and confused. She had been so certain that he felt toward her exactly how she felt toward him. "So soon? Why? Did I say something wrong?"

He shook his head and got up. She rose to face him as he began gathering up the blanket and picnic basket. "If you're worried about what grandfather would think, you should know he just wants me to be happy."

They got back in the boat and Cash began to row away from the shore. "Don't you find me attractive?" she asked with unusual directness.

He looked at her with a bittersweet expression that caught at her heart. "You know I do, Minnie Louise. You're as bright as you are lovely, and I've no doubt that you see exactly how I feel about you."

"Then . . ."

"It has nothing to do with you. I've made some serious mistakes in my life that caused a lot of people, including myself, much pain. I'm a great deal older, and, I hope, a little wiser now. I won't do that again."

"Why would it be a mistake for you and I to . . . to become closer?" she asked, feeling hurt and rejected.

"You have your entire life ahead of you, my dear girl. Most of my life is behind me."

"But surely it isn't the amount of time two people share, but the quality of the time they spend together."

He smiled ruefully. "Only someone young could feel that way."

She looked desperately unhappy now. He felt sorry for her – and even sorrier for himself. He knew enough of life to be certain that she would recover from her wounded feelings and go on to feel the same way about someone younger and more appropriate. Whereas he was sadly certain that he would never feel this way about anyone again.

"We can be friends . . ." he began carefully.

"Friends!" Her derisive tone was eloquent.

"Don't underestimate the importance of friendship. If my wife and I had been able to be each other's friend, we would still be married."

"Perhaps," she said hopefully, "friendship can grow into something more."

If only that were possible, he thought. Aloud, he said, "I'll be going home tomorrow. And unfortunately I doubt that we will have an opportunity to see each other again. But I would very much like to correspond with you, Minnie Louise. And share my life, both past and present, if you think you might be interested."

"I would be very interested, Cash. And if you don't mind, I'll write back to you, and share my life."

"I'd like that very much."

They had arrived at the dock near her grandfather's house. Cash got out then reached out a hand to help her. As she took his hand

and stepped onto the dock, they were very close for an instant. She looked up at him. He looked down at her. Neither spoke. Cash had no idea what she was thinking at that moment. But he was thinking how cruel the passage of time was.

One week after Cash returned to White Hall, he wrote to Minnie Louise. Sitting at her desk, she opened the envelope eagerly and found a valentine that he had made. It read, "Lady, I've looked upon thy face and beauty, kindness, virtue, grace were all combined to make thee fair. O may thy fortune be as bright as are those eyes whose gentle light thy features now so softly wear."

She smiled slowly. Then reached for her ink plume and dipped it into the ink bowl.

A few weeks later, Cash sat in the library at White Hall, reading her third letter to him. "Dear Cash, I have enjoyed your letters to me very much, especially the poetry. Sometimes I am sorry you ever met me, for probably you would have given another more worthy of you, and better suited to you, the deep regard you have bestowed on me."

Oh, no, he thought. That wouldn't have been possible.

Six months later, he sat in the same place, holding her latest letter. He had a somber look on his face as he read, "I should tell you that there has been another suitor who did not show me the same restraint shown by yourself. He has twice asked me to marry him. That causes me to seek your advice as to whether one should ever consider marrying someone you do not passionately love, but who is capable of giving you a very pleasant life."

He was surprised at the depth of his pain on reading this. He had told himself that what he felt for her would lessen in time. This proved how wrong he was. "By the way," her letter continued, "it has been six long months since we were together. I wonder if you can even remember what I look like."

He pulled out his writing materials and wrote furiously, "My little friend, I am not often given over to that passion of fallen hopes – envy – but I cannot but feel some touches of the green-eyed monster when I hear of others enjoying your society, and I, excluded by distance, cannot. Do I remember your features? Does one forget the sun or the moon or the stars when they do not shine? I am sorry that I have not been able to see you, but I felt it best to love you through my letters."

He paused, thought hard for a moment then continued, "It is implied in your letter that our ages are the true objection to a nearer alliance. Unfortunately, that is true. I love you. But my love cannot change the harsh reality of where you are in your life and where I am in mine. You talked of the possibility of marriage to another. I cannot advise you on that matter. My feelings toward you are not objective enough to do so. But I wish you all the happiness in the world and pray that you find it."

The letter was signed, "Believe me with undying love, Your C.M.C."

When Louise read this letter, she was in tears. He loved her as deeply as she loved him. But he wouldn't allow her to give herself to him. And that left only one choice.

Cash was alone in the library, drinking heavily, when Launey came home on a break from school. Giving his son a look of hopeless longing, he said, "She's married."

Launey didn't know what to say. He knew to whom his father referred. He had been aware of the correspondence and hadn't approved of his elderly father's apparent infatuation with a much younger woman. With the callousness of the young, Launey assumed that his father should have put all thoughts of romance aside long ago. After all, love was for the young, not the old.

Launey had felt confident that his father was doing the right thing in insisting on merely being a friend to this young lady. But seeing how distraught his father looked now, he was surprised to see that the old man was still capable of profound romantic feelings and yearnings.

Launey loved his father with a fierce devotion that bordered on hero worship. He hated seeing him this unhappy. For the first time Launey wondered if it had truly been wise for his father to dismiss the young woman's attraction to him, or merely caving in to convention. He would never know for sure. All that was certain was that if there had been a rare opportunity for his father to find true love one last time, it was lost now.

CHAPTER THIRTY-EIGHT

One year later Cash took the train to Boston for Launey's college graduation ceremony. In the dining car, Cash chatted with the other passengers over dinner. In the dark windows flashed the occasional lights of small hamlets that the train was passing through. After dinner, he returned to his seat. It was late now, and the train was quiet.

He nodded off for awhile then awoke to find the young woman next to him leaning against him, using his arm and shoulder as a pillow. Cash looked down at her then looked out the window at the night.

His eyes were filled with sadness, loneliness and a yearning he tried hard to avoid thinking about. There was something very poignant about the fact that this stranger next to him was the first woman to touch him in a long time – and she was unaware of their closeness.

He closed his eyes and tried to sleep. But it was a long time before he nodded off again.

Cash was jolted awake by the sound of the train's whistle piercing the early morning quiet. "Time to wake up, folks," the porter announced. "We'll be in Boston in ten minutes."

The young woman next to Cash stirred, then opened her eyes. Realizing that she was leaning against Cash, she pulled away abruptly, embarrassed. The porter continued, "Anyone like a cup of coffee?"

"I'll have cocoa," the girl said.

"Yes, miss, one cocoa comin' up. And you, sir?"

"Coffee. Strong and black," Cash answered. He focused on looking out the window at the passing scenery. But he missed the feel of the girl's cheek against his shoulder. For a man who had always been so physical, he found himself at this late stage of life rarely experiencing the reassuring feeling of a simple touch.

After the ceremony, Cash made his way through the crowd to join Launey and his pretty young fiancée. Despite the fact that Cash was in his eighties now, he was still strong and upright and vigorous.

"Congratulations, son," Cash said proudly. "I suppose now you'll be moving on to the music conservatory. Or," he added hopefully, "maybe you'd like to help me at home with the sheep business."

"I've been offered a position with the Revenue Service. Daphne and I are going to be married next month. I want to go into something steady and secure so we can start a family."

Cash's financial experiences with the government hadn't proven to be all that secure, but he didn't say so to Launey. He tried to be happy for his son. But the truth was he'd desperately counted on Launey returning to White Hall at some point and raising a family there. Cut off for the most part from his other children, and his grandchildren, he'd hoped Launey would one day fill the empty mansion with the delightful laughter and exuberant actions of children.

Now it looked like Cash would remain alone in the big, silent house for the rest of his days.

Back at White Hall, Cash, Abraham and Orelia were busy shearing sheep. "That's the last of 'em," Cash said with relief. "Thank God. Ten hours a day for a solid week is about all I can take of this."

"These fellows keep multiplyin' like they have," Abraham said, "and we're gonna have to hire some extra help, 'specially when you're off on one of your speaking tours."

"They keep multiplyin' like this, and I won't have to go out on any more speaking tours." Cash went on, "Why don't you take one of these rascals home for your table? They'll go good with all those vegetables you've been growing."

"I get the hint, Mr. Cash. Why don't you join us for dinner?"

"I'll be over as soon as I clean up and change."

An hour later Orelia and Abraham were in their garden, picking vegetables for dinner, in the dim light of early evening. At first they didn't notice the group of men coming over the nearby ridge. The torches the men carried illuminated their white hoods and robes. The head Klansman's robe was set off with red piping, as were the eye-holes in his hood. This gave him a particularly sinister look.

Glancing up, Orelia saw them first. She froze. Noticing her expression of abject fear, Abraham looked to see what she was staring at. Panic raced through him. Grabbing Orelia's hand, he pulled her toward the house, about fifty feet away. She stumbled and fell. Abraham stopped to help her up, but before he could do so, the men were upon them.

The leader grabbed Orelia, ripped her dress and threw her to the ground. He was about to rape her, when Abraham pulled out the pistol Cash had given him and fired, hitting him. But the others were on him before he could fire again. They grabbed both Orelia and Abraham. Gesturing to their dead leader, one of the men said, "Gather him up." Then he turned to Abraham. "We're takin' you in, nigger. You're gonna be tried and hung, legal-like."

Cash was riding toward Abraham and Orelia's house when she came running toward him, hysterical. "Mr. Cash! They took Abraham!"

Cash dismounted. "Who took him?"

"The Klan! They were comin' at us and Abraham shot one of 'em - - the sheriff! They said he'll be hung!"

"The sheriff was with the Klan?"

"He was the leader!"

One week later, one of the Klansmen, who was a sheriff's deputy, was testifying at Abraham's trial. "Like I said, we were just ridin' down the road an' that nigger up an' shot the sheriff."

Orelia, who sat behind Abraham, started to protest, but Cash, sitting beside her, stopped her.

"Your witness," the prosecutor said to the defense attorney.

The attorney didn't even get up. "No questions."

Orelia and Cash exchanged a look of disbelief.

"The state calls Deputy Clarence Higgins," the prosecutor called out.

A second deputy took the stand and was sworn in.

"Can you tell us what happened that day?" the prosecutor asked.

"Like Deputy Clark already said, the nigger shot Sheriff Walker for no reason."

"No further questions, Your Honor."

As the deputy left the stand, the prosecutor said, "The state rests its case."

"The defense may call its witnesses," the judge said.

The attorney remained seated. "The defense calls no witnesses, Your Honor."

Cash had tried to remain patient and hopeful, but this was too much. He jumped to his feet and bellowed in outrage, "Your Honor, this trial is a sham! The defense attorney isn't doing his job! There is a witness – the defendant's wife! She was there! The sheriff was trying to rape her!"

The judge banged his gavel. "Were you there, Mr. Clay? Did you witness the events?"

"No, but Orelia was. She can testify to what happened."

"Folks in these parts are well aware of your sympathies towards the negras, Mr. Clay. You know full well that they can't testify in court."

Cash was livid. "And you know full well that congress has given them the same rights that we all have, including the right to testify at a trial."

Ignoring that, the judge said, "This is a clear case of murder. My job is to make sure justice is done. If the counsel for the defense so desires, he may bring up my ruling all the way to the Supreme Court."

"Yes, Your Honor," Cash said with a sarcastic tone. "But I'm sure he won't so desire! And even if he did, the defendant would be long dead from hanging! Even if you won't let his wife testify, you can't stop the defendant from speaking on his own behalf!"

The judge had had enough. "Bailiff! Take this man out of here and lock him up! Mr. Clay, I declare you in contempt of court!"

Cash wasn't accustomed to losing, not with something as important as this. For the first time in his long life, he felt weak and useless, and he was sickened by that feeling. What good was he any more, if he couldn't help a good and innocent man like Abraham?

As the bailiff dragged Cash away, he turned back to the judge and shouted, "And I declare you the biggest scoundrel who ever sat on the bench!"

"That'll cost you ten days in jail, Mr. Clay!"

Two weeks later, Cash was sitting under one of the big magnolia trees at White Hall. He looked up when he heard the sound of horses approaching. Orelia and her children were riding in an old buckboard that was piled high with all their belongings.

As she got down from the buckboard, Cash went to her and hugged her tightly. "I'm so sorry, Orelia."

"You have nothin' to be sorry about, Mr. Cash. You did everything you could to save Abraham." She pulled herself together and went on in a bleak tone, "I stopped by to thank you for buyin' our place at such a generous price."

"What are you going to do? Where will you go?"

"North, to Cincinnati. Goin' to use the money for me to go to nursin' school. There's a place there that takes black women." She added in a voice that seemed to hold all the pain in the world, "The South has taken the two men I loved. I won't lose anyone else to this damn place."

Cash knew this was a permanent goodbye. He would never see Orelia again. She had been part of his life for so many years, since she and George were married. At that moment he felt that everyone he had ever cared for was gone.

One of the children called out, "Ma, we'd best be goin' if we're gonna be out of the county by nightfall."

Cash understood the urgency of this. The Klan roamed at night.

"Goodbye, Orelia," he said simply.

"Goodbye, Mr. Cash."

She climbed back up onto the buckboard seat and drove off. Cash watched them until they were out of sight.

CHAPTER THIRTY-NINE

1894

S everal months later Cash stood in Orelia and Abraham's old house, showing it to the new tenant, Tom Richardson and his family. With Tom were his wife, Loretta, and baby and his brother, Klell. There was also a tall young woman Cash hadn't met previously. She was of medium height, long, luxuriant black hair plaited in a braid that hung to her waist, and dark eyes. She was far from pretty, but there was something about her – a vulnerability and shyness – that caught Cash's attention.

As Tom, Loretta and the young woman went through the rooms upstairs, Cash turned to Klell. "Who's the young lady with you?"

"My sister, Dora. We came to live with Tom and Loretta when our ma was killed in a train wreck."

Cash realized the young woman might very well be looking for employment. Since Orelia had left, he'd been without a full-time servant, and the house was beginning to show neglect.

He said to Klell, "Do you think she might be willing to come work for me? I could use a housekeeper."

"She'd have her own room there?" Klell asked bluntly.

"Of course." Cash was taken aback at the suggestion of impropriety.

Klell called up to his sister. "Dora! Come on down here! You're gonna live in the big house with Mr. Clay!"

A few minutes later, Cash, with Dora sitting behind him, rode up to White Hall. "Here it is," he said proudly. The three-story brick mansion was especially impressive on this beautiful spring day. Flowers were in bloom, as were the magnolia trees, covered with large white blossoms. Around it, dozens of sheep grazed peacefully, presenting a lovely pastoral scene.

"You live here?" Dora asked in awe.

"Sure do. And now so do you. That is, if you can cook. You can cook, right?"

"A little. But I could learn to do more if you'll show me."

Cash wondered if he'd been a bit rash in offering this girl the position of housekeeper without knowing anything about her background. But it didn't really matter. The truth was, he was desperate for someone to take care of the house, and him.

When they walked inside, Dora looked around with wide-eyed amazement. Her appreciation of the place he'd come to take for granted, made him see it with new eyes. Over the last few years, since Launey had been gone, and now with Orelia gone, too, Cash had come to view it as a lonely, isolated spot. Dora's enchantment with it was delightful.

He led her upstairs to her room. She stopped in the hallway to admire the sword that hung on the wall and the jeweled cane in a glass cabinet along with other memorabilia.

"What a beautiful sword! Are you a knight?"

Cash chuckled. "No, nothing like that. Sometime I'll tell you the story of how I came to have that sword."

"I'd love to hear it, Mr. Clay. My mama used to read me stories before I'd go to sleep at night."

"I'm afraid it won't be as exciting as the stories your mama read to you, Dora."

When she saw the bedroom with its canopy bed and fireplace, she was beside herself with excitement. She'd never lived in such nice surroundings before. "Oh, I love it, Mr. Clay! Thank you so much for letting me stay here. Is there anything I can do for you right now?"

"You can stop calling me 'Mr. Clay.' Just plain Cash would be better. Feel free to have a bath, if you'd like, and get settled in. Then come downstairs and make me some tea."

She looked puzzled. "Bath? You mean, in a tub in the kitchen?"

"You have your own bath here." He led her into the adjoining bathroom. " To receive the hot water, you just pull down this chain. The water from the copper tanks on the roof releases the water into the tub."

Dora's expression revealed that this was something she'd never seen before. "I always had to bathe at the creek or in a tub with water heated on the stove."

For the first time, Cash fully appreciated how simple Dora's background had been. He hadn't paid much attention to how she was dressed, but now he took in her worn and faded dress. "Feel free to look in the other rooms up here and see if you can find any clothes my daughters left behind. You're welcome to them."

"You have daughters?"

"Yes, but I don't see much of them anymore." Nor of his sons, Cash thought sadly. He went on, "I'll leave you to get settled then."

An hour later Cash was in the library, going over his accounts, when Dora came in, carrying a tray with tea things. She looked cleaner than before, and she wore a pretty cotton dress that Cash remembered seeing Mary wear. It was a bit short on her, because she was taller than Mary, but it was a distinct improvement on her previous clothing.

The shortness of the dress revealed her bare feet. And he realized with a start that she might not possess a pair of shoes. "Looks like you could use some shoes, as well, Dora. Did you find any with the dresses?"

"No, sir."

"Then we'll have to go into town and buy you a pair."

Her face lit up with delight. Cash felt a surge of happiness. It made him feel good to do things for this simple girl, who appreciated them so much. She was a breath of fresh, unspoiled air in his house and in his life. Perhaps, he thought, there might yet be more to life than growing old and being alone.

The relationship between Dora and Cash developed quickly. She idolized him and he adored her. At first, he wanted to do things for her purely for the satisfaction of making her happy. It didn't occur to him that someone as young as she was could feel anything more for him than gratitude. After all, he was old enough to be her grandfather. He envisioned spending what was left of his life with her taking care of him, and him providing for her.

They went to one of Louisville's finest women's wear shops. From experience with Mary Jane, Cash knew that shopping could take awhile. He left Dora to the ministrations of the clerk and went across the street to a men's wear shop to get some new clothes for himself. Somehow he felt like sprucing up a bit. Before returning, he got a haircut and had his beard trimmed. He felt more spry than he'd felt in ages.

When he returned two hours later, Dora said, "Why, don't you look handsome." He beamed at the compliment. She held up two pairs of shoes and said, "I can't decide between these two."

"We'll take them both," Cash said to the clerk.

Dora was speechless with gratitude at his generosity.

An hour later, Dora was still trying on dresses. Every time she tried one on, she came out and modeled it for Cash, who enjoyed her obvious pleasure in the beautiful clothes.

"You look beautiful!" he told her with more heartfelt sincerity than objective accuracy. Despite the new clothes, Dora remained rather plain. And because she was so tall, she was a bit gangly and ungraceful. But to Cash, the transformation wrought by the new clothes and by her expression of delight, made her enchanting.

Finally, the shopping spree was over. Cash settled the large bill, then took Dora out to dinner at one of the finest restaurants in the city. They sat at a table set with crisp white linen and the best china and crystal. He enjoyed a cognac while Dora tasted champagne for the first time. She had no idea what to order, so he ordered for her, the priciest items on the menu. Everything was new to her, and more delicious than she'd ever imagined food could be.

He told her stories of his amazing life and she hung on every word. She especially liked hearing about Russia and royalty and the gilded lives they lead. Recounting his exploits to this eager and adoring listener reminded Cash of something he'd nearly forgotten – he'd lived a life of rare fullness.

When dinner was over, they went dancing. As with most things, Cash had to show her how to do it. He held her up in his arms that were still surprisingly strong, so that her feet were barely touching the floor. She had her arms around his neck and her face pressed against his shoulder. He moved her around the dance floor like a ballroom dance teacher with a brand new pupil.

It was a magical evening and when they returned to White Hall, Dora kissed him goodnight on his cheek. Cash smiled down at her then suddenly she kissed him again, this time full on the lips. He was shaken by the contact, and by her unabashed attraction to him.

276

"Dora," he began, gently pushing her away. "We mustn't . . ."

She looked chagrinned. "I'm not good enough for you, Cash. I know that, but I hoped . . ." She stopped then looked away in embarrassment. "Goodnight," she whispered, and ran up to her room.

Cash went into the library and built a small, cozy fire. He sat there, thinking hard, late into the night. His mind churned with questions of propriety versus desire, selfishness versus love. He felt younger than he'd felt in years. Was he just trying to recapture his youth in the arms of a young woman? But he kept thinking of Minnie Louise and the possibility of love that he had rejected. It seemed now as if fate was offering him one last chance to love and be loved again.

By the time he finally went to bed, he had made up his mind that only one person's opinion of all this mattered. And that was Dora's.

The next morning Cash found Dora in the kitchen, making breakfast. Her cooking skills had been very basic, but she'd gradually learned to do enough to satisfy Cash. When he came in, she couldn't quite look him in the eye. She was horribly embarrassed about throwing herself at him the night before, and suffering the humiliation of being rebuffed.

"Breakfast is about ready," she murmured, concentrating on the eggs frying in the pan.

He took her by the shoulders and turned her to face him. "Dora, I'm going to tell you a new story. About an old man who falls in love with a young woman. He doesn't know what to do about it."

"Is this a true story?" she asked hopefully.

"Yes. It's our story. About you and me."

"You mean – you love me?" she asked, hardly daring to speak the words.

"I love you very much. You've brought more joy to my life than I thought possible. The question is whether you could love me."

"But I do. I do love you, Cash. You're the nicest, most generous, wisest, strongest . . ." She paused to take a breath, and Cash chuckled. She smiled, delighted to see that her awkwardness amused him. "I just didn't think someone like you could love someone like me."

"I could. And I do. And I want to marry you."

Dora was speechless. She hadn't dared hope that he could feel she was worth marrying. "Oh, Cash," she whispered in a trembling voice.

Taking something from the pocket of his coat, he held it out to her. It was a beautiful ring with a large ruby and the double eagle of the Romanoff's carved in the gold band. Dora stared at it, speechless. When she didn't take it, Cash took her hand, put the ring in her palm, and curled her fingers around it. "Every girl should have an engagement ring when she becomes betrothed," he said with a smile.

Then his expression turned serious. "There are certain realities we must discuss, my dear. I am a great deal older than you. I don't care what the world thinks of that. But I do care about your feelings."

"It doesn't matter," she insisted.

"There are things that do matter. I want you to know that when you become my wife, I will do everything I can to make you happy. And I will see to it that you are protected financially. You will never have to want for anything again."

"I don't care about that, Cash."

"But I do."

He gazed at her with utter adoration. "Now," he said, "I think I'll kiss you, if it's all right with you."

She nodded, unable to speak through her tears of happiness. She lifted her face to his and he kissed her tenderly.

That day he went to Tom Richardson and formally asked for his sister's hand in marriage. At first Tom was shocked and disapproving. "She's still in her teens!" he said angrily. "And you're an old man!"

Cash was taken aback by this news. Dora looked much older. He'd assumed she was in her late twenties or early thirties. He realized that her life had been hard, and it showed in her complexion and demeanor. But he was still determined to let nothing come between them.

"Not so old that I'm incapable of love," Cash retorted. "And I love your sister. I have sworn to take care of her and to do everything within my power to make her happy."

Tom frowned. He wasn't happy about this. Not happy at all.

Cash went on, "We would like your blessing. It would mean a great deal to Dora. But understand this – I mean to marry her. And no one can stop me."

Tom had no doubt that Cash meant it. And he knew he had no legal power to stop this wedding. The age of consent was twelve, and Dora was well beyond that. It was common for young women to marry older men who could provide financial support and social status. Tom could be as angry as he wanted to be, but it would do no good.

He glared at Cash. "You'd better treat her right, Cash. Or you'll have me and Klell to answer to."

"She'll never have cause to complain of my treatment of her, Tom. I promise you that."

When Cash left, Tom was still angry. But he had accepted the inevitable, and promised that Dora's family would be at the wedding.

The wedding was the talk of all of Kentucky, and indeed much of the nation. The difference in ages, and the position of the bridegroom, made the match such a controversial one, that newspapers wanted to cover it.

The ceremony was described in the Lexington newspaper by a reporter who witnessed it: "The scene was a touching one. Never before and probably never again to be equaled in American life, the ceremony began, and the man who had led thousands to victory in a crusade for human victory, who had joyously faced death in innumerable personal hand-to-hand encounters, who in his youth the perfect Apollo in appearance, if not a Napoleon in the cause of freedom, whose portrait hangs in the palace of the dead Russian Emperor, stood as meekly as a little child with an expression of unspeakable happiness upon his time-worn but still fresh and youthful features.

"By his side stood that simple country girl, as shy as a gazelle, knowing as little of the great world in which her venerable husband had played so conspicuous a part as the most untutored daughter of nature. The ceremony was very brief, and when it was over the General gave her a vigorous kiss, which she bashfully but willingly returned."

In a pointed reference to gossip that Cash must be senile, the article continued, "Cassius Clay is in excellent health, erect and muscular as an Indian, and bids fair to live many years if he will only quit fighting. He walked me to the door, talking in his agreeable and courtly way. My rather hefty hand was lost and helpless in the grasp of that enormous paw now so gentle, which had laid such violent hold upon so many luckless adversaries.

"'Goodbye, my young friend,' he said. 'Tell all my friends and also my enemies' – there was just a fleeting grimness in his smile as he said this – 'that I love my little bride better than any woman I ever saw. She is a good and virtuous girl, and I believe she will make me a good and loyal wife.'

Some think the old General is crazy", wrote Lane in his newspaper account of the wedding. "But I do not think so. His mind is clear as a bell. I do not even think he is in his second childhood, but if he is, I shall hereafter have no fear of growing old."

CHAPTER FORTY

T he day after the wedding, Cash, Dora and her older sister, Louella, were having lunch at the dining room table. Louella had come to the wedding with her three children, including a new baby. Dora had been holding the baby and playing with him happily. She looked at Cash. "Would you like to hold him?"

Cash took the little boy from her. The baby immediately reached up and tugged at his white beard. Cash laughed happily. It had been too long, he thought, since he'd held a baby in his arms. He rarely saw his grandchildren, because of the estrangement from his children after the divorce. And Launey and his wife hadn't had children yet.

"His name is Simon," Louella said. "Like in the nursery rhyme."

"He looks pretty bright to me," Cash responded with a laugh, and Louella joined in.

Dora didn't get the joke. She looked at her sister and her husband, and felt like an outsider.

Just then the new housekeeper Cash had hired brought in dessert. Dora hungrily dug into the delicious pecan pie. Watching her, Louella winced as she saw Dora hold the fork awkwardly with her fist wrapped around it instead of between her fingers.

"If you two will excuse me, I'll skip dessert and go over some business in the library." He turned to Dora. "When you get a chance, there's something I'd like to talk to you about."

When he was gone, Louella said to Dora, "Let me show you something." She held a fork between her fingers. "This is the proper way to hold a utensil."

Dora felt horribly embarrassed. "Is that what you and Cash were laughing about?"

"What? Oh, no. We were laughing about 'Simple Simon.' You know – 'Simple Simon met a pie man.'"

But Dora didn't know. She'd never heard the nursery rhyme, and she could only read at a very basic level.

"I need to ask Cash something," she said, and left.

Louella watched her unhappily. Without meaning to, she'd made her sister feel inferior and inadequate.

In the library, Dora said to Cash, "What did you want to talk to me about?"

"Your sister mentioned that she was a teacher, before she had the children."

"She had to give it up when all the young 'uns came."

Cash said gently, "You never finished school, did you?"

Dora flushed and shook her head.

"What if I hired her to help you finish your schooling?"

"You don't think I'm good enough for you," Dora said miserably.

"I will pay her to teach you, not because I think I'm better than you, but because I love you and don't want you to miss out on your education."

"Can she bring the children?" Dora asked, brightening.

"Yes. It will be wonderful to have children around here again."

"Soon we'll have our own children, Cash."

Hearing the excitement in her voice, Cash felt a twinge of concern. He hadn't thought about the issue of children when he'd asked her to marry him. Now he realized he should have. It was only natural that she would want a family. Seeing her with Louella's children, especially the baby, it had been obvious how naturally maternal she was. Cash only hoped that he would be able to give her children.

Weeks later, Louella came to Cash and told him there was no use in trying to continue to tutor Dora. She had absolutely no interest in education. All she cared about was becoming a mother. And that wasn't happening.

Louella said frankly, "I'll tell you honestly, Cash, if she doesn't have a child soon, you'll lose her."

Cash had been thinking the same thing. He felt guilty at the thought of depriving Dora of something she wanted so badly, and terrified at the thought of losing her.

Two years after their wedding, Cash said goodbye to Dora as she got into the carriage in front of the house. She said she was going for a brief visit to Louella, who had moved to a neighboring town. She would only be gone a few weeks. But Cash had sensed for some time that her unhappiness at not getting pregnant was affecting their relationship. He suspected that she didn't want to see her sister so much as she wanted to be away from him.

Weeks turned to months. It was winter and the flowers were long since dead and the leaves had blown off the trees. White Hall had a bleak appearance reflected in the atmosphere within the house.

Cash sat in the library, writing to Dora. "My dearest Dora, life is not the same without you. It has been six months since you left. Do you not miss me as I miss you? Please come home. Your loving husband, Cash."

When Dora received the letter, she asked Louella to write a response, that she dictated. "Dear Cash, Louella is writing this for me so I cannot say everything that is in my heart. I have had time to think about us and what we must do now. You know that all I wanted more than anything was to have your child. That hasn't happened, and I have given up hoping that it will. I am sorry but I have decided to stay here until I can find work and take care of myself."

As Cash read the letter, his face crumpled, and suddenly he looked all of his more than eighty years as he threw the letter in the fireplace.

One year later, on a similarly cold and dreary winter day, Cash was in his attorney's office in Lexington, signing the final divorce papers. "This marriage cost you plenty," the attorney said with a frown of disapproval. "By the time you figure the house in Richmond, with the extra lot, and the monthly stipend . . ."

"She asked for nothing," Cash said tersely. "That was my departing gift to her."

"Along with the majority of the shares in your estate."

"She deserves it. I promised to take care of her and I will do so."

Cash could tell by the way the attorney was looking at him that he was thinking there's no fool like an old fool. He was probably right. But Cash couldn't find it within his heart to regret loving Dora or marrying her. She'd given him one last burst of hope and joy. And for that he would be eternally grateful.

At Dora's house in Richmond, her brother, Tom Richardson, pounded on the front door. When it finally opened, he was shocked to see how bad Dora looked. She was pale and thin.

He entered the house, then rubbed his hands briskly together as he looked around. "My God, it's freezing in here. Where's the rest of your furniture?"

She didn't want to tell him that she'd broken it up and burned it for heat. But he could figure it out for himself. "What do you do with the money Cash sends you?"

"I buy things," she answered slowly. "Dresses, shoes . . ."

Tom shook his head in disapproval. But he knew there was no point in lecturing her. "Cash heard that they had cut off your coal supply. He asked me to bring this money to you. I have a ham from the farm, too. I'll bring it in."

Opening the envelope, Dora looked at the bills stuffed inside. As always, Cash had been generous. She shoved the money in the pocket of her dress, then looked defiantly at Tom. "I met someone at a dance recently. We want to be married."

"Fine," Tom said curtly. "What's stopping you?"

"According to the divorce agreement, I'll lose the house and my monthly allowance."

"Can't this new man provide for you?"

"He's young, Tom. Just getting started. He's a handsome Irishman. Riley Brock's his name."

"Can't he at least buy coal to keep you from freezing?"

"He'll have a job soon. In the meantime, would you talk to Cash? See if I can keep the house and the allowance."

That was the last thing Tom wanted to do, considering how generous Cash had been to all of them. But Dora was his little sister, and he was worried about her welfare. She clearly wasn't capable of taking care of herself. "You'd be better off talking to Cash yourself, Dora. He still loves you, and I suspect he'd put your happiness above his own feelings. That's the kind of man he is."

Dora didn't care what kind of man her ex-husband was. She was totally focused on a handsome young Irishman with wavy, red-gold hair. "You're right," she said slowly. "I probably could talk him into it."

"He may want to meet this Irishman of yours. As a matter of fact, so would I."

"I'll wake him up."

Tom is dumbfounded. "He's still asleep? It's two o'clock in the afternoon!"

"He was up late last night, planning the business he wants to start."
She laughed awkwardly. "I'm afraid he had a bit too much to drink."

"What kind of lout are you thinking of marrying, Dora? He can afford
whiskey, but he can't afford coal or food?"

"At least he doesn't act like he's better than me. And he wants to have
a family."

Tom just looked at her helplessly. There was no way to get through to
her that she was not only taking advantage of Cash's generosity and
caring, but making a terrible mistake.

A few days later, Dora sat in the library at White Hall with Cash. He
was trying very hard not to let her see how much it hurt him to hear
her talk of marrying another man. "Why do you come to me? You
don't need my permission."

"He wants to start a printing business with his brother, Allen. We
can't afford to get married if I lose the house and my allowance." She
went on before he could argue, "I know he'll make me happy, Cash!
He's waiting outside, if you want to meet him."

That was the last thing he wanted to do. But he felt he needed to do it,
for her sake. He nodded, and Dora ran out to get Riley.

A moment later, she returned. Looking at the debonair young man,
Cash felt not only envy, but deepening concern. He could see why
Dora would fall in love with Riley. But he could also see that this was
not a young man to be trusted.

"Pleased to meet you, sir," Riley said, extending his hand. "Dora has
told me so many nice things about you."

You mean, she's told you that she depends on my money, Cash
thought. He said carefully, "I understand you want to go into the
printing business."

"Yes, sir. My brother and I have worked in the business before, and
our prospects are good. But it will be tight at first. That's why we
could use Dora's allowance for a bit longer."

He didn't say that he and his brother had been in the counterfeiting
business before, and their prospects are good because they had
contacts who would fence the phony bills. Both Riley and Allen had
done time for bootlegging and passing phony currency.

Riley went on, "We'll pay you back with interest, sir, as soon as we get
the business off the ground."

Cash had confronted many scoundrels, and worse, in his long life. He
felt in his bones that Riley was one. And he feared for Dora's
happiness and welfare.

285

But he knew there wasn't a thing he could say to change her opinion of this young man. She was clearly as besotted with him as Cash had been with her.

"Very well," he said slowly. He gazed tenderly at Dora. "I promised to take care of you, and I will. Always."

Dora was too focused on the relief she felt at knowing she and Riley could afford to marry to be aware of how painful this was for Cash. Ignoring her ex-husband, she smiled happily at the new love of her life.

Months later, in the sheriff's office in the state capitol of Frankford, Kentucky, Sheriff Anderson was carefully examining a pile of brand new bills. He turned to his deputy. "All of 'em have the same serial numbers. Get a hold of the revenue boys. They're gonna want to find the source of this money."

The deputy said, "I hear most of 'em are bein' passed in Lexington and Richmond. Must be comin' from somewhere around there."

Riley and Allen were riding up to an old barn in the woods when they saw revenuers taking the printing press and distillery equipment out on a wagon. They quietly turned their horses around and rode off fast.

Back at Dora's house, Riley stuffed a wad of new bills into a duffle bag. "Where are you goin?" she demanded.

"To Cincinnati to get new equipment," he lied.

She shoved a legal document at him. "What about this? The banks' taking back my house because you haven't paid back the money you borrowed against it."

Ignoring the document, Riley said, "Some men may come around lookin' for me an' Allen." He grabbed her roughly by the arm. "Don't tell them anythin', you hear?"

"I don't understand, Riley." She tried to hold onto him, to keep him from leaving, but he shook her off. When she grabbed him again, he slapped her hard, sending her sprawling on the floor. Then he left.

As he hurriedly left, she screamed, "Riley!" But he ignored her.

She lay there, sobbing, knowing he was abandoning her forever. What was she to do? How would she survive?

Then she realized there was still one person she could turn to.

CHAPTER FORTY-ONE

It was a stormy night at White Hall. Between flashes of lightning and crashing thunder, the shutters could be heard slamming against the brick walls. Inside, Cash went to the front door in response to a loud pounding on it. Opening it, he found Dora, soaking wet and looking physically battered and emotionally distraught, standing there sobbing. She threw herself into his arms.

"My God, Dora! What happened to you?"

"Riley's run off. Can I stay here?"

"You have a house . . ."

"The bank's taking it." She pulled herself together enough to explain about the unpaid debt.

Cash frowned. Unfortunately, he wasn't surprised. He was more bothered by Dora's appearance than her financial situation. "He hurt you, didn't he?"

She didn't answer.

He said tightly, "We'll talk about this in the morning. In the meantime, you can sleep in my room. There's a fire going and it's warm. I'll sleep in a guest room."

The next morning Cash sat Dora down in the library and got the whole story out of her. It was all he could do to control his rage at Riley. He was comforting her when his housekeeper, Irma, came in and said there was a man out front wanting to see Dora. He said he was her husband.

Telling Dora to wait there, Cash went out to confront her no-account husband.

Riley was waiting in the vestibule, hat in hand, looking suitably chagrinned. Without saying a word, Cash belted him hard, sending him flying against the wall. He slumped down on the floor, fighting not to lose consciousness.

Dora came running out of the library and fell to the floor beside Riley. "Don't hurt him, Cash!" she screamed.

She seemed unaware of the irony in begging an eighty-five-year-old man not to hurt a thirty-year-old one.

Riley said slowly, "I don't blame you for that, Mr. Clay. I deserve it. I just came to tell Dora how sorry I am for what I done to her and to beg her forgiveness."

Cash couldn't believe Dora could still love such a worthless young man. But clearly she did.

"You ever lay a hand on this young lady again, and I'll kill you. Do you understand?"

Riley nodded silently.

Dora said to Riley, "Of course I forgive you. But where will we live now?"

Riley had no answer. That was actually why he was there. He knew the revenuers were looking for him, and he needed a place to hide out. When he went back to Dora's house later the previous night, and learned she had gone to White Hall, it occurred to him that this was the perfect place to lay low for awhile.

When Riley said nothing, Dora looked at Cash pleadingly. He hesitated. But it was no good. He couldn't send her away, homeless. "You can stay in the tenant house until you two can sort things out."

Dora gave him a smile of such gratitude that it touched his heart. He still loved her, God help him. And he always would.

Cash put Riley and his brother, Allen, who had turned up, to work shearing sheep. Dora helped Irma in the house. She was perfectly happy to be there, but Riley and Allen hated the hard physical labor. They were determined to leave just as soon as it was safe to do so.

Six months later Dora gave birth to a healthy baby boy. She named him Cassius Marcellus Clay Brock. Riley was furious, and accused Dora of being unfaithful. No matter how much she denied it, he didn't believe her.

Cash knew this couldn't be his child. Still, he was profoundly touched by Dora's gesture. He had never told her about the murder of his son. Somehow, her desire to give this baby Cash's name, made him feel almost as if he had his namesake back again.

Cash visited his lawyer once more. Again, the man was flabbergasted, as he often was by this unusual client. "You want her to have the house in Pinkard?" the lawyer asked in disbelief. "And a large share of your estate in the event of your death? And upon her death, it's to go to her son?"

Cash nodded. Shaking his head, the attorney thought, Now I've seen it all. Ah, well. There's no fool like an old fool.

At White Hall, Riley pulled a weak Dora, who was recovering from giving birth, out of bed, while Allen stood guard with a gun. She held onto the newborn baby as Riley dragged her by the hair out the door. "You're comin' with me, bitch!" Dora screamed in terror as Riley dragged her down the stairs.

Hiding in the kitchen, Irma shook with fear.

When Cash rode up that evening, Irma came running out to meet him. "Mr. Cash! Thank God you're back!"

"What is it? Is it Dora? The baby?"

"Those Brock brothers drug her off. She didn't want to go, but they made her. They had guns!"

Cash thought fast. "I'm going to write a note to Dr. Perry. You take it to him just as fast as you can. He'll know what to do." Perry was Cash's closest neighbor.

Cash ran inside, hurriedly scrawled a note then Irma raced off with it.

Taking the Bowie knife and the Lincoln pistol down from the wall where they were mounted, he prepared to wait for what he expected to happen. He didn't think Riley would be satisfied with just taking Dora. He would probably want to exact revenge on Cash, as well, for his suspicions about the baby.

At the tenant house, Riley tied Dora to the bed. "I'll be back to take care of you," he said through clenched teeth. "But first I'm gonna finish off that old bastard."

He and Allen ran out of the house, jumped on their horses, and raced off toward White Hall.

At Dr. Perry's house, Irma waited anxiously while the doctor read the note. "The Brock brothers have taken Dora and the baby. My gut tells me they'll be back. Come at once! Bring guns!"

Perry shouted to his servants to grab their guns.

Riley and Allen approached the house quietly. It was in total darkness now. Inside, with only the glow of the embers of a dying fire lighting the room, Cash waited. He held the Bowie knife in one hand, and the revolver in the other. He heard the sound of the front door opening slowly . . .

At the tenant house, Dora managed to get one hand free from the ropes. She untied herself quickly, grabbed "little Cash," and headed for the door.

Dr. Perry and his servants had reached the entrance to White Hall, where they saw two horses loosely tied to a post. They raced through the open front door and into the library. There they saw an amazing sight. Cash sat in his old rocker, perfectly calm.

"There's a dead man on the floor," shouted one of the servants. "He's been shot."

"Another dead one over here," a second servant said. "A knife stuck in his gut."

Just then Dora came rushing in, holding the baby. "Is he all right?" she asked hysterically. Then, seeing Cash, she ran over to him and dropped to the floor at his feet. "Thank God! Oh thank God!"

Dr. Perry just shook his head in reluctant admiration. Cash Clay was still more than a match for any man, even at nearly ninety.

CHAPTER FORTY-TWO

1900

Apassenger train made its way through the lush green countryside of Kentucky. As it neared Pinkard, Cash looked anxiously out the window. He knew Dora would probably be waiting for him. She was usually good about being on time. But he was always just a little nervous. Because his life at White Hall was so lonely, he looked forward to these visits with an almost pathetic eagerness.

He held an expensive hand-painted vase filled with a dozen red roses picked from the garden at White Hall. The porter noticed the roses and smiled at Cash. "Special day?"

"It's my ninetieth birthday!"

"My, my. You sure don't look ninety, sir."

Cash thought, I don't feel ninety, either, not in my heart anyway. It's just my body that's beginning to act so old. But I've lived every one of those ninety years to the fullest.

He wondered if Dora had read the letters from the Methodist Church that he had asked the minister to send to her. Her future happiness, and that of the little boy he thought of as a son were of primary importance to him, and her eternal salvation was critical to that happiness.

He thought of Dora's last letter to him. "Dear Husband – I received your loving letter. Please come and visit. I would come to you, but I only got six dollars." It was signed, "Your dear wife, Dora."

They weren't husband and wife, of course, but she liked to refer to him that way, and he didn't mind. It made him feel less alone. He knew the reference to money was a blatant attempt to wangle some more financial support out of him. And he knew she'd sell

291

the vase. He didn't mind that, either. He'd promised to take care of her, and he was keeping that promise.

Dora, the son she'd named after Cash, and Launey were the only family he was close to. He loved them dearly. His children with Mary Jane had severed all ties with him. They were so furious that he was leaving the bulk of his estate to Dora, little Cassius, and Launey, that they were trying to get him declared legally insane so they could challenge the will. He was confident they wouldn't succeed. He might be many things, he admitted ruefully to himself, but crazy wasn't one of them.

He'd long since been ostracized by Lexington society because of his support of the black cause. Now that he was over ninety, his world had shrunk to the grounds of White Hall, and an occasional trip to Pinkard to visit Dora and Cassius.

As the train pulled to a stop, Cash saw a small, horse-drawn buckboard with Dora and little Cassius sitting in it. They waved gaily at him. When he walked over to the buckboard, the little boy grinned happily and hugged him.

Handing the vase to Dora, Cash said, "I grew these roses in my garden just for you."

"Oh, Cash, they're beautiful."

He got up onto the buckboard seat and they set off for the five-mile drive to the house he had provided for them.

Watching them leave, a woman who'd been on the train with Cash asked her lady friend who'd met her at the station, "Who is that distinguished looking elderly gentleman? You can tell he must've really been something when he was younger."

Her friend sniffed disdainfully. "Don't you recognize him? He's that old rascal, Cassius Clay. A nigger lover and a damned republican."

The woman had heard stories about the famous – some said infamous – old man. She stared at him now with even more interest. She agreed with her friend's dismissive comments about him, of course. Both women would have been appalled to realize that Cash would have found that description of him both accurate and something to be proud of.

In the buckboard, Cash Jr. asked the man he called "papa" about something he'd heard. "My teacher says you were an abo . . . abo . . ." He stopped, unable to pronounce the word.

"Abolitionist," Cash finished for him.

"Yeah. What's that, papa?"

Cash thought for a moment, then he said slowly, "It's someone who believed that God made us all in his image. And nothing else mattered. Especially not the color of our skin."

The little boy looked perplexed, but accepted the explanation. Smiling down at him, Cash knew that the boy didn't really understand. But that was all right. Some day, God willing, he would.

EPILOGUE

Cassius Marcellus Clay died in 1903, at ninety-three years of age, his health ultimately ruined by injuries inflicted presumably by the Brock brothers although never tried and proven. That night a tornado took down trees all over Lexington and threw wagons into the air. It took rooftops off buildings and snapped the head right off a statue of Cash's more famous cousin, Henry Clay.

Some said he was a prophet. Others called him a madman. He would have been the first to admit he was far from perfect. He gave in to his share of temptations. But like King David, he was a man after God's heart. Like David, he tried harder than many people to do the right thing, even though he failed at times.

To some people, he was their hero, their champion. Another great champion and fighter for freedom, the boxer Cassius Clay, later known as Muhammad Ali, was named after Cash Clay. Some say that Ali's great-grandfather was one of the slaves freed by Clay long before the Thirteenth Amendment freed all the slaves.

Muhammad Ali writes in his autobiography The Greatest "If there is any white blood in me it's because some white man raped a black slave woman."

Muhammad Ali does have white blood in him according to genealogists. His mother's maiden name was Grady an Irish name because, according to these same genealogists, Odessa Grady Clay was the great-granddaughter of the freed slave Tom Morehead and of John Grady of Ennis, whose son Abe had emigrated from Ireland to the United States.

We do know for a fact that Muhammad Ali/Cassius Marcellus Clay Jr. father's name was Cassius Marcellus Clay.

Did his father perhaps have the famous abolitionist's blood in him? A direct blood connection is impossible as his father was born in 1912 some nine-years after the original Cassius Marcellus Clay died.

It can only be surmised that his father was named after the plantation owner that freed his grandfather, or his father was simply named after the Cassius Clay who is the subject of this novel.

It is more likely than not that his father had the name passed down to him because his grandfather was named after the slave owner that freed him just as Ali's mother's great-grandfather Tom Morehead took the name of the slave-owner who freed him.

A large tombstone in the cemetery at Richmond, Kentucky, bears the name of Cassius Marcellus Clay, the date of his birth and death, and the words, "Knife Fighter." Clay didn't choose that inscription. All he wanted on his tombstone was one word – Alaska.

It was the accomplishment of which he was most proud. Not because he had any idea that the area would one day become a rich addition to the United States, but because it played a pivotal role in the victory of the Union over the Confederacy. And thus led to the fulfillment of his greatest dream – freedom for an oppressed people.

When Cassius Clay changed his name to Muhammad Ali in 1964, he said, "Why should I keep my white slave master's name visible and my black ancestors invisible, unknown, unhonored?"

It is our hope as authors of this novel that Muhammad Ali will read this account and realize that his namesake the white, plantation owner who gave up a son, his marriage and even happiness; and instead lived despised by many of his neighbors because of his dedication to abolish slavery, and he is the one perhaps who has been to the general public invisible, unknown and unhonored.

Whitehall

Young Cash

Bust of Cassius Clay

"Cassius Clay the legislator and newspaper publisher."

"Mary Jane (Warfield) Clay"

: "True American" First Anti-slavery newspaper in the South.

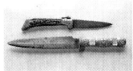

"Cash's pistols."   "Clay's knives."   "One of
                                          Cash's cannons."

Sword from Tiffany's inscribed "Presented by the citizens
of Fayette and Madison County. "Don't kill the men,
they are innocent, I alone am responsible."

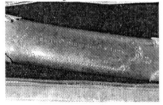

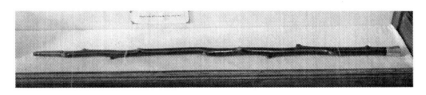

: "Ceremonial cane presented by the Governor inscribed
"Cassius Clay, friend to the poor."

"Cassius Clay Major General
before returning to Russia
as our Ambassador."

: "Tsar Alexander II.
Freed 23 million white slaves
or serfs. Like Abraham Lincoln
he, too, was assassinated."

"Marie, the Russian ballerina."

. "Launie, Cash and
Marie's son."

"Old Cash."

"Dora, Cash's 15 year old bride."

Meeting of Frontiers exhibit in the Library of Congress.
Cassius Marcellus Clay
SIGNIFICANCE

* minister to Russia, architect of "strange friendship" with Czar Alexander II
* prevents mediation efforts of Napoleon III and Palmerston
* represents Lincoln's war aim of abolitionism

Kentucky Abolitionist

* cousin of Henry Clay; veteran of Mexican War; governor of Kentucky
* married Mary Jane Warfield of Lexington 1832
* fought duel with Samuel Brown 1843, bullet deflected by his silver knife case, always carried bowie knife, formal 18-in. blade with pearl handle or street blade with bone handle
* published *True American* newspaper 1845
* abolitionists upset he volunteered to fight against Mexico 1846, but he was a militant patriot
* helped create Republican Party, served on the first National Committee in 1856
* sought VP nomination 1860, but lost to Hannibal Hamlin of Maine
* lived near Lexington at Whitehall

Minister To Russia 1861-62

* Lincoln rewarded Clay with appointment
* Clay from key border state, yet too volatile for Cabinet
* instructed to win support of Russian government with an "athletic Western argument"
* left for Russia May 1, 1861 with wife, children, nurse, bowie knives
* instructions: support Russia with "athletic Western argument"
* mingled well with aristocracy, lavish parties, duels
* met "liberator" Czar Alexander II July 14, after czar had issued his edict Feb. 19 liberating 40 million serfs, giving land to the village (mir), creating in 1864 district assemblies (zemstvo), and in 1870 municipal councils (soviet).

Poland Rebellion 1862

* Foreign Minister Gortchakov - needed U.S. friendship
* expansion southeast into Caucusus, northeast into Poland
* Czar suppressed revolt by Jan. 1863, ended Polish autonomy
* Napoleon appealed to Brit., Austria, U.S. for intervention
* Garibaldi revolt in Italy, hero in U.S. to Italian brigades
* French troops withdrawn from Italy
* to face Bismarck, new president of Prussia Sept. 1862
* Prussian and Austria invade Denmark 1864

Minister to Russia 1863-69

* Russian fleet sent to U.S. July 26, 1863
* Brit. and French fear alliance - cartoon Nov. 21, 1863
* Atlantic Fleet under Admiral Lisovski arrived NYC Sept. 24
* Russian sailors photographed by Brady
* Pacific Fleet under Admiral Popov arrived in San Francisco Oct. 12
* Popov on alert in Dec. against possible CSA attack
* but Gortchakov instructed Popov to stay neutral
* Welles: "God bless the Russians"
* cartoon - Dr. Lincoln to Smart Boy of the Shop: "Mild applications of Russian Salve for our friends over the way, and heavy doses - and plenty of it - for our Southern patient"
* Clay returned to US 1869 with Russian boy Launey Clay who was the offspring of one of his Russian extramarital affairs
* divorced Mary 1878, married 15-year-old servant Dora Richardson at age 84 in 1894, divorced in 1898
* died at Whitehall July 22, 1903

"The Negro freedom movement would have been historic and worthy even if it had only served the cause of civil rights. But its laurels are greater because it stimulated a broader social movement that elevated the moral level of the nation. In the struggle against the preponderant evils of the society, decent values were preserved. . .

. . . Moreover, a significant body of young people learned that in opposing the tyrannical forces that were crushing them they added stature and meaning to their lives . . .

. . . The negro and white youth who in alliance fought bruising engagements with the status quo inspired each other with a sense of moral mission, and both gave the nation an example of self-sacrifice and dedication."

MARTIN LUTHER KING JR.

THE AUTHORS

Pamela Wallace, a native Californian with a degree from UCLA, is both a novelist and a screenwriter. She co-wrote the screenplay "WITNESS," for which she won an Academy Award, a Writers Guild award, and the Mystery Writers of America award (the Edgar).

Three of her twenty-nine published novels have been produced as made for television movies: Tears in the Rain; Love with a Perfect Stranger; Dreams Lost, Dreams Found. Others have been optioned to be produced as television movies or as a television miniseries.

Ms. Wallace wrote the award-winning HBO film, If These Walls Could Talk, produced by and starring Demi Moore. She also wrote Borrowed Hearts, starring Roma Downey, which was the highest-rated TV program of the week it aired and the ABC movie of the week, Lovers of Deceit, an adaptation of a non-fiction true-crime book. She also co-wrote the screenplay for the movie If the Shoe Fits.

Most recently she has stepped into the role of producer, producing Getting Back to Kansas for the Lifetime Network from her own screenplay and has written another movie entitled Straight From The Heart, which was shown on the weekend preceding Valentines Day, 2003 on the Hallmark Network. It received the highest rating ever achieved on that network. As both writer and/or producer, Ms. Wallace has several projects in development with various production companies.

Richard Kiel is best known for his memorable role as Jaws in the James Bond movies The Spy Who Loved Me and Moonraker, and for his appearance in other notable films such as The Longest Yard, Pale Rider, Force 10 From Navaronne, The Silver Streak, Cannonball Run II, So Fine, and Happy Gilmore.

He has also appeared in nearly 100 television shows including The Wild, Wild, West, The Man From U.N.C.L.E., I Dream of Jeannie, The Monkees, Gilligan's Island and many more including the Paul Bunyan Show which he wrote and produced.

Kiel has written and/or co-written several screenplays: The South Shall Rise Again, With Wings As Eagles, Escape From Paradise and Consider The Ravens.

He has also stepped into the role of producer, co-producing and co-writing The Giant of Thunder Mountain, a theatrical film which garnered five-star reviews and a Family Film Award of Excellence from the Film Advisory Board.

His humorous and entertaining autobiography, Making It BIG In The Movies was published in 2002 by Reynolds & Hearne in London, England and was also reprinted in hardcover.

This is Kiel's first novel, Cassius Marcellus Clay, the Kentucky Lion, full of action, romance and history; it is a labor of love based upon over twenty-five years of research.

Printed in the United States
200297BV00007B/190-240/A